Socialization and Values in Canadian Society

Socialization and Values in Canadian Society
Volume One
Political Socialization

Edited by Elia Zureik and Robert M. Pike

The Carleton Library No 84
McClelland and Stewart Limited

THE CARLETON LIBRARY

A series of Canadian reprints, original works
and new collections of source material relating
to Canada, issued under the editorial supervision of the Institute of Canadian Studies of
Carleton University, Ottawa.

DIRECTOR OF THE INSTITUTE
Davidson Dunton

GENERAL EDITOR
Michael Gnarowski

EXECUTIVE EDITOR
James Marsh

EDITORIAL BOARD
B. Carman Bickerton (*History*)
Dennis Forcese (*Sociology*)
David Knight (*Geography*)
J. George Neuspiel (*Law*)
Thomas K. Rymes (*Economics*)
Derek G. Smith (*Anthropology*)
Michael S. Whittington (*Political Science*)

© *McClelland and Stewart Limited, 1975*

ALL RIGHTS RESERVED

0-7710-9784-0

The Canadian Publishers
McClelland and Stewart Limited
25 Hollinger Road, Toronto 374.

Printed and bound in Canada

Contents

Volume 2: Socialization, Social Stratification and Ethnicity

Preface

THE idea for this two-volume anthology arose directly from a research project which Elia Zureik, one of the editors, was undertaking into the nature of the basic value premises which underlie the structure and functioning of Canadian society. During the course of the project, it became evident that there was a very limited amount of published material concerned with the patterns and processes of socialization in Canada, although, on the other hand, there was a good deal of valuable but unpublished data on socialization available in the form of research papers, graduate dissertations and privately-circulated reports. Hence, it appeared to us to be a highly worthwhile task to bring together some of this unpublished material within the covers of a book (or more correctly, two books) which would focus around the interlinkage between socialization and certain major facets of Canadian society. In accordance with this goal, the first volume of this anthology is devoted to the theme of political socialization, and the second volume is centred around various aspects of the interrelationship between socialization and social stratification in the context of a society which is officially dedicated to the preservation of a mosaic of ethnic groups.

To be more specific, Volume One of the anthology includes papers in the following areas of study—the internalization of political norms, the role of textbooks as agents of political socialization, some aspects of an apparent alienation and radicalization amongst young people, perceptions of the political process and of the nation by the young and, finally, basic issues in research on political socialization. Volume Two includes studies of the learning of stratification norms and ideologies, of class and ethnic variations in value-orientations, of the impact of institutional change on young people's educational and occupational aspirations and, finally, of patterns of culture contact and cultural adaptation resulting from the influence of the majority society on various minority groups. All the empirical papers in both volumes cover patterns and processes of socialization occurring during the earlier years of the life-cycle, and in particular from the early school-going age groups to the college-going years. This focus on youth is deliberate for, although socialization is a continuing process which spans the entire life-cycle of the individual (and we certainly do not intend to deny the importance of adult socialization), we would like in this anthology to lay stress on the importance of early experiences in structuring subsequent attitudes and behaviour.

As will be apparent from our comments in the first paragraph above, one of the basic purposes of this anthology is to act as a vehicle for the dissemination of ideas and research findings pertaining to socialization in Canada which have not, up to this point in time, been available to a wide academic audience. Thus, nine of the ten papers contained in Volume One have not previously been published, while the remaining paper has been substantially revised by its contributor prior to republication. Again, of the eleven papers in Volume Two, none have previously been published. In addition, in the performance of our editorial task, we have found it desireable to precede the contents of each volume with a lengthy introduction and overview which is written by the editor whose research interests lie closest to the broad theme of that volume. It is hoped that these introductions will provide the reader with some insight into the various questions of a general theoretical or empirical nature which are raised through our contributors' papers, as well as underlining certain sub-themes which recur amidst the apparent diversity of subject matter in each volume. Needless to say, the editors accept joint responsibility for the selection and organization of all papers included in the anthology.

If one of our basic purposes in preparing this anthology has been to fill a gap in the published material pertaining to socialization in Canada, another has been to use our broad themes of political socialization and stratification/ethnicity as analytical frameworks within which to highlight certain major characteristics of Canadian value-systems and social structure. We would not claim that these characteristics are uniquely Canadian, in the sense that we could not find parallels in other countries; nonetheless, they point to a social cleavage perspective of Canadian society which, in our view, offers a far more meaningful interpretation of social realities in this country than would a perspective which views equilibrium and social consensus as the "normal" state of society. Thus, along with a number of other academic observers of the Canadian social scene, it would seem to us that the following characteristics are peculiarly relevant to an understanding of our history and of our present social condition:

1. A weak sense of national identity accompanied by a strong sense of regional identification. In the case of certain provinces and regions (for example, Quebec), the regional identification is interlinked with particular ethnic group loyalties.
2. A hierarchical social class structure which is associated with the existence of class-based inequalities in educational and occupational opportunities.
3. An ethnic stratification system based on familial, religious

and linguistic allegiances which is intertwined with existing class structure.
4. An official ideology which espouses the doctrine of cultural pluralism rather than assimilation.

The ways and means whereby young Canadians acquire certain images of, and orientations towards, their society and its institutions —including the norms, values and patterns of behaviour which under-lie the first three of the above salient characteristics of the society —form an important thematic feature of this anthology. The fourth characteristic—the ideology of cultural pluralism—is more rarely a topic of direct discussion by our contributors, but their research find-ings, where relevant, tend to throw some doubt on the widely-held view that Canada is much less assimilationist-oriented than the United States.

The above comments raise three further points relating to the orientation towards the study of socialization which is taken in this anthology. First of all, in line with a consensus conception of society, it is often the case that a discussion of socialization implies an emphasis on social control, conformity and the passing on of sanctioned values and norms. Although this is true of our conception of socialization to the extent that we are certainly interested in finding out *who* transmits *what* and to *whom*, and the circumstances under which such transmis-sion occurs—that is, with the agents of socialization, with the contents of what is learned, with those being socialized and, finally, with the "social setting" of socialization—the treatment of socialization in this anthology should, nevertheless, not be seen as limited to its more conservative "pattern maintenance" aspects. Hence, in looking at socialization we are concerned not only with the transmission and acquisition of values characteristic of the dominant groups in the society (which are generally accepted as the "societal values"), but also with the emergence of new sets of values which need not coincide with existing norms; and, perhaps most important, with the varying degrees to which the members of Canada's various ethnic minorities have been able to maintain, or make a functional adaptation, of tradi-tional values in the face of powerful pressures for assimilation to the so-called "Anglodominant" (or in the case of native peoples, Euro-Canadian) culture. Indeed, although a society presumably cannot sur-vive without a certain degree of agreement among its members as to the "rightness" of core societal goals and values, there is a recognition in this anthology that different social and ethnic groups may also adhere to their own value systems which will influence the behaviour of the members of these groups in particular institutional spheres.

Second, whilst we have suggested that a society requires a certain consensus on core values and goals if it is to survive, some of the papers contained in this anthology would seem to indicate that such a consensus is not achieved in Canadian society without substantial efforts being made by and through the major agencies of socialization to foster amongst the young an acceptance of the legitimacy of the existing social order. For example, whether it is the bland middle-class consensus view of Canadian society presented in many social studies textbooks, or the role which the school is seen to play in persuading Indian youth of the innate superiority of white culture, one is frequently confronted with a vision of the maintenance of consensus through coercion. By coercion we mean the utilization by dominant groups of manipulative socialization in order to foster an internalization of particular perceptions of social reality to the exclusion of alternative viewpoints. Such an approach to the analysis of the bases of social consensus in the society has, in our opinion, more in common with the sociology of Karl Marx than that of Talcott Parsons. As an important strand of thought in an anthology on socialization, it is unique enough to merit our special mention.

Finally, since continuity and change in the functions of a society's major social institutions can be regarded as having a major impact in the realm of social values, neither we nor our contributors have attributed a paramount importance to behavioural and motivational aspects of socialization at the expense of the institutional perspective. It is our hope, therefore, that those papers in this anthology which pursue an institutional approach, insofar as they examine the interlinkage between changes in the structure and role of institutions and changes in the value-orientations of the young, will succeed in showing the relevance of this approach to the study of socialization.

Having looked at the orientations to socialization taken in this anthology, we should now mention a few other considerations which lay behind our choice of papers and also (as is the obligation of all good editors) note some of the gaps and omissions in our offerings. First of all, as will be evident from our previous comments, the substantial emphasis which has been laid in English-Canadian and French-Canadian socialization studies on specific authority patterns within the family, and on child-rearing practices and the subsequent value-orientations of young people (see, for example Elkin, 1969: chap. 5 *passim*; Lambert, Yackley and Hein, 1971; Tremblay, 1973) is not very apparent in the contents of this anthology. This particular field of investigation appears to us to have been reasonably adequately dealt with in the Canadian sociological and psychological literature, and we have preferred, therefore, to complement studies in this field by looking rather at the ways in which young people's membership in certain wider social groups and categories come to affect their perceptions of the society, and of their social positions within it. We are not, of course, intending to depreciate thereby the profound importance of studies of family relationships and child-rearing practices for a better understanding of the socialization process. Second, it has been our aim to provide the reader with access to research findings drawn from studies undertaken in various parts of Canada, for it is our belief that "what is learned" in the process of socialization (and particularly in the area of politics) is hardly likely to be uniform across a country where regional loyalties run strong. Thirdly, we have been concerned to include studies which look at salient aspects of socialization occurring amongst the members of a variety of ethnic groups; a purpose which is in line with our interest in the maintenance or adaptation of traditional values in the face of pressures for assimilation. Fourthly, we have tried to answer the "who" part of the question "who transmits what and to whom?" by seeking out papers which look into the socialization impact of the major agencies of socialization which should ideally have included the aims of the mass media. Unfortunately, however, our pursuit of Canadian studies on the mass media was not as successful as we would have liked it to be, and consequently the absence of papers on the socialization impact of the media (unless we count books as "mass media") is, in our eyes, the most glaring gap in the anthology. We can only plead the absence of—or possibly our ignorance of—suitable or readily-available empirical research in this area during the period of time (1971-72) when we were soliciting papers for inclusion in the anthology. Similarly, the phenomenological and social linguistic studies which have recently assumed a place of particular importance in socialization research (see Dreitzel, 1973) are not represented amongst the papers, although issues arising from such studies are touched upon in the editor's introduction to the first volume.

In conclusion, we should note that our rationale for dividing this anthology into two volumes rests primarily on the substantial number, and relatively large average size, of the papers which it contains. On the other hand, our rationale for dividing the anthology into two relatively *self-contained* volumes, the contents of each of which are heralded both by this preface and a lengthy editor's introduction, rests primarily on our desire to facilitate the utilization of each volume by teachers and by students without the explicit need arising for reference to the contents of the others. We hold this purpose of allowing each volume to "stand by itself" as it were, to be a desirable one in the light of possible differences in the kinds of academic audience to which the major themes of each of the two volumes will appear. (Volume One is, for example, likely to have more appeal to political sociologists than Volume Two). On the other hand, we would certainly not wish thereby to play down what we see to be a very real degree of complementarity in the contents of the two volumes. Indeed, it is our hope that many readers will find it desirable to treat them as a "partnership."

Robert Pike
Elia Zureik
April, 1974

Bibliography

Dreitzel, H.P. *Childhood and Socialization* (New York: Macmillan, 1973).

Elkin, F. *The Family in Canada* (Ottawa: Vanier Institute of the Family, 1971).

Lambert, W.E., Yackley, A. and Hein, R. "Child Training Values of English Canadian and French Canadian Parents," *Canadian Journal of Behavioural Science*, Vol. 3, No. 3 (1971), p. 217-236.

Tremblay, Marc-Adelard. "Authority Models in the French Canadian Family," in G.L. Gold and M.A. Tremblay, *Communities and Culture in French Canada* (Toronto: Holt, Rinehart and Winston, 1973), p. 109-122.

Acknowledgements

THIS anthology was originally accepted for publication by a reputable Canadian publishing house in 1972. However, about a year after the initial acceptance, we were informed by the directors of the publishing house that an over-extension of its financial commitments necessitated a period of retrenchment; and that the anthology would regrettably be one of those publishing commitments which "could not be met in the foreseeable future" (a euphemistic phrase which meant, in actuality, that the anthology was being given the axe because it did not offer swift short-run profits). We were, therefore, left in a condition to which editors and authors appear to be peculiarly vulnerable—that is, being left high and dry with a copy-edited manuscript just a few months before the scheduled publication date. Thereafter, the reportedly depressed state of the academic book market (combined, it seems, with a certain unwillingness amongst book publishers in Canada to publish manuscripts containing material written in both official languages) hindered our efforts to attract another publisher for some months.

Given this unencouraging history, we are naturally grateful to the Carleton Library, and particularly to its sociology editor, Professor Dennis Forcese, for publishing the manuscript at a time when the springs of hope were beginning to run dry. However, we also recognise that there might have been no manuscript left for the Library to publish, if our contributors had not possessed the singular patience and fortitude which was required to remain faithful to what must often have seemed to them to be a totally lost cause. Hence, we wish to express our appreciation for the encouragement and support, both tacit and active, which we received from the contributors to this anthology. We fervently hope that none of them has ever to wait so long again for the publication of a paper.

Finally, we acknowledge a debt of gratitude to Marion Meyer of the Queen's Department of Sociology for her help in editing the French Language papers. Our wives, for their part, have succeeded in maintaining their sense of humour during a peculiarly difficult period.

Robert Pike
Elia Zureik

Kingston, May 1974.

Vol. 1

Political Socialization

Introduction
And Overview

Elia T. Zureik

Introduction

THE purpose of this overview is to sketch the main strands which best describe existing political socialization research and show how the collection of papers in this volume contribute to our understanding of one aspect of Canadian society, namely the acquisition of political values; we hope that the contributions in this volume provide useful grounds for testing cross-culturally some of the ideas encountered in political socialization research, but which have been developed in other political settings.

Although there are numerous claims suggesting that early political learning plays a significant role in structuring subsequent political attitudes, the discussion of key issues in my other contribution to this volume should make it apparent that it is still not clear what the precise nature of this learning process is, and what bearing early socialization has upon later attitudes and behaviour. Yet, students of politics have found it essential to consider in some detail the nature of the political learning process and, in particular, how young people orient themselves to legitimating political symbols, both personal and institutional. For example, Max Weber's (1957) discussion of charisma and later David Easton's (1965) notion of personal legitimacy provide two similar ideas related to political identification as a source of political legitimacy. In Easton's words:

> But regardless of the direction of affect, I am proposing that the child in any stable system may find a focus in some prominent or central figure of authority—and the feeling so generated with regard to this personal embodiment of authority may be subtly transferred to other institutions of political authority. We would not expect that this is the only mechanism at work in forming the bonds between children and their political norms and structures . . . But we can discern in this process a possible source for

nurturing sentiments of legitimacy in children, viewed as members of a system.[1]

While it is true that a great deal of political socialization research has concerned itself with legitimacy, i.e. how young people learn to support dominant norms in society, our perspective on political socialization is rather more encompassing. We view political socialization in terms of acquisition as well as rejection of established political norms.

Approaches

Approaches to the study of early political attitudes have been eclectic in nature, drawing on various behavioural disciplines. Merelman's (1970) characterization of the dominant approaches in political socialization research is stated in the following words:

> One group, whom I call developmentalists, believes there is an enduring link between the psychology of child development political socialization, and adult political orientations. A second group, intermediate in character, is composed of environmentalists, who feel that political orientations are largely the product of social stimuli which act forcefully on the psychological processes of development. . . . Finally, a third group believes that political socialization is primarily autonomous, dependent principally upon experience with the political system rather than upon psychological forces or social stimuli. This latter group, which believes the gap between political socialization and developmental psychology unbridgeable and unimportant in any case, we call autonomists.[2]

It is clear from the above quotation, which is an accurate portrayal of most American approaches to political socialization research, that there is little room for considering the relevance of the socio-historical perspective, a point on which I elaborated in another contribution to this volume. In the light of this, we have chosen to work within the following three main groupings: the psychological, social and autonomous approaches. They correspond in a rough way to Merelman's typologies, except that in our case the social refers to both the environmental and historical correlates of political attitudes.

Autonomous Approach

As Merelman sees it, the autonomous approach has its origins in the Eastonian framework of systems analysis. Because of the prominence of systems analysis in current political socialization research, we find it essential to delineate the main features of this approach.

In an attempt to formulate a "political theory of political socialization," Easton and Dennis (1969) view political socialization in terms of two basic models of politics: the allocative model and that of systems persistence. The former addresses itself to the problem of political allocations and the processes by which binding decisions are reached in the polity. The allocative model seeks to explain how the citizen relates to the outputs of the political system and how he develops his orientations to central issues facing him. Most of contemporary political socialization research could be classified as falling within the systems persistence domain. We know more about the means by which support is generated toward the various levels of the political system than we know about how young people develop, or fail to develop, an awareness of, and involvement with, specific policy outcomes and issues in society.

Basically, what is involved in the systems persistence model is an assessment of how support, both diffuse and specific, is generated toward the three levels of the political system: the political community, the regime and authorities. Political socialization thus becomes the basis of support directed toward the three levels of the political system. Writing with Dennis, Easton reiterates his earlier definition of the political community as "that aspect of a political system which . . . can [be] identified as a collection of persons who share a division of political labour."[3] Patriotism, national identification and belief in the right of every citizen to partake in the political life of a country are examples of support at the political community level. "The regime describes that part of the political system that we may call its constitutional order in the very broadest sense of the word."[4] In this respect, the regime refers to the norms of political participation, the values which govern the activities of members of the political community and the structure of authority roles. In terms of operational concepts, the regime covers the sense of political efficacy (norms), moral premises of society (values) and the scope of authoritative roles (structure of authority). Finally, "the authorities are those members in whom the primary responsibility is lodged for taking care of the daily routine of a political system."[5] The emphasis in this type of support is on the incumbent of a role and not on the role itself. Occupants of authoritative roles include elected representatives, members of the bureaucratic apparatus and other key political figures. These types of political support are interrelated as Muller (1970) finds in his study of American students. His relevant finding is that personal legitimacy counts as the most important source of effective support provided by favourable intentions to the regime.

According to Easton and Hess (1961), a political system is likely to persist and absorb changes in its structure if cleavages and dissensus are first directed toward the authority level, thus causing minimum stress to either the regime or the community. Considering identification with partisan leaders to be one feature of authority level support, Easton and Hess offer the following explanation for their previous claim:

> Change of party identification is morally acceptable, if not desirable from time to time. But with regard to regime and community, not only are members reluctant to tolerate moral alternatives, but the whole weight of the practical democratic ethic puts beyond doubt the pale of respectability, even the discussion of the desirability of a radical change.[6]

From this they go on to distinguish between the extent of attachment at the community and the authority levels of the political system:

> For these reasons we might certainly be justified in expecting the research would reveal that orientations at the community level are much more deeply seated and therefore less easily displaced, than those at the authority level.[7]

While it is true that loyalty to country and adherence to basic political norms are more deeply rooted than identification with partisan authority figures, it is apparent from the research carried out— subsequent to the time that Easton and Hess made the above remarks—that identifications with political personalities, as well as political parties, also manifest themselves early in life. To begin with, the child forms an affective attachment to salient political symbols such as political leaders, to be followed later on with the articulation of orientations to regime and community levels. But, as we shall note later on in this paper, what is significant about this early affective orientation is that it could shape later cognitive attitudes.

If valid, this observation is particularly pertinent to the Canadian case since the results of more than one study point to the existence of cleavages at the regime and community levels of the political system. Reilly (1971) in his study of law students at McGill University found that Anglophones were likely to orient themselves to the federal level of government whilst Francophones identified to a larger extent with the provincial level of government. Indeed, in Reilly's study, close to two-thirds of the Francophones endorsed the idea of an independent Quebec whilst the corresponding proportion amongst the Anglophones was nil. This can be contrasted with Rioux's (not dated) study of Quebec 18-21 year-olds carried out in 1964, which found that only 14 per cent favoured separatism and 20 per cent endorsed economic independence of Quebec (although 55 per cent thought that Quebec would eventually separate from the federal system). The shift in political attitudes of young Quebecois towards espousal of separatism is apparent, and we find further confirmation to this is Lamy's* study conducted in 1968. In contrasting the political attitudes of French- to English-Canadians, Lamy discovers a strong sense of regionalism and marked sympathy with separatist movements among the Francophone group, while the Anglophones showed a positive orientation to the federal level of government. It must be emphasized, however, that this sense of regionalism is not confined to French Canada. Skogstad's* study of Alberta youth revealed a sense of western regionalism as well.

It should be stated that there are obvious shortcomings to the "political system" concept, in spite of its operational utility. This is not the place to go into a detailed assessment of the above approach; suffice it to state here two main reservations. The first centers on what is meant by political. In the Eastonian scheme it is clearly stated, for the political system is that which is concerned with the authoritative allocation of "valued things" by means of societally binding decisions. Moreover, the political is distinguished from the so-called non-political, the economic for example. In our view, both of these assumptions are limiting. For us, the political implies more than that which is associated with the formal outputs of the political system. We are also concerned with those processes which act to legitimate the dominant ideologies, but which are not, on the face of it, formally linked to political system outputs. This perspective necessarily leads us to view political socialization as a process of system legitimation whereby individuals are assigned differential access to power resources in society. Overall, we are in agreement with Miliband (1969) who takes to task the systems analysis approach to political life for its failure to deal with power. Indeed Miliband quotes Easton as saying that "neither the state nor power is a concept that serves to bring together political research."[8] Cohen's* definition of what is political is wider in scope and is in line with ours, for he says: "I propose to regard activity as political which relates to attempts to create, maintain or change systems of unequally distributed valued social resources."[9]

Our other objection to the Eastonian framework is also related to its formalistic treatment of political decision-making:

*Papers included in this volume will be referred to with an asterisk.

When they appear as statements, authoritative allocation [of values] take the form of verbal indications of the binding rules that are to guide the performance of tasks. They are decisions on the part of the authorities that certain actions should be or will be taken. In a legal system, they appear as laws, decrees, formal legislation, regulations, or administrative and judicial decision. In non-legal systems, they may simply be the opinion of a council of elders or of a paramount chief, about what ought to be done under the circumstances. But whatever the specific form, they stand on authoritative outputs since they indicate that activities will be undertaken to maintain or modify the distribution of some valued things in society.[10]

Where we depart fundamentally from Easton's framework is in the labelling of those acts which either legally or non-legally are defined in the public eye by means of legitimating ideologies as decisions, thus ignoring what Bachrach and Baratz call "non-decisions." The latter are acts which are not undertaken by the authorities for fear of undermining their legitimacy. Thus, in this sense non-decisions *are* decisions.

More recently, attempts have been undertaken to incorporate in a more direct fashion the reciprocal effect the political system has upon learning of political norms. A starting point would be Abramson's (1972) notion of "political reality" which we discuss in our other contribution to this volume. Instead of viewing the emergence of political attitudes in the context of socialization experiences and psychological make-up of the individual, this approach looks at political attitudes in terms of the *experience* and *image* young people have of their political environment.

Focussing on political efficacy and participation as areas of political behaviour which are most likely to be affected by the actual structure of the political environment, Form and Huber (1971), working with an adult sample, confirmed the existence of a relationship between a low level of political efficacy and a corresponding belief among their poor black respondents that the political system is basically inegalitarian and dominated by power elites. "Thus, for the blacks, feelings of political efficacy result from a realistic appraisal of how the political system works."[11]

Weissberg's (1970) study of adolescent experience with policemen is an attempt to assess the reciprocal effect which the political system has on the attitudes of American youth. His findings show that a positive evaluation of the police is accompanied by a supportive attitude. Yet Rodgers and Taylor (in Nimmo and Bonjean, 1972) revealed that although black youngsters distrusted policemen, this distrust was not generalized to other political authority figures. Upon examining public opinion data for both adults and school children, Abramson (1972) noted a rise in the level of distrust between the period 1966 to 1970, thus attributing this decline in support to changes in the political environment during this period. Furthermore, he noted an interesting relationship between political knowledge and the sense of political efficacy; for the blacks, an *increase* in political knowledge implied an awareness of the shortcomings of the political system in terms of an incongruency between expectations and the actual political reality.

Psychological Approach

Hess and Torney (1967), two leading exponents of the psychological approach to political socialization research, offer four models to explain the processes by which political learning takes place. They refer to the accumulation, interpersonal-transfer, identification and cognitive developmental models. We shall utilize these models as the bases for our elaboration on the relevance of the psychological approach to political learning.

Briefly, the accumulation model deals with direct learning whereby the child acquires information in an additive fashion irrespective of the logical relationship among the information acquired and how the absorption of this information is contingent on the personality make-up of the child. A characteristic feature of this type of knowledge is that it is devoid of any critical or evaluational thought. Political concepts are assimilated on the basis of their face-value. And what is more significant about this learning process is that it is likely to persist through the adolescent years. Remmers (1963) in his study of tolerance among young Americans found that while the majority of these adolescents are capable of regurgitating the Bill of Rights, thus demonstrating that they have at least succeeded in "accumulating" political knowledge, few would be prepared to extend the meaning of the Bill of Rights to specific minority or political groups. Merelman's (1972) more recent findings on American high school students provide partial support of Remmer's (1963) results. Merelman finds that although with age there is an increase in the appreciation of freedom of speech as a democratic principle, this is true "when these rights are stated in the abstract." Zellman and Sears (1971) go one step further by documenting the presence of similar attitudes among both adults and adolescents. Consider the following conclusion from their study on tolerance of dissent where the generational similarity is highlighted:

The combination of widespread support for the abstract principle of free speech, alongside opposition to its extension to concrete situations, is a crucial characteristic of both children's and adult's opinion. Our data indicate further that it holds as a dominant pattern at both the aggregate and individual level of analysis.[12]

The conclusion to be drawn so far is that there are limitations to the psychological approach as a whole (a point to which we shall return later on), for in this instance it is difficult to explain the absence of generalized and evaluational thought among adults on the basis of developmental factors alone. It is essential to view the learning of political concepts in terms of their content and how this relates to the dominant ideologies and the social climate of the time. It is quite unrealistic to expect the prevalence of tolerance on a generalized basis extending to each and every specific group in society if such a mode of thinking is not part of the ethos of that society to begin with.

Moving to the interpersonal-transfer model, here the child generalizes his experiences with immediate authority figures, parents for example, to relate to remote political authority. The logic behind this approach is expounded by two social learning theorists: "Learned patterns of response tend to generalize to situations other than those in which they were learned, the extent of generalization being a function of the degree of similarity . . ."[13]

A fairly recent and vigorous attempt to put to test the transference hypothesis is the one reported by Abramson and Inglehart (1968). The main theme of their argument runs as follows: children usually tend to idealise their parents although such an idealisation declines with age. The early parental idealisation is later transferred onto heads of state. It reaches the point of personal identification when there is a congruency between the two types of roles as perceived by the child. For this reason, leaders who are associated with "political" or "bureaucratic conflicts" do not arouse affective orientation generally attributed to familial authority figures. It therefore follows that in comparing monarchical to republican systems "a stronger idealisation of hereditary monarchs than of non-partisan but elected chiefs of state, and a stronger idealization of the chief of state than partisan politicians will ensue."[14] When applied to the U.S., the Netherlands and France, it is noted that there is a positive correlation between indices of parental trust and positive perception of political leaders.

In spite of the above systematic treatment of the transference hypothesis, Froman (1962) argues that such an analysis obscures the influence of other socialization agencies and does not account fully for the process by which attitudes are assimilated and how these various attitudinal dimensions are linked to each other.

Jaros and his colleagues (1968) isolate an additional factor which further underlines the shortcoming of the transference hypothesis. They find no confirmation to the authority hypothesis among Appalachian children in the U.S., and that there is no significant correlation between the child's trust in familial authority and his reaction to political authority figures. Moreover, they find, contrary to previous evidence (Greenstein, 1965; Hess and Torney, 1967), that these poor, white children from the southern U.S. manifested a "malevolent," rather than the well-known benevolent, image of the President. Recent studies of political attitudes of black children have further substantiated the serious limitations of the benevolent-image hypothesis. (Orum and Cohen, 1973; Green, 1972; Greenberg, 1970). Interestingly enough, in a study by Tolley (1972) of American children's attitudes to the Vietnam war, both black and white children are distrustful of President Nixon, with distrust increasing with age. Among black children this distrust extends to 77 per cent of this group, compared to 55 per cent among white children.

How does the Canadian evidence compare to the American? A study of British Columbia children carried out by this author (1971) showed the British Columbia children adhering to a benevolent image of Prime Minister Lester Pearson. It is difficult to generalize from this particular finding to the perceptions of Canadian children as a whole. Although Rush's (1972) and Cohen's* findings do not specifically deal with perception of key political leaders in Canada, they nevertheless demonstrate disaffection from political leadership in at least two specific settings, the former in British Columbia and the latter in Newfoundland.

The discussion so far should make it apparent that although the child's initial attachment to the political system is facilitated through identification with personal political symbols, it is not exactly clear how the various background factors contribute to this identification and the extent to which such a process reflects a benevolent image of leaders. It could well be that in addition to the mediating psychological and social factors, the political structure itself and the young person's experience with it are equally relevant factors. We dealt with these points earlier on in our discussion of the autonomous model.

Imitation, the third type of learning singled out by Hess and Torney, focusses on emulation by the child of those significant others around him. Again, it is not clear from the literature how the actual modelling is accomplished. Does learning take place in a "behavioural" or "observational" context? Modelling through behavioural imitation implies that "the copier must slowly bring his response to approximate that of a model and must know he has done so, that is his act is an acceptable reproduction of the model act."[15]

But Danziger (1971) points out, and rightly so, that it is probably the latter type of social learning which is supported by empirical findings:

> There is overwhelming evidence that children learn complex acts through cognitive processes based on observation rather than being trained by external reinforcements administered by either parent.[16]

Danziger bases his conclusions on Bandura's work in which he adopts a rational conception of man. In the latter's view observational learning is "highly prevalent among homosapiens, exceedingly efficient and, in cases where errors are dangerous or costly, becomes an indispensible means of transmitting and modifying behavioural repertoire."[17] The relevance of this type of learning for political socialization is quite obvious. Very few young people engage in either political or even quasi-political activity. Some of these, however, imitate the behaviour of their parents, especially when it comes to party identification.

But before we proceed to demonstrate the applicability of this model to specific political situations, it is worthwhile referring in brief to the ideological premises underlying the stimulus-response model which is really the basis of all learning theories. Implied in Bandura's statement above is a utilitarian conception of man which in turn assumes a voluntaristic theory of action. The latter implies that people's values and behaviour are to a large extent free from coercion and all that is needed is to seize upon available information and utilize it to maximize their gain and minimize their loss. Like the theory of free-market competition, here too the existence of monopoly over the acquisition and dissimination of information is overlooked. It is thus imperative to view the stimulus-response model in the context of certain constraints, the most important of which centres around the notion of manipulative socialization which we discuss elsewhere in this volume, and the relationships between the individual's experience in social structure and the range of stimuli available to him.

The above is not intended to minimize the importance of this learning model to our understanding of social behaviour, yet, placing the emphasis on rational behaviour obscures the importance of inciden-tal form of learning. According to Wilson (1970), what distinguishes the imitation model is that "A major aspect of this stimulus association is a rather unconscious modelling of behaviour after some other indi-vidual. Often, of course, this model is one with whom the child has established a relationship, but very complex patterns of behaviour can also be developed by emulating a model with ahom no prior relation-ship has been established."[18]

The significance of this learning process is apparent in studies of prejudice formation and party identification. Bearing in mind that up to the age of seven or eight the child internalizes the moral codes of the significant others around him, such as his parents, Tajfel (1969) points out that during this stage "the value pronouncements are judged by the source rather than by their content."[19] From the point of view of developing democratic values and moral principles, it is important that in going through this stage the child be exposed to different sources of information, or "significant others" so to speak, in order to facilitate the development of critical moral judgements.

Likewise, students of politics have singled out the mediating influence of parental role-modelling in facilitating for identification with political parties at an early age. We are not implying that this identification is either stable across the life span or that the process of transmission of party identification from parents to children is achieved with one-to-one correspondence, a point which I elaborated upon elsewhere.* What is significant about this process is that the initial attachment to political parties is achieved on the basis of affective and not cognitive knowledge (Hyman, 1964; Greenstein, 1965). In comparing the political socialization experiences of Canadian and American party activists, Kornberg, Smith and Bromby (1969) noted similar patterns, that is, that many American party activists and some Canadians identified with a party before becoming politically aware.

The underlying assumptions of the cognitive developmental model, the last to be dealt with within the context of the psychological approach, are to be found in Piaget's (1968) writings on intellectual and moral development of the child. Basically, Piaget argues that there is a universal sequence in the development of the child's thought processes and that this sequence is best understood in terms of age progression. Thus, the child progresses from learning social codes devoid of any sense of obligation, to a recognition of adult constraints manifesting itself in a unilateral acceptance of rules and obligations, to a stage where the child's moral judgement is no longer a mere reflection of adult authority, rather it is dictated by expectations of reciprocity.

Such a conception of the thinking process has implications for emergence of political thought and how the child relates to the world of politics. Adelson and O'Neil (1966), drawing on Piaget's framework, note in their study of American adolescents that it is not until the age of 13 that the adolescent begins "to transcend personalized modes of discourse" by exhibiting a greater subjective involvement with non-personal social issues which eventually leads him to develop a communal view of society. By the time the young person reaches the age of 15, he should have managed to comprehend abstract political notions and is able to deduce particular information from generalized principles. The *rate* of political development, however, is a function of the child's level of intelligence as well as his social background (White, 1968), though it is extremely difficult to disentangle the interrelations among these two factors (see Jackman, 1970).

Investigation by this author (1970) of the moral judgement of a sample of British Columbia children concerning the Vietnam war has revealed that maturity, high level of intelligence and middle-class background are associated with an anti-establishment view of the war. Children with those characteristics tended to blame the U.S. and South Vietnam for the war more so than children in the rest of the sample.

Tolley's (1972) results based on a sample of American children add further evidence bearing upon the relationship between moral judgement and background variables. Children attending Friends schools come out the least accepting of the Vietnam war compared to children attending public and parochial schools. When considering race as a variable, "poor blacks express less support for wars in defence of American freedom or against communism than lower and middle income whites."[20]

A more refined developmental model which has been tested cross-culturally and applied to concrete social situations is the one developed by Kohlberg and Tapp, (1971). According to Kohlberg, there are three main levels of cognitive development associated with moral maturity: a) preconventional level, b) conventional level, and c) post-conventional level. The preconventional level has two stages to it, one of which explains obligation to moral codes in terms of deference to power based on sheer physical punishment, while the second state explains the child's actions in terms of personal utilitarianism, i.e. that actions are carried out to satisfy the personal needs of the child. There is resemblance between this conception and that depicted in Piaget's early stage of moral development. Both seem to single out the relevance of egocentrism of the child to internalization of moral codes. Moving to the second level of Kohlberg's scheme, it is typified by adherence to fixed authority rules and conformity to external norms. Out of the second stage, the child begins to develop "autonomous moral principles." The ability to think causally and inductively are at the core of the postconventional level. It is here that the young person, though guided by utilitarian behaviour, begins to take cognizance of social constraints and realize the consequences his actions might have for the rest of society. A final important feature of this last level of moral development is the emergence of ethical considerations in which the child's decision of right and wrong is based on "logical comprehensiveness, universality and consistency."

In testing this model, Kohlberg and Tapp (1971) verified the presence of the above developmental sequence. Working with American data in which the sample covered a wide age range, from the kindergarten to the college years, it was discovered that while postconventional reasoning was almost non-existent in the primary school sample, it was characteristic of the mode of reasoning of the college sample. With slight variations this pattern held cross-culturally. (See also Gallatin and Adelson, 1971)

The process of cognitive maturity has also been extended to account for the child's transition from a personal to an impersonal form of identification with the political system. Easton and Dennis' conclusions, which highlight this point, are typical of other findings on political identification of American children. They state:

> As he passes through grades 2 to 8, the child begins with a rudimentary notion of government, represented by a few high ranking and visible leaders. But as he grows older, the child sees government in less personal terms. He becomes increasingly aware of its group character and its major institutions; he learns something about the norms (for example, voting) of a representative government and popular democracy.[21]

The situation with respect to Canada is not all that clear cut. A study of British Columbia children by this author (1971) using identical items to those used by Easton and Dennis detected a similar pattern. Pammett's (1971) results based on an Ontario sample portray a contrasting picture:

> American studies report that political knowledge is personalized at young ages and that it tends to form around some strong figure seen as the epitome of the political process. In contrast, a striking fact that emerges from this study is that Canadian children's knowledge of some of the *institutions* of government is as high as that about the more personalized roles in government.[22]

Lamy's* findings support those reached by Pammett. Yet, it must be stressed that Johnston's (1969) study of national sample of young Canadians supports the original premise concerning the priority of affective political knowledge. It could very well be that the differences in results are due to regional variations and that the geopolitical proximity of the Ontario samples in both Pammett's and Lamy's surveys might have accounted for the results delineated above.

An important feature of the development of political thought is the relationship between cognitive and affective orientations. Jennings (1967), in a study of American high school students, found that a greater level of factual knowledge about the international system is accompanied with a high level of interest in international organizations such as the U.N. Another group of researchers (Johnson, Middleton and Tajfel, 1970) have underscored the importance of affect in terms of structuring the content of cognition. Working with an adolescent English sample, the above authors show how factual knowledge about other nations was conditioned by favourable or unfavourable attitudes to the nations in question. Tolley's (1972) study to which we referred earlier also documents the emergence of the affective dimension of attitudes towards the Vietnam war prior to the crystallization of cognitive ones. For example, although few of Tolley's sample possessed factual knowledge about the war, a large proportion of the sample expressed an affective attitude toward it.

Although Kohlberg and Piaget allude to the relevance of environmental factors to moral judgement, the stress in both schemes is on the independent development of structures of thought. It is important to bear in mind that culture, social class and specially schooling have an important bearing on the rate in which the various stages of thought develop. Ehly's* paper highlights the interrelationship between socio-cultural factors and moral thinking (see also Jahoda, 1963). A group of Canadian researchers (Beck, Sullivan and Taylor, 1972) have shown how the transition from one stage of moral development to the next is facilitated by the teaching method and the content of what is being taught (See also Bidwell, 1972). With a similar shortcoming in mind, Merelman (1972) remarks that "the theory of cognitive development does not take into account the motivational aspect of political socialization." This observation is supported by a recent study of Canadian children. Schleifer and Douglas (1973) find that the development of the moral judgement of the child is more a function of his emotional maturity than it is of his level of intelligence.

Social Approach

A great deal of research has dwelt on the differences between working and middle-class cultures. Writing about Britain, Klein (1965) presents an adequate summary of both class cultures in terms of two major dimensions of socialization, "impulse following/impulse renouncing" and "arbitrary learning/problem solving." The first dimension has to do with choosing a "less valuable goal whose impact is heightened by the immediacy or obviousness and intrinsically more valuable goal whose psychological attractiveness is reduced by remoteness and obscurity."[23] The second dimension refers to learning based on rigid presentation of codes of behaviour in contrast to socialization into norms that are adequately explained. In the words of Klein, this has a long-term effect:

> We may argue that an arbitrary type of child-rearing tends to produce one of the characteristics of many traditional societies, cognitive poverty. One may say with equal justification that this type of socialization is likely to make for an adult personality which is heavily dependent on group tradition.[24]

Referring to the relationship between these forms of socialization and social class, Klein points out that in contrast to the middle-, the working-class child is socialized into norms which stress impulse following and arbitrary type of learning (see also Dervin *et al*. 1970).

Extending a similar type of reasoning to politics, Hess and Torney argue that because of the abstract nature of politics, middle-class children are likely to develop faster than their working-class counterparts. The explanation they advocate below is similar to that advanced by Klein above:

> Working-class children also personalized their view of the government. The social class difference may follow from the tendency of working-class parents to emphasize rules and the enforcement of rules rather than offering rationale which are more impersonal and abstract guides for behaviour.[25]

Greenstein (1965) has also noted that once the class-based contrast in political development crystallizes, it takes longer for a working- than for a middle-class child to shed his unrealistic image of politics.

Considering the joint effects of age and social class upon the rate of political development, Easton and Dennis (1969) postulate three possibilities. First, it is possible that differences which appear early —and which show the child from higher socio-economic status to be well ahead in his political development compared to the lower socio-economic child—will persist into later life. Second, it is likely that differences in the rate of political development will narrow down with maturity. And third, if the class cleavages are deep rooted, it is likely that early differences in political development might persist and increase as the child proceeds through life.

However, Easton and Dennis remark that regardless of which of the above processes takes place, some lasting effects on political development are likely to be felt.

1. The higher status child will have learned his lessons earlier,

and thus such lessons may well have taken root more firmly.
2. If the lag for the lower-status child postpones some political learning beyond the most plastic period of childhood,
many political orientations may be unlikely to strike deep
roots.[26]

The social class lag theory as applied to political development is
not supported by Percheron's French study (1972). On the contrary, she discovers that in a politicized culture working-class children
develop their political orientations earlier than middle-class children.
And with respect to Britain, one cannot help but agree with Hoggart's
(1969) impressionistic treatment of the two social class perspectives to
politics in which he differentiates between personal and concrete values, on the one hand, and abstract values on the other. The first typifies
the working class and the second the middle class. Hoggart singles out
Royalty as that aspect of political life which appeals to the working
class because it can be easily translated into personal and concrete
terms.

An equally relevant factor which separates the working-class child
from the world of politics is his socio-linguistic experience. Relying on
Bernstein's (1972) ideas concerning the social class bases of linguistic
and communicative development, it would be surprising indeed to find
the working-class child, who possesses a restricted and public code,
capable of relating and decoding the elaborate, formal language of
politics, which is shaped by the experience of the middle class.

Heeding Bernstein's findings, Enstwistle (1971) warns of the
likely failure of the schools' role in attempting to rectify the lack of
political information among young people:

Bernstein, for example, has popularized the notion that children
from lower working class environment may speak a language
whose syntax is quite different from that normally required by the
traditional school. In the same way, those who argue the greater
efficacy of political socialization over deliberate attempts to provide political education are making the useful point that children
often learn from their social environment a language of politics
which differs from the rational and academic discourse of political
theorists.[27]

What is implied in the above discussion on values-cum-politics is
that the working-class child is surrounded by a culture and value system
which make it difficult for him to develop the skill needed to engage in
political participation. Thus, the onus in this type of argument is put on
the individual, who, in this instance, has failed to adapt to the dominant

styles of political thought. This line of argument is reminiscent of the ''culture of poverty'' debate in which it is upheld that the poor individual is basically trapped into a way of thinking and style of life which make it impossible for him to transcend the vicious circle of poverty. Again, the stress here is on the subjective, motivational level (values, norms, etc.) of the individual actor and not on the objective economic conditions which are conducive to conditions of poverty (see Hofley, 1971). With respect to political behaviour, it is worthwhile quoting Form and Huber (1971) who express succinctly the point we raised:

> Likewise, the assumption that psychological attitudes, such as a sense of efficacy and citizen duty, explain why people participate politically involves a bias in favour of existing conditions because people are thought to be ''free'' to act as they choose. This assumption is similar to that mode in classical economics, where a man was ''free'' to garner whatever rewards he could garner, and if he failed, it was clearly his own fault. That assumption is no longer popular among social scientists, but the attempt to explain political behaviour in terms of individual motivation is logically similar and, so far as we can ascertain, still fairly popular.[28]

It is interesting to note the nature and prevalence of ''value'' analysis in Canadian sociological writings. Consider the contribution of Richer and Laporte (1971) in discussing the cultural and cognitive bases differentiating between the English and French-Canadians in terms of competitive behaviour. It is more or less a repetition of an earlier works by Rosen (1959) and Strodbeck (1959) regarding the relationship between achievement orientations and ethnicity.

Richer and Laporte argue that in contrast to the English-Canadians who are urbanized, have an egalitarian family structure, endorse the protestant ethic and are future oriented, the French-Canadians are portrayed as past oriented, collectivists, dominated by religious ideology and lacking the protestant ethic. No attempt is made by these authors to link the mode of thinking and aspirations of each group (specially with respect to competition, the authors' area of concern) to the actual position of that group in society in terms of inter-group power relations (see Milner and Milner, 1973). Lambert (1970) gives a more direct expression to the role of early socialization in structuring achievement levels: ''The contrast in socialization values of French-Canadian and English-Canadian parents . . . suggest that the French-Canadian pattern of family interaction may contribute both to relatively low achievement needs, and in turn, to unrealistic expectations.''[29]

We are not arguing here that the study of values is unimportant. What we are saying is that it is equally important to investigate the institutional mechanisms which give rise to and sustain these values.

Of the various socialization agencies, the school and mass media are central in terms of their legitimating roles. While the research regarding the former is substantial, the latter is barely researched from the point of view of assessing its impact on political attitudes of young people. This is particularly important if one singles out the place of television in the life of the young. As early as pre-school years, ages 3 to 5, children spend a total of 64 per cent of their waking time viewing television (Caron, 1971). Another survey of fourth and fifth graders in the U.S. showed that lower-class children spend between 6 to 7 hours per day watching television, compared to upper-class children whose viewing time ranges from 4 to 5 hours per day (Greenberg, 1970). The same study showed that when asked to identify with a person whom they have seen on television, and with whom they would want to be like, every white child identified with a white, and 31 per cent of the black children also chose a white person.

Summarising the findings of another study, Greenberg (1970) describes the powerful influence of television on lower-class children this way:

> Use of television as a means of finding out what life is about was a more important function among the lower-class respondents than among those in the middle class. This was even more true for the black teen-agers than the white lower-income teens.[30]

The reality confirming function of television is also apparent in the study of the impact of advertising on children. Caron's (1971) review of the literature showed how at a younger age children have difficulty in distinguishing reality from fiction when viewing commercials, although their sense of discrimination increased with age. In one of the few studies assessing the impact of the mass media on political attitudes of children, Chaffee and his colleagues (1970) comment that as far as political knowledge is concerned the mass media has an influence; this is not the case with respect to overt political behavior. Tolley's (1973) study to which we referred earlier documents the differentiated impact television has on the attitudes of American children to the Vietnam war by showing that viewers who exhibited a higher level of political knowledge tended to endorse the Vietnam war more so than non-viewers. Hartman and Husband's (1974) study of the impact of British television on racial attitudes of young Englishmen reveals a limited effect on the development of prejudice when compared to situational and experience-related factors.

Turning to the influence of school, the literature is more voluminous on the subject, though less consistent. Hess and Torney's (1967) claim that in the United States the public school is the most important politicizing agency has been seriously questioned by Sears (1968) on methodological grounds; likewise, the assumption put forward by Dreeben (1968) that the school is the main agency responsible for inculcating universalistic norms has been challenged by Davis.* His study of a sample of British Columbia children residing in a remote area of the province revealed that in this instance it is the home, and not the school, which is responsible for transmitting universalistic norms.

The school has also been viewed as a training ground for participatory norms. However, Ziblatt's (1965) and Merelman's (1971) studies failed to confirm a positive relationship between participation in extra-curricular activities within the school system and specific political attitudes.

Empirical works from the United States, England and Canada demonstrate clearly the legitimating role of the schools. Edgar Litt (1963), in an analysis of civic education programs in the United States, found that a form of platonic code was in operation in American schools. That is to say, it was only in the upper-class schools that children were encouraged to take an active role in politics. In lower-strata schools, the teachers were more concerned with encouraging the children to be passive citizens. A pilot study by this author of teachers' attitudes in England towards political education produced not too dissimilar results. Only nine per cent of the teacher sample were in favour of encouraging children to take an active role in politics and only 35 per cent favoured teaching children that the political system is not permanent and immutable but can be changed by them if they wish it. In a separate English study, Lister (1969) found that even among the cream of secondary students in Britain quite a few had insufficient factual knowledge regarding key political concepts.

With respect to Canada, Hodgetts' (1968) nation-wide study of history education depicted the apolitical image young Canadians have of their country. Attachment to Canada is defined in terms of the physical attributes of the country, and not necessarily in terms of its political institutions. This emphasis on the landscape is, as we point out later on, not unique to writings directed to the young.

Another aspect of the interpretation of Canadian society, according to Hodgetts, is that "the content of Canadian history courses is [marked] by the total absence of any conflicting or controversial material."[31] In this respect, Hodgetts is concurring with Pratt's* conclusions. Whenever conflicting views appear they are associated with the two different interpretations of Canadian history, the French- and English-Canadian versions. (See also Trudel and Jain, 1970)

A more recent study by Stager and Sullivan (1970) portrays a different picture concerning the image young Canadians have of their society. Working with a significantly smaller regional sample than that used by Hodgetts, the above authors discovered a greater sense of national identity, loyalty and awareness of Canada's problems among the youth in their sample. The contrast between the two findings could be explained in terms of the timing of the surveys. The latter survey was carried out at a time when the issue of history teaching was debated, presumably as a result of Hodgetts' findings. It would be interesting to find out if the findings f Stager and Sullivan are typical of Canadian children as a whole and whether or not these feelings have lasting effects.

It must be stated, however, that the "bland consensus" version of Canadian history which emerged from the studies by Pratt and Hodgetts is not all that inconsistent with the conventional interpretation by Canadian historians of Canada's history, as well as the novelist's portrayal of Canadian social values. Mealing's (1965) discussion of the "absence of social class as a concept" in the works of Canadian historians is in line with McDougall's (in Mandel, 1971) assertion that social class does not play a significant role in Canadian fiction. But as Careless (1969) notes social class awareness is constrained by regional identification. "At any rate," he says, "industrialism and urbanism have not yet here created strong national awareness of common class interests. Socio-economic strains have tended to be expressed in largely regional terms, or at most in non-enduring regional alliances of disadvantaged elements."[32] Regionalism is not the only factor which has inhibited a generalized expression of class feelings. Preoccupation with the land and environment has been a dominant theme in Canadian fiction. It is no accident, for example, that Atwood's (1972) recent thematic treatment of Canadian writings have centered around the notion of survival. It would be a useful exercise in the sociology of literature to try and account for this overemphasis by Canadian writers on the landscape, ethnic relations, attachment to the land and so on at the expense of social class. McDougall provides a starting point when he attributes the absence of proletarian literature and general discussion of social class relations to the actual social origin of the writers who have tended to be middle class and associated with academia. In addition to this, one could also attempt to locate a correspondence between the social climate of the time and the values expressed in Canadian novels, and whether or not changes in the former have been accompanied by changes in the latter.

Notes

[1]D. Easton, *A Systems Analysis of Political Life* (New York: John Wiley and Sons Inc., 1965), p. 307.

[2]R.M. Merelman, "The Role of Developmental Psychology in the Study of Political Socialization: Some Hypotheses and Some Data" (Paper delivered at the Sixty-Sixth Annual Meeting of the American Political Science Association, 1970), p. 2.

[3]D. Easton and Jack Dennis, *Children in the Political System: Origins of Political Legitimacy* (New York: McGraw Hill, 1969), p. 58.

[4]Ibid., p. 59.

[5]Ibid., p. 60.

[6]D. Easton and R. Hess, "Youth and the Political System," in S.M. Lipset and L. Lowenthal, eds., *Culture and Social Structure* (New York: Free Press, 1961), p. 227.

[7]Ibid.

[8]R. Miliband, *The State in Capitalist Society* (London: Wienenfeld and Nicholson, 1969), p. 2.

[9]A.F. Cohen, "The Political Context of Childhood," p. 164.

[10]D. Easton, op. cit., p. 354.

[11]W.H. Form and J. Huber, "Income, Race and the Ideology of Political Efficacy," *The Journal of Politics*, Vol. 33 (1971), p. 685.

[12]G.L. Zellman and D. O. Sears, "Childhood Origins of Tolerance for Dissent," *Journal of Social Issues*, Vol. 27, No. 2 (1971), p. 118.

[13]Bandura and Walters, in R.W. Wilson, *Learning to be Chinese: The Political Socialization of Children in Taiwan* (Cambridge: M.I.T. Press, 1970), p. 9.

[14]R. Abramson and R. Inglehart, "The Development of Systemic Support in Four Western Democracies," *Comparative Political Studies*, Vol. 1, No. 1 (1968), p. 424.

[15]Quoted in H. Hirsch, *Poverty and Politicization* (New York: Free Press, 1971), p. 21.

[16]Ibid., p. 34.

[17]Ibid, p. 22.

[18]Wilson, *op. cit.*, p. 8.

[19]H. Tajfel, "Cognitive Aspects of Prejudice," *Journal of Social Issues*, Vol. 25, No. 4 (1969), p. 87.

[20]H. Tolley, *Children and War* (New York: Teachers College Columbia University Press, 1973), p. 41.

[21]Easton and Dennis, *op. cit.*, p. 127-128.

[22]J.H. Pammett, "The Development of Political Orientations in Canadian School Children," *Canadian Journal of Political Science*, Vol. IV (1971), p. 136.

[23]J. Klein, *Samples from British Culture*, Vol. 2 (London: Routledge and Kegan Paul, 1965), p. 503.

[24]Ibid., p. 535.

[25]R. Hess and J. Torney, *The Development of Political Attitudes in Children* (Chicago: Aldine, 1967), p. 134.

[26]Easton and Dennis, *op. cit.*, p. 329.

[27]H. Entwistle, *Political Education in Democracy* (London: Routledge and Kegan Paul, Ltd., 1971), p. 20.

[28]W.H. Form and J. Huber, "Income, Race and the Ideology of Political Efficacy," *Journal of Politics*, Vol. 33 (1971), p. 686-687.

[29]W.E. Lambert, "What Are They Like, These Canadians? A Social-Psychological Analysis," *The Canadian Psychologist*, Vol. II, No. 4 (October, 1970), p. 321.

[30]B.S. Greenberg, "Summary of Findings and Future Research Directions," in B.S. Greenberg and B. Dervin, eds., *Use of the Mass Media by the Urban Poor* (New York: Praeger, 1970), p. 77.

[31]Hodgetts, *What Culture? What Heritage?* (Toronto, 1965), p. 24.

[32]J.M.S. Careless, "Limited Identities in Canada," *Canadian Historical Review*, Vol. 50, No. 1 (1969), p. 8.

Bibliography

Abramson, Paul R. and Inglehart, Ronald. "The Development of Systemic Support in Four Western Democracies," *Comparative Political Studies*, Vol. 1, No. 1 (1968), p. 419-442.

Abramson, Paul R. "Political Efficacy and Political Trust among Black School-children: Two Explanations," *The Journal of Politics*, Vol. 34 (1972), p. 1243-1269.

Adelson, J. and O'Neil, R. "The Growth of Political Ideas in Adolescence: The Sense of Community," *Journal of Personality and Social Psychology*, Vol. 6, No. 2 (1966), p. 295-306.

Atwood, Margaret. *Survival* (Toronto: Anansi, 1972).

Beck, Clive, Sullivan, Edmund and Taylor, Nancy. "Stimulating Transition to Postconventional Morality: The Pickering High School Study," *Interchange*, Vol. 3, No. 4 (1972), p. 28-37.

Bernstein, Basil. "A Brief Account of the Theory of Codes," in H.P. Dreitzel, *Childhood and Socialization* (New York: MacMillan, 1973), p. 213-239.

Bidwell, Charles E. "Schooling and Socialization for Moral Commitment," *Interchange*, Vol. 3, No. 4 (1972), p. 1-27.

Careless, J.M.S. "Limited Identities in Canada," *Canadian Historical Review*, Vol. 50, No. 1 (1969), p. 1-10.

Caron, Andre. *The Effects of Advertising on Children* (Le Publicite-Club de Montreal Inc., 1971).

Chaffee, Steven, Wasel, L. Scott and Stephen, Leonard. "Mass Communication and Political Socialization," *Journalism Quarterly*, Vol. 47 (1970), p. 647-659.

Danziger, Kurt. *Socialization* (Harmondsworth, Penguin Co., 1971).

Dervin, Brenda *et al*. "Summary of Related Research Findings," in Bradley S. Greenberg, and Brenda Dervin, *Use of the Mass Media by the Urban Poor* (New York: Praeger, 1970), p. 89-117.

Dreeben, Robert. *On What is Learned in School* (Reading, Mass.: Addison-Wesley, 1968).

Easton, David. *A Systems Analysis of Political Life* (New York: John Wiley and Sons Inc., 1965).

Easton, David and Dennis, Jack. *Children in the Political System: Origins of Political Legitimacy* (New York: McGraw Hili, 1969).

Easton, David and Hess, Robert. "Youth and the Political System," in Seymour Martin Lipset and Leo Lowenthal, eds., *Culture and Social Structure* (New York, The Free Press of Glencoe, 1961), p. 226-251.

Entwistle, Harold. *Political Education in Democracy* (London: Routledge and Kegan Paul, Ltd., 1971).

Form, William H. and Huber, Joan. "Income, Race and the Ideology of Political Efficacy," *The Journal of Politics*, Vol. 33 (1971), p. 659-688.

Froman, Lewis A., Jr. "Learning Political Attitudes," *Western Political Quarterly*, Vol. 15 (1962), p. 304-313.

Gallatin, J. and Adelson. "Legal Guarantees of Individual Freedom: A Cross-National Study of the Development of Political Thought," *Journal of Social Issues*, Vol. 27, No. 2 (1971), p. 93-108.

Greenberg, Bradley S. "Summary of Findings and Future Research Directions," in Bradley S. Greenberg and Brenda Dervin, eds., *Use of the Mass Media by the Urban Poor* (New York: Praeger, 1970), p. 73-80.

Greenberg, Edward S. "Orientations of Black and White Children to Political Authority Figures," *Social Science Quarterly*, Vol. 51, No. 3 (1970), p. 561-571.

Greene, Eugene. "The Political Socialization of Black Innercity Children," in Anthony M. Orum, ed., *The Seeds of Politics: Youth and Politics in America* (Englewood Cliffs, N.J.: Prentice-Hall, 1972), p. 180-194.

Greenstein, Fred. *Children and Politics* (New Haven, Conn.: Yale University Press, 1965).

Hartman, Paul and Husband, Charles. *Racism and the Mass Media* (London: Davis-Pynter, 1974).

Hess, Robert and Torney, Judith. *The Development of Political Attitudes in Children* (Chicago: Aldine, 1967).

Hirsche, Herbert. *Poverty and Politicization* (New York: Free Press, 1971).

Hodgetts, A. B. *What Culture? What Heritage?* (Toronto: Ontario Institute of Education, Prentice-Hall, 1965).

Hofley, John R. "Problems and Perspectives in the Study of Poverty," in John Harp, and John Hofley, eds., *Poverty in Canada* (Scarborough: Prentice-Hall, 1971), p. 101-115.

Hoggart, Richard. *The Uses of Literacy* (Hammondsworth: Penguin, 1969).

Hyman, H. *Political Socialization: A Study in the Psychology of Political Behaviour* (New York: The Free Press, 1969).

Jackman, Robert. "A Note on Intelligence, Social Class and Political Efficacy in Children," *The Journal of Politics*, Vol. 32, No. 4 (1970), p. 984-988.

Jahoda, Gustov. "The Development of Children's Ideas about Country and Nationality, Part I: The Conceptual Framework," *British Journal of Educational Psychology* (1963), p. 47-60.

Jaros, Dean, Hirsch, Herbert and Fleron, J. Frederic Jr. "The Malevolent

Leader: Political Socialization in an American Sub-Culture," *American Political Science Review*, Vol. 62 (1968), p. 564-575.

Jennings, M. Kent. "Pre-adult Orientations to Multiple Systems of Government," *Midwest Journal of Political Science*, Vol. 11 (1967), p. 291-317.

Johnson, N.B., Middleton, Margaret R. and Tajfel, Henri. "The Relationship between Children's Preferences for and Knowledge about Other Nations," *British Journal of Social and Clinical Psychology*, Vol. 9 (1970), p. 232-240.

Johnstone, John C. *Young People's Image of Canadian Society*, (Study No. 2 of the Royal Commission on Bilingualism and Biculturalism, 1969).

Klein, Josephine. *Samples from British Culture*, Vol. II (London: Routledge and Kegan Paul, 1965).

Kornberg, Allan, Smith, Joel and Bromby, David. "Political Socialization of Canadian and American Party Officials: A Preliminary Report," *Canadian Journal of Political Science*, Vol. II, No. 1 (1969), p. 64-68.

Lambert, W.E. "What are They Like, These Canadians? A Social-Psychological Analysis," *The Canadian Psychologist*, Vol. II, No. 4 (October, 1970), p. 303-333.

Lister, Ian. "Political Education and the Schools," *New University and New Education* (May, 1969), p. 23-25.

Litt, Edgar. "Civic Education, Community Norms and Political Indoctrination," *American Sociological Review*, Vol. 28 (1963), p. 69-75.

Mankoff, Milton. "Power in Advanced Capitalist Society: A Review Essay on Recent Elitist and Marxist Criticism of Pluralist Theory," in Milton Mankoff, ed., *The Poverty of Progress* (New York: Holt, Rinehart and Winston, 1972), p. 82-93.

McDougall, Robert L. "The Dodo and the Cruising Ark: Class in Canadian Literature," in Eli Mandel, ed., *Contexts of Canadian Criticism* (Chicago: University of Chicago Press, 1971), p. 216-231.

Mealing, S.R. "The Concept of Social Class and the Interpretation of Canadian History," *The Canadian Historical Review*, Vol. XLVI (1965), p. 201-218.

Merelman, Richard M. "The Adolescence of Political Socialization," *Sociology of Education*, Vol. 45 (1972), p. 134-166.

Merelman, Richard M. *Political Socialization and Educational Climates* (New York: Holt, Rinehart and Winston, 1971).

Merelman, Richard M. "The Role of Developmental Psychology in the Study of Political Socialization: Some Hypotheses and Some Data (Paper delivered at the Sixty-Sixth Annual Meeting of the American Political Science Association, 1970).

Miliband, Ralph. *The State in Capitalist Society* (London: Weienfeld and Nicholson, 1969).

Milner, Sheilagh Hodgins and Milner, Henry. *The Decolonization of Quebec* (Toronto: McClelland and Stewart, 1973).

Muller, Edward N. "Correlates and Consequences in the Legitimacy of Regime Structures," *Midwest Journal of Political Science*, Vol. XIV, No. 3 (1970), p. 392-412.

Orum, Anthony M. and Cohen, Roberta S. "The Development of Political Orientations among Black and White Children," *American Sociological Review*, Vol. 38 (1973), p. 62-74.

Pammett, John H. "The Development of Political Orientations in Canadian

School Children," *Canadian Journal of Political Science*, Vol. IV (1971), p. 132-141.

Percheron, Annick, "Political Vocabulary and Ideological Proximity in French Children," in Jack Dennis (ed.), *Socialization to Politics: A Reader* (New York: John Wiley and Sons Inc., 1973), p. 211-230.

Piaget, Jean. *The Moral Judgement of the Child* (London: Routledge and Kegan Paul, 1968).

Reilly, Wayne C. "Political Attitudes among Law Students in Quebec," *Canadian Journal of Political Science*, Vol. IV, No. 1 (March 1971), p. 122-131.

Remmers, A.H., ed. *Anti-Democratic Attitudes in American Schools* (Evanston: Northwestern University Press, 1963).

Richer, Stephen and Laporte, Pierre. "Culture, Cognition and English-French Competition," in Jean Leonart Elliot, ed., *Minority Canadians*, Vol. 2 (Ontario: Prentice Hall, 1971), p. 141-150.

Rioux, Marcel. *Attitudes des Jennes du Quebec Ages de 18 à 21 Ans* (Unpublished report submitted to the Royal Commission on Bilingualism and Biculturalism, undated).

Rodgers, Harrell and Taylor, George. "Pre-adult Attitudes toward Legal Compliance: Note Toward Theory," in Dan Nimmo and Charles Bonjean, eds., *Political Attitudes and Public Opinion* (New York: David McKay Co. Inc., 1972), p. 215-227.

Rosen, B.C. "Race, Ethnicity and the Achievement Syndrome," *The American Sociological Review*, Vol. XXIV (1959), p. 47-60.

Schleifer, Michael and Douglas, Virginia. "Moral Judgements, Behaviour and Cognitive Style in Young Children," *Canadian Journal of Behavioural Science*, Vol. 5, No. 2 (1973), p. 133-144.

Sears, D.O. Review of *The Development of Political Attitudes in Children*, by R. Hess and J.V. Torney, *Harvard Educational Review*, Vol. 38 (1968), p. 571-577.

Stager, Mary and Sullivan, Edmund. "Conception of Canada in Secondary School: An Exploratory Study," *The Canadian Journal of History and Social Science*, Vol. 6, No. 2 (1970), p. 21-29.

Strodtbeck, Fred L. "Family Interaction, Values and Achievement," in D.C. McClelland, *et al.*, ed., *Talent and Society* (Princeton: D. VanNostrand, 1958), p. 135-194.

Tajfel, Henri. "Cognitive Aspects of Prejudice," *Journal of Social Issues*, Vol. 25, No. 4 (1969), p. 79-97.

Tapp, J.L., and Kholberg, L. "Developing Sense of Law and Legal Justice," *Journal of Social Issues*, Vol. 27, No. 2 (1971), p. 65-91.

Tolley, Howard J. *Children and War* (New York: Teachers College Columbia University Press, 1973).

Trudel, Marcel and Jain, Genevieve. *Canadian History Textbooks* (Study No. 5 of the Royal Commission on Bilingualism and Biculturalism, 1970).

Weber, Max. *The Sociology of Social and Economic Organization* (New York:

The Free Press, 1964).

Weissberg, Robert. "Adolescent Experiences with Political Authorities," *The Journal of Politics*, Vol. 34 (1972), p. 797-824.

White, Elliot. "Intelligence and Sense of Political Efficacy in Children," *Journal of Politics*, Vol. 30 (1968), p. 710-731.

Wilson, Richard W. *Learning to be Chinese: The Political Socialization of Children in Taiwan* (Cambridge, Mass.: MIT Press, 1970).

Zellman, G.L. and Sears, D.O. "Childhood Origins of Tolerance for Dissent," *Journal of Social Issues*, Vol. 27, No. 2 (1971), p. 109-136.

Zibblatt, David. "High School Extra-curricular Activities and Political Socialization," *The Annals*, Vol. 361 (1965), p. 20-31.

Zureik, E. "Children and Political Socialization," in K. Ishwaren, ed., *The Canadian Family* (Toronto: Holt, Rinehart and Winston, 1971), p. 186-203.

Zureik, E. "The Child's Orientation to International Conflict and the United Nations: A Review of the Literature and an Analysis of a Canadian Sample," *Proceedings of the International Peace Research Association Third General Conference* Vol. III (Assen, the Netherlands: VanGorcum and Comp. 1970), p. 171-189.

1.

Major Issues in Political Socialization Research

Elia T. Zureik

UNLIKE most of the contributions to this volume, the present paper is essentially theoretical, and deals with what Zureik considers to be the main issues in the proliferating field of political socialization research.

Zureik addresses himself to the following key problems in the field: how to predict adult political behavior from early socialization experiences, why is it essential to study political socialization of the mass as well as that of the elite, what is the nature of the relationship between attitudes and behavior, to what extent is developmental psychology useful in explaining the emergence of political attitudes and how to incorporate historical analysis in the study of young people's political development.

Essentially, Zureik sees political socialization developing along non-historical lines, confining itself to a consensus view of society and still being unable to isolate the precise link between early and late attitudes and behaviour.

Introduction

ALTHOUGH political socialization research has been on the increase and enjoyed a secure position in the last decade, it has been subjected recently by both critics and advocates to a more sombre assessment regarding its utility in explaining political behaviour. Our purpose in this paper is not to review the literature on political socialization, but rather to clarify some of what we consider to be central issues in political socialization research, and show how it might be possible to tackle the problems we raise below.

While there are as many as ten recognizable problem-areas of research in the field (Dennis, 1968), we shall focus our attention on the following central themes which we think are crucial to the current debate. First, it is yet to be shown empirically that as a result of knowing early political attitudes we can predict later political behavior. Second, the current emphasis in studying mass, rather than elite values has been criticised on the ground of its limited utility in explaining the operation of the political system. It is argued, if the objective is to find out how political decisions are reached, it would make more sense to unravel the experiences of the elites than it is of the masses who are in the whole disinterested in politics and have little impact in affecting the course of political events. Third, so far little attention has been devoted to determining the nature of the causal link between attitudes and behaviour. Fourth, a great deal of political socialization research has suffered from the structural-functional stigma through its overstress on those early socialization experiences conducive to the creation of system-support orientations. Fifth, assuming that we are able to establish the link between early and later political attitudes, it is not clear what the relative contributions of the various socialization agencies are, not to mention the difficulty in isolating specific personality correlates which would account for the emergence of specific types of political attitudes and not others. Sixth, most of existing political socialization research, like other attitudinal studies, has been ahistorical. The empirical evidence gathered through the use of survey research has been interpreted in terms of localized socialization experiences taking into account, in most cases, the attitudes of a specific group in one setting and at one point in time. Whenever cross-national comparisons have been carried out, there has been a tendency either to ignore or underestimate the relevance of the historical factors peculiar to specific national settings, factors which would account in part for apparent cross-national variations in political attitudes.

The Missing Links

The essential question facing researchers in the area of political socialization—and socialization in general, one might add—is "Why study the political attitudes of young people in the first place?" In other words, "Could we learn anything unique and valuable by examining political attitudes of young people which we could not have obtained by doing standard opinion research on the adult population?" It is customary to brush aside this question by recalling that since time immemorial political thinkers such as Plato and Aristotle have recognized the importance of early training for future citizenship. For this reason, the argument implies, the study of early political socialization is bound to be important! However, as Steintrager (1968) remarks, this strange marriage between classical political theory and contemporary political science has been carried out with a crucial distinction, namely that contemporary empirical research in politics has dissociated itself from the normative bias of classical theory. Whether or not this claim of objectivity in political socialization research has been achieved is not difficult to verify as will be demonstrated later on in this article (see Connell and Goot, 1972; Zeigler and Peak, 1970; and Miliband, 1969).

A more convincing synthesis of the various problems listed earlier is needed, if we are to advance our research into the genesis of political attitudes beyond the casual association of our work to that of the giants. A fairly recent review of three standard works in political socialization highlights the problem of linkage with which we are concerned here:

From the point of view of trying to determine whether there is a linkage [in political attitudes] the normal study tends to create an unfalsifiable proposition: it tends toward hypothesis saving. The researcher studies children of various ages, he discovers an apparent evolution with age, the older children moving closer to the views that are known to exist among adults. On another attitudinal dimension, he finds that the older children resemble the adults less so than do the younger ones. In the former situation, the researcher concludes that the socialization process has been virtually completed for that dimension. In the latter case, he suggests that at some age level beyond the oldest stratum he has studied the attitudes characteristic of adults in that society are adopted by the youth. Most significantly, throughout this process he *avoids* specifying the conditions under which attitudes will persist, will be subject to transformation or will actually change.[1]

The gist of the above argument is that certain early political attitudes which have occupied researchers so far are unstable, and have little bearing upon adult attitudes. Building his case with the aid of Converse's argument (1971), Schonfeld goes on to suggest that it would be more helpful in explaining adult political behaviour if socialization research focuses on early authority of a non-political nature. Thus, questioning young people about remote political objects with whom they have had little personal experience, such as heads of State, is bound to produce unfruitful results since this is likely to elicit "non-attitudes." Instead, and here Schonfeld brings Eckstein (1966; 1969) into the picture, the researcher is better off if he focusses on the extent of congruency between political and non-political authority experiences. According to Schonfeld, the stress should be put on tapping behaviour and not attitudes, for "political behaviour so qualified is essentially authority behaviour."[2] Examples of non-political authority experiences cited by Schonfeld which could be located in primary socialization institutions and which have their parallel in the political sphere include "participation, responsiveness, compliance, directiveness and affect."[3]

To some extent, Schonfeld's ideas regarding structural parallelism among institutions are not new. We have seen a similar approach adopted by Almond and Verba in the *Civic Culture* (1963), with the exception that their data were retrospective and did not include all the authority dimensions delineated by Schonfeld. They did, however, investigate the relationship between early participation in decision-making activities in the home and school, on the one hand, and sense of political competence on the other, bearing in mind that in this instance competence denotes a psychological trait centering around the predisposition to act, and not behaviour itself. Their conclusions show that early socialization experiences of the type singled out above are secondary in explaining the tendency of adults to get involved in politics. Rather, it is adult experiences in the work-place which account for crucial types of adult political orientations such as sense of political competence.

Thus, it is not clear why Schonfeld would suggest examining the nature of authority patterns in the home and school, bearing in mind that Eckstein, as well as Almond and Verba, converge in concluding that the closer the socialization institutions are to the political authority structure, the more relevant socialization experiences within these institutions become to explaining political behaviour.

In commenting on the same problems of linkage, Greenstein (1970) suggests that the best way of detecting the sources of variations or reinforcements in the transmission of political values is to look at those cases where "integenerational discontinuity is *sharp*—or when the continuity is specially strong."[4] Addressing themselves to the same problem, Searing, Schwartz and Lind (1973) have undertaken to test an earlier proposition put forward by Greenstein, namely "the more important a political orientation is in the behaviour of adults, the earlier it could be found to emerge in the learning of the child."[5] The above authors extended the applicability of this statement by arguing that since benevolence preceeds cynicism in the age sequence of political learning, it is logical to expect adult trust in public officials to show the highest level of correlation with other political orientations. While by empirical verification the proposition is not borne out, the orientations chosen by the authors for examination, though seem to be important according to their estimate, need not be the central political orientations from the point of view of the respondent. (Clarke and Kenski, 1973).

Another alternative is the one adopted by Easton and Dennis who view orientation changes in terms of the identification process itself which, during the early years, begins along personalistic lines (in the sense that the child first establishes his political attachment in terms of personal identification with leaders) and, as a result of cognitive development, substitutes institutional identification for a personal one. The difficulty with this latter type of explanation, as Hirsch rightly asserts, is that by focussing on authority perception Easton and Dennis might "be tapping the dimension of authoritarianism rather than support for the political system."[6] Another methodological shortcoming of the Easton-Dennis study is that their propositions or arguments are not presented in a falsifiable fashion (Schonfeld, 1971). In other words, by concentrating on discovering diffuse support among American children for the political system, Easton and Dennis ignored possible sources of strain and disaffection during adolescence and college years.

One obvious way out of this dilemma, though impractical to implement, is to carry out a longitudinal research project in which an attempt is made to construct a socialization profile of the individual actor across the relevant life span. This way it will be possible to assess the extent of attitudinal changes over time. Kagan and Moss' (1962) longitudinal study of eighty-five children over a twenty year period is one of the few instances where researchers have attempted to trace attitudinal change among the same subjects over time. Their conclusions confirm the importance of early learning to structuring subsequent behaviour. However, it must be pointed out that in adopting this strategy the researcher has little control over the societal changes taking place during the period in question, which could very well play a significant role in affecting behaviour patterns, overshadowing the influences of early socialization experiences.

Another theoretical alternative by which it is possible to tap the link between early and later attitudes, we suggest, is to focus on early socialization, not necessarily confined to familial authority patterns per se, which structures future orientations, political and otherwise. In particular, we propose that political socialization research focus on the child's perception of social structure in general and his image of himself in terms of the social stratification system in particular. What we are arguing for here is the need to incorporate *anticipatory* socialization as a necessary variable towards establishing the link between early and later political attitudes. The more crucial this process is for the future role performance and status position of the young, the more likely that its impact will be detected early within the child's value system. Socialization for future occupational roles is one form of anticipatory socialization which is relevant for understanding political attitudes, because it implies some sort of an awareness of the authority position the adolescent is likely to occupy in the social hierarchy.

Working within the socialization framework, Turner (1964) documented the primary influence anticipatory socialization (in the form of occupational choice) has upon the emergence of social attitudes. Stinchcombe (1969) makes a similar argument in his study of American adolescents. He finds occupational expectations to be directly correlated—more so than social class—with alienation from the school system. Indeed, in a study of English youth by this author

(Stradling and Zureik, 1973), occupational expectation is shown to be a powerful predictor of the sense of political competence.

Although the notion of anticipatory socialization is part of the formidable literature on reference group theory, its application to political socialization research has been limited. Dawson and Prewitt (1969) have considered this notion on the theoretical level, while Tapper (1971) was more explicit in applying it in his research on English children. More recently Steinitz *et. al.* (1973) have applied Turner's ideas in a qualitative fashion to deal with the ideological development among working-class American youth.

Elite-Mass Dichotomy

At the core of empirical political theory lies the issue of political participation and democratic stability. Classical political theorists as well as contemporary ones have detected a common pattern in the political behaviour of citizens. In summarizing the findings of a host of studies, Milbrath (1965) isolates apathy, indifference and disinterest in politics as dominant features among the masses of Western regimes. Milbrath is quick to concur with others that this is not necessarily a bad thing for "despite the low level of political interest and activity, democratic governments continue to flourish and provide reasonably satisfactory governance for their citizens."[7]

To rectify this shrtcoming on the mass level, the focus is shifted to the elite segment of society. It is argued that political systems could be made responsive to the demands of the public as long as there is a fair competition and circulation among elites. Whether or not this is actually accomplished is far from settled, and we do not intend to deal with this controversy here. Our interest in the elite-mass dichotomy is from the point of view of political socialization research.

If it is the case that the public at large lack structured belief systems, a point stressed by Converse (1971), that these beliefs show little consistency over time, and that, in any case, the public have little say in shaping major political decisions, why not limit political socialization research to the study of elites, which is Marsh's (1971) suggestion as expressed in the following words:

> If their [students of political socialization] interest is in the operation of the political system and some people's behaviour is more influential than that of others, then this concentration or aim to achieve a representative sample would seem misguided. It seems to me that bearing in mind the purpose of political socialization research we should study the behaviour (not the attitudes) of the

elite (not the entire population) as their behaviour is likely to have most influence on the operation of the political system.[8]

Our objection to this elitist position is two-fold. First, it is a moot question whether or not the fragmentation in the belief systems among the public is so impressive not to merit consideration. From Luttbeg's (1968) study as well as that of Clarke and Kenski's (1973) it is apparent that those who either advocate shifting the emphasis in political socialization research to study elites exclusively, or those, such as Searing *et al*. (1973), who question the entire utility of socialization research seem to overlook two main factors. First, the choice of attitudinal items to test the constraint thesis, i.e. that attitudes cluster along recognizable dimensions and in turn they influence behaviour, have tended to assume that what is salient for elites holds true for the public at large, a point Luttbeg shows need not be true. In other words, the political attitudes of the public, especially their ideological orientations, seem to exhibit a different picture of attitudinal clustering compared to that of the elites. Witness, for example, how the choice of foreign policy issues in the Searing's *et al*. study overlooks the results of other studies which have demonstrated the low saliency among the public of issues related to foreign affairs, compared to those related to the domestic scene. Merelman's (1972) comments are pertinent here:

> For example, although most mass attitudes rarely influence political events, some orientations are continuously powerful, for example, those involving race. Moreover, adult racial attitudes undoubtedly depend heavily upon socialization during childhood and adolescence. . . . This example indicates that theory relating socialization to the political system must become more discriminating about the sorts of orientations likely to influence the political behaviour of the mass public normally only peripherally involved in politics.[9]

The other factor usually overlooked in testing the constraint thesis is the heterogeneous composition of the mass public. Regional, ethnic, generational and other sub-group characteristics which would account for possible variations in attitudinal configurations are usually ignored. Searing and his colleagues, though they do not pursue this line of investigation in their study, are nevertheless aware of it:

> It should be noted that our results can be generalized only to a national population. It is, of course, still possible that some orientation/issue-belief relationships may be presented for distinct groups within this population. Thus far, socialization research has

usually been directed toward orientations learned by all members of a society. If research were focussed upon orientations particularistic to subgroups, however, the structuring principle's validity would bear further investigation in these contexts.[10]

Second, let us assume for the sake of argument that the elitist position is empirically tenable, should it not be then the paramount task of political socialization research to explain the conditions which give rise to disinterested and inarticulate masses whose support of the political system seems to be more a function of resignation and accommodation than it is of active participation and consensus? One is also justified in saying as Connell and Goot (1972-1973) do that "the way mass political consciousness is formed is of particular importance to revolutionary and socialist movements quite as much as to the staffs of establishment orders."[11] This in turn leads to posing important questions which have not been tackled by political socialization theorists:

> The way people acquire factual detail about politics is interesting, but not very problematic. What is constantly problematic is the acquisition of political delusions or distortions, or patterns of belief which act against the interest of the person holding them.[12]

We shall deal with the problem of false consciousness in our concluding section of the paper.

Attitude-Behaviour Dichotomy

Another area of concern for attitudinal researchers in general is the exact direction of the causal link between values and behaviour. While this whole controversy revolving around the value/behaviour dichotomy is far from being settled, our purpose in discussing it here is to give some concrete examples of how it is possible to disentangle the causal link between the two. In discussing the logical assumptions underlying political behaviour research, Barry notes: "Values are at best the last link in the chain of causation before behaviour itself. They are not independent variables. A good explanation [of the performance of the political system] may incorporate values as intervening variables, but the values themselves must be explained."[13] Hence, there is need in doing research of this sort to view values in the context of the institutional matrix; it is quite plausible to infer values from institutional structures rather than assume that values always structure institutions and behaviour. An illustration of this plausible causal argument is provided by Budge in his comment on the relationship between political stability and values. Referring to a study of political values of

English youth which concluded that because the youth in question expressed critical evaluation of political life in England, this must signify a decline in political support, Budge (1971) suggests that the attitudes of these youth are better explained as the *outcome* of a stable political set-up which has as one of its main characteristics tolerance of dissent and criticism.

In all fairness to behavioural and motivational research, few competent researchers of this persuasion would want to generalize from the study of random sets of attitudes and values to behaviour in general. The tendency is to focus on a cluster of interrelated attitudes, consider these attitudes as comprising some sort of a personality syndrome, and then resort to accounting for behaviour in terms of personality configuration. But here again the findings are not all that consistent. Marsh (1972) cites two longitudinal studies of young people which showed a decline in the magnitudes of correlations among the various personality dimensions across time, thus showing that personality traits are not necessarily stable. More recently, Weinstein (1972) attempted to establish the link between attitudes and behaviour through empirical testing. He confirmed the hypothesis that for an attitude to be predictive of behaviour it has to meet two conditions: (1) attitudes are likely to be reliable predictors of behaviour if they are considered in terms of *both* the assessment of a certain issue and the tendency to act toward that issue; and (2) negative affect or pre-disposition towards an issue is likely to be accompanied with actual behaviour more so than if the attitude reflected a positive affect to begin with.

Kolson and Green (1970) raise another important methodological issue when they show that basically children are reluctant to give a judgement on matters with which they are unfamiliar. More importantly, when confronted with unfamiliar situations the tendency would be to avoid giving negative responses, in order to reduce the chance of suffering from cognitive dissonance.

Also, it might very well be that what appears to be inconsistency in attitude formation is rendered comprehensible in the light of situational and other factors. Three separate studies come to mind for illustration purposes. The first study is by Schuman (1972) who contrasted the distribution of responses from a U.S. national sample to three attitudinal items dealing with racial discrimination, yet revealing significant inconsistencies. Thus, while 13 per cent of the respondents were willing to endorse discrimination if portrayed in abstract and general terms, the proportion rises to 50 per cent when the reference is to concrete situations. It appears that discrimination is endorsed by a larger proportion if it is described as necessary to insure economic success, or that it reflects the sentiment of the white majority. What is suggested here is that values be regarded in relative rather than in absolute terms. This is in line with Kavanagh's (1972) comment concerning the linkage between political attitudes and political behaviour. He has written that in trying to assess the systemic consequences of political values and attitudes, some weighting for factors such as the information, intensity, and political weight attached to the opinions seem necessary.

Another piece of evidence which demonstrates the utility of distinguishing between abstract and situational contexts of attitudes is the way a Canadian sample reacted to incoming immigrants. Thus, while the majority of Canadians prefer to admit professional and white collar immigrants, compared to skilled and unskilled labourers, the picture is reversed when it comes to actual contact with immigrants. Few of the Canadians sampled, if they had the option, would want to use the services of the professional immigrant strata such as doctors, and lawyers (Jones and Lambert, 1959).

Finally, an example from the area of personality and politics could serve our purpose. Bearing in mind that authoritarianism goes hand in hand with intolerance of out-groups, Greenstein (1965) refers to a study which showed students who scored high on the authoritarian scale to react deferentially to blacks. What appears to be inconsistency in attitudes in this instance is explained by considering the impact of the setting. The students in the sample were chosen from a liberal, Northern campus in the United States, and the responses given were dictated in a large measure by the social climate of the campus, including a fear of sanctioning by the peer group if prejudiced attitudes were expressed.

The Functional Bias

In part, the reason for defining political socialization as a system-maintenance process is due to the genesis of the concept of socialization which appeared first in anthropological, and, later, sociological writings. Without going into great detail into the history of the concept, suffice it to state here that the current meaning of socialization is largely dominated by the Parsonian model which views social control and socialization in more or less similar fashion, namely, that both are necessary means to insure the stability and functioning of the social system: "The two main classes of mechanisms by which motivation is kept at the level and in the direction necessary for the continuing of the social system are the mechanisms of socialization and social control."[14] Hence, for those who extend the relevance of the concept to the political domain, "all political systems tend to perpetuate their culture and structures through time, and they do this mainly by means of the socializing influence of the primary and secondary structures through which the young of the society pass in the process of socialization."[15] The obvious shortcoming of such a functional definition is that it does not account for those processes which fail to perpetuate existing dominant norms, or, even more important, to create counter-norms which threaten the existing political institutions (See Furby, 1971). And if the phenomenon of social change is dealt with at all, it is often portrayed as an ephemeral or deviant case.

What characterizes most of the earlier and more recent works in political socialization is their consensual approach to political life. In the words of one of its practitioners and critics:

> What is the case is that when trying to formulate general statements about political socialization, its theorists almost always fall back on tacit assumptions of consensus and indeed some kind of consensual collective control. Specific power groups, their interests, and the ways propaganda serves their interests, drop out of sight.[16]

Miliband's assertion regarding the ideological function of the political socialization process is worth mentioning here, since he also views the dissemination and management of political knowledge to be a part of a larger process of system-legitimation, a process usually undertaken by the infra-structure of society, e.g. the schools and the mass media. The aim of this process is to interpret the world in a manner which to a large extent would insure the continual functioning of society. In this respect, political knowledge becomes functional, although it is rarely questioned from whose point of view. Zeigler and Peak also note the undue emphasis given to consensus as the outstanding feature of American political life, a factor which has led American political scientists engaged in this type of research to draw a highly unrealistic, and maybe an ideal-type, image of the American political scene. In these authors' view—and their concern is primarily with the impact of the school as a socializing agency—political socialization research ought to examine not only the manifest, but also the *latent*, content of the information transmitted.

> In advanced industrial societies, especially stable democracies, the important thing about socialization is not the explicit content of political education programmes; implicit assumptions are more important. We need to address ourselves to the question of what is *not* told to American children as well as what is told to them.[17]

Superficial treatment of concepts, such as democracy, freedom, equality of opportunity and so forth, ideas which underlie the basic premises of the liberal-democratic society, are not sufficient to guarantee the development of critical thought among the young. It is only when the teaching process undertakes the task of assessing the feasibility of actually attaining these above mentioned ideals in a society in which the stratification system—in the political-economic sense—makes it impossible for power to be diffused to reach all members of society on a reasonable basis, can we then talk about socialization into norms of competence.

Though Canadian society is significantly more pluralistic, especially along ethnic and regional lines, which makes the study of the political socialization process more difficult to handle, the evidence of a case study substantiates the picture drawn above. Pratt's* paper is a significant contribution in this direction. Through content analysis of history textbooks he found that the treatment of social classes and political groups is quite revealing in projecting a powerful legitimating image of the dominant ideology.

> Poverty, unemployment and economic disparity rarely feature in textbook accounts of the contemporary Canadian scene. Hard work, respectability and the deferment of gratification are seen as the means to success which is measured in terms of property and financial affluence.[18]

Pratt concludes his discussion of social classes by remarking that, on the whole, and in spite of a recent improvement in presenting a balanced view of political and social life in Canada, the balance tips in favour of the middle-class interpretation of society. It is worth quoting him at length again, since his conclusions stand in antithetical form vis-a-vis the espoused governmental ideology of pluralism:

> Canada is viewed as a white, Christian, homogeneous, middle-class country where liberal democracy and free enterprise have combined the ideal country. That society may not remain static, but may be transformed, does not concern the textbooks, for none of the subjects taught in school consider the future a legitimate part of their subject matter. Students whose aspirations differ from this monolithic model are likely to be considered, and to consider themselves, misfits.[19]

In spite of the fact that a critical examination of political socialization approaches reveals the presence of powerful forces insuring the perpetuation of a consensual image of politics, another equally relevant fact appears: these forces are not always successful; radicalism and dissent, though they are the properties of a small portion of the youth population, are social facts which need explanation.

A passive view of the individual, or to use Wrong's (1961) well-known phrase the "oversocialized conception of man," is not all that consistent with human reaction to social norms. Our intention in the remaining part of this section is to present an alternate perspective on socialization which might yield useful insights in coping with change and conflict.

While it is true, as stated above, that socialization is essentially a process of social learning which centres around the internalization of norms and values, it is important to bear in mind that this process is cumulative throughout the life-cycle and does not take place on the objective level alone; the individual actor does not perform his role according to a set of prescribed criteria. There is another subjective dimension involved which has to be considered if the socialization process is to be fully accounted for. This is the dimension of interpretation and reflection in which both the individual's reference groups and his perceptual world play important roles in mediating between the objective reality and the self. To use Rafky's definition, ''Socialization is the process wherebs the objective, i.e. external and coercive world of social objects, norms, institutions and legitimations become subjectively real to the individual.''[20]

In this respect, the phenomenological perspective on socialization stresses the need to incorporate the actor's subjective interpretation of his actions, and that the totality of the individual's experiences, which shape his so-called life-space, is what determines his interpretation of, and reaction to, social events. New roles and norms are interpreted in the light of previous experiences and situational contexts. Thus, the process of socialization is facilitated by the extent to which meanings of roles are intersubjectively shared with other individuals considered to be significant for the socialized person. In this respect, socialization is best understood in terms of four main aspects:

First, socialisation requires other people—significant others —with whom the child interacts. Second, the child's identity is a system, either additive or integrative, of the roles, attitudes [and] identities . . . which significant others display vis-a-vis him when relating to him. Third, and most important, socialization is continuous. It is not useful to conceive of socialisation as a process that ends at some point in the biography of the individual. Thus, a change in significant others leads to a change in identity: a child interacts with significant others and, therefore, makes additions to the sediment of his self-system or identity . . . [fourth] the self is situated in that other people and objects (social and physical) are necessary for the experience.[21]

A recent commentator on the state of political socialization research attempted to draw the attention of students in this area to the need to incorporate some of the above points if we are to avoid what he calls the ''Spatio-temporal bias'':

Many of the behavioural (including political socialisation) studies rest on interviews, opinion surveys, and interviews with individuals. As with political systems, which are constantly changing. . . , the life-space or perceptual field of the individual is constantly changing. Yet inferences drawn from political socialisation studies tend to neglect this factor (or, perhaps, cannot account for it); they accept what the individual states *now* as a "given" in terms of his recollections of his political socialisation and of the events which influenced or shaped him.[22]

Cohen's* phenomenological definition of socialization which we quote below from his contribution to this reader is chosen to illustrate what we have in mind:

Socialization is done an injustice if regarded simply as a process in which children come under the influence of pre-existing structural contexts and cultural practices: children have a dynamic and reciprocal relationship with those socializing forces, making and unmaking them, as well as being made by them.[23]

Another illustration of the relevance of ethnomethodological and phenomenological approaches to the study of children's political attitudes is alluded to in Connell's critique of American political socialization, to which we referred earlier in this essay. It is erroneous, Connell says, to assume that there exists a "community of meaning" among children and adults in terms of their perception and interpretation of political life. For this reason, Connell argues, and rightly so, that the subjective meaning a child associates with a political symbol is a function of the child's experience, and is therefore radically different from that held by adults. (Connell and Goot, *opcit*.; and Connell, 1971). An identical issue is raised by Marsh, though not couched in experiential terms. He criticized the tendency of researchers to superimpose their conceptions of abstract political concepts, the notions of democracy and freedom, for example, and then proceed to put into categories the reactions of young people to such concepts according to some adult notions of objective criteria.

Working within the tradition of symbolic-interactionism, Brooks (1972) approaches the study of political ideology through applying the ideas of Cooley and Mead. He postulates, and confirms, a relationship between the perception of the self, the "I," and its relationship to institutions, the "Me." He finds that those students who identified themselves as right-wingers, tended to anchor themselves and center their lives within societal and communal institutions such as the family, occupation, church and state. On the other hand, those who perceived themselves as left-wingers reacted negatively to the institutional framework of society. In other words, the political role the individual assigns to himself in terms of orientations to institutions is linked to the image he has of himself.

Inasmuch as phenomenology has been gaining ground lately in so-called critical social science writings, it is important to bear in mind its limitations; they are elaborated lucidly by Dreitzel (1970). The basic criticism which is levelled against the phenomenological perspective is that it shifts the emphasis from studying the way reality *originates* to the way it is *constructed* in people's minds. Although it is important to understand the interpretative process (a point which we have stressed above), it is more important in our view to investigate the genesis of social reality. To do so, one has to examine how outside structures and power distribution in society determine and legitimate the rules of conduct and modes of interaction. Not to do so would be to reduce human interaction to its idiosyncratic, subjectivist level.

Abramson's (1972) notion of "political reality" is instructive in this regard, for he takes cognizance of the relevance of the so-called objective factors to the study of political attitudes. According to Abramson:

> Political scientists have usually considered feelings of political effectiveness and political trust to be largely a function of either sociological or psychological attributes. They have less often considered the way such feelings are affected by actual political power and by the trustworthiness of political leaders.[24]

The obvious difficulty in extending this approach to the study of young people is that very few at a younger age have had any direct experiences with the political system. In Abramson's words, "Children, unlike adults, have little or no opportunity to engage in reality testing with their political environment."[25]

Developmental Aspects and Agencies of Socialization

It is becoming increasingly clear now that not all political attitudes appear simultaneously and early in life. There is a distinct progression in the way the child orients himself to the world of politics. Ideological orientations which are contingent on cognitive maturity and the ability to think causally do not begin to appear till after the age of 11. Thus, the comprehension of certain democratic values and rationalization of individual behaviour does not emerge in substantial form till mid or even late adolescence (Adelson, 1971). This is in contrast to affective identification and attachment to leaders and political parties which appear as early as the age of 5 to 7 (Greenstein, 1965; Hess and Torney, 1967; Easton and Dennis, 1969).

A useful chronological delineation of political thinking based on empirical research is the one suggested by Connell. He singles out four stages of development: intuitive thinking, primitive realism, construction of the political order and, finally, ideological thinking. Over all, what these stages signify is a gradual progression from the simple concrete stages of thought to the more differentiated complex forms. Whereas during the first two stages, up to the age of nine, the child views politics in a disconnected fashion, during the latter stages his perspective of the political world is characterized by awareness of the complex relationship between thought, preference and action (1971).

Connell underlines the difference between Piaget's (1968) scheme of cognitive development and his own in the sense that the developmentalists focus primarily on structures of thought. In the case of Piaget with his bio-social model, the emphasis is laid upon the inherent autonomy and, to a large extent, universality of the cognitive development among children in general (culture and values are assigned secondary place in this respect). The rigidity of Piaget's model is due mainly to the fact that it originally developed out of research on the child's conception of space, number and physical environment, things which are not socially bound. The situation is different in the case of socio-political thought where subjectivity dominates, and the form of thinking is dictated to a larger extent by ideological orientations inherent in the socialization processes. To quote Connell, political thought is typified by "intrusions of adult thought forms into the child's thinking, because in fact adult thought is here the stuff of the children's construction."[26]

It should be stated, however, that Piaget's stages of development, in spite of their cross-cultural shortcomings, have been shown to be valid on the whole, including examination of the moral and political development of young people's thoughts (See Ehly*, Merelman, 1970; Adelson, Green and O'Neil, 1969; Adelson and O'Neil, 1966; and *Journal of Social Issues*, 1972). Thus, in more than one study, the evidence shows that there are discrete, though sometimes overlapping, stages of cognitive development associated with political thinking. In developing sophisticated political thought, the child passes through the imitative, ego-centric and finally logical sequence of thought development. In other words, the child progresses from a concrete and personalistic view of the world to adopting a more abstract and reciprocal view of social and political life, a view in which the ego is not the centre of the self, but rather evolves as an extension of communal relationships.

From the point of view of political socialization research where traditional theories of social learning and crude versions of the Freudian schemes have characterized most of the current research, there is room for a consideration of the psychological learning model *a la* Piaget. In a sense the latter could be complementary to the former. If one starts from the developmentalist perspective anticipating to find certain forms of thought in terms of an identifiable age sequence, yet fails to establish this presence, it becomes necessary to look at the socio-cultural factor which impeded the anticipated development. Ehly,* in her study of the development of the concept of peace among Canadian, English and American children, notes that compared to the American girls in the sample, both the English and Canadian counterparts lagged behind in developing a corresponding image of peace. This lag, Ehly explains, could not be sought in biological or purely developmental explanations, but rather has to be accounted for through examining the nature of socialization experiences.

One of the socialization agencies which has received substantial attention in political socialization research is the family. This has been particularly the case in the area of partisanship where for a long time it has been inferred on the basis of aggregate comparisons between parents and children that the latter usually grow up to mirror the party image of the previous generation (Hyman, 1969). Upon closer examination of the results, the extent of congruency in the case of party identification has been overestimated. This has been shown to be true cross-culturally, as well. A study by this author of party identification among young Englishmen revealed on the basis of parent-child comparisons (rather than that of separate, independent comparisons) that resemblance in party identification extended to about one-half of the sample only (June, 1974; as well as Dowse and Hughes, 1971). This has also been the case among Australian (Anderson, *et al*. 1972) and American samples (Jennings and Niemi, 1968). Published Canadian data are yet to be made available. However, drawing upon unpublished data, the results of a 1965 national survey, where adults were asked to recollect the party identification of the father, yielded a congruency of around one-third among the entire sample. Upon controlling for those who recalled the father's party identification, the percentage rose from 32 to 53.† Pammett's limited case study of a Kingston sample supports our claim. He finds, for example, that by the eighth grade, only 45 per cent of his public school and 54 per cent of the separate school children identify with a political party. This could be attributed to two factors. First, weak parental transmission of party identification, and second, the structure of the party system in Canada which is characterized by

†Thanks are due to professor William Irvine of Queen's University who provided the author with the above data.

plurality rather than by a simple two-party system, not to mention the fact that the provincial and federal systems of party structures lack the one-to-one correspondence present in the American system. And the more complex political symbols are, in this instance political parties, the less likely that they will act as focal points of identification. A somewhat different picture is presented by Rush (1972). He remarks that to a very large extent the children from his North Vancouver sample mirror their parental party image. It is difficult to assess this type of evidence since Rush does not provide any details on whether or not his conclusions are based on independent or pair-wise comparisons.

It must be stressed, however, that in spite of the relatively low level of correlation between parents and children in the area of partisanship, it is still the highest compared to other areas of political behaviour.

A final piece of evidence which casts further doubt on the undue emphasis put on the family as a politicizing agency springs from a stock-taking exercise of empirical research findings, mostly American over the 35 year period, 1930-1965. Connell concludes his synthesis of the various studies by saying:

> It appears from a substantial body of evidence that processes within the family largely have been irrelevant to the formation of specific opinions. It appears that the two generations have developed their opinions in parallel rather than in series, by similar experiences in a common way of life. The only case when family inheritance of specific opinion can be said to be strong is where the family's communications are clearly shaped by institutions outside it.[27]

On broader social and ideological issues the extent of parent-child agreement is much weaker as noted by a host of comparative studies. (In addition to the sources cited above, see Friedman, et al., 1972; and Martinussen, 1972).

Historical Factors

So far there have been no serious attempts to apply some of the useful insights encountered in the sociology of knowledge writings to interpret the gathered evidence concerning the nature of political ideas among young people. This is the more curious, since the main thrust behind some of the original writings of the sociology of knowledge as expounded by Mannheim (1960) and others is to try and provide a general framework for explaining political knowledge.

One of the few places in which we come across indirect reference to the socio-historical forces in a discussion of political socialization research is in the notion of generational influences. Thus, there is a passing mention of the relationship between the political climate of a certain period, such as that of the Depression and the Cold War, and the impact these events might have had on the way parents compare to their offspring on various political dimensions (Jennings, 1967).

Lambert (1972) provides an interesting alternative to this in attempting to draw together two diverse approaches to account for political consciousness. Relying on the works of Piaget and Mannheim, Lambert constructs a framework which explains the emergence of political consciousness by applying ideas from the literature on moral and cognitive development, and by noting the significance of the phenomenon of generations. Following Piaget's writings, he argues that the age span 18 to 26 is the most crucial phase in the life-cycle of the individual in terms of handling sophisticated and abstract political ideas. It is during this period, Lambert contends, that the person is capable of engaging in rationalistic thinking involving cause-effect relationships which is an essential ingredient for ideological thinking. This has an implication for socialization theories, since the emphasis here shifts from childhood to adolescent experiences. Thus late adolescence exerts greater influence in shaping political consciousness than early childhood socialization. Noting the centrality of the age span 18-26, Mannheim's notion of generations becomes important, since it forces the researcher to focus on rather specific historical events which have taken place during the life-cycle noted above.

Nevertheless, we fail throughout this approach to detect the tracing of the rise of specific styles of thought taking into account more enduring historical phenomena such as capitalism and its impact on the development of political consciousness among the young. Moreover, the process suggested by Lambert is rather static in terms of relating early to later socialization. What bearing would early socialization into specific class and ethnic norms have on the *interpretation* of these historical events? If we are to link history, as depicted in the concept of generations, to thought and action it is important that Lambert take cognizance of the process of meaning-cum-experience, factors which would not be accounted for in Piaget's theory of psychological unfolding.

To return to the main theme of this section, it should be stated that the lack of interest in the relevance of historical factors to explaining the emergence of political attitudes is due to two main factors. The first is inherent in the sociology of knowledge approach itself which has suffered from the lack of an operational and coherent framework of analysis. Second, most of the approaches discussed in the previous sections of this paper have had their intellectual origins in contemporary empiricism, both the sociological and psychological writings.

With respect to the second factor, the literature here lays too much stress on the individual and fails in consequence to recognize, as Mannheim (1960) shows, that it is not men as individuals who think but men in certain groups who have developed a particular style of thought in an endless series of responses to certain typical situations characterizing their common position. Even where groups such as social classes are treated as something more than just useful "control variables" which account for a certain amount of variance and offer statistical relationships, political socialization research still tends to treat them as ahistorical entities. No attention is paid to the fact that the ideas which are transmitted to children by their social class or other social groupings have emerged in response to specific historical situations and as such portray the cumulative experience of that group (Moore: 1969). More will be said about this point later on.

The former approach associated with the sociology of knowledge tends, whenever used, to lead one to adopt a uni-dimensional view of how political thought is acquired. For example, some sociologists of knowledge and Marxists claim that the individual's political thought is a "reflection" of the socio-economic group or class to which an individual belongs. And all that is necessary to understand if we are to find out the way political thought develops is to determine the person's social position.

However, there is an element of an oversimplification in such an argument, for it is not the case that all members of the social class adopt the view of their particular class. Middle-class radicalism and working-class conservatism are some of the well-known phenomena which have occupied political sociologists a great deal. But it is precisely in this area that political socialization research is justified in drawing upon the historical analysis, in addition to traditional approaches, to account fully for such "deviations."

What areas of political thought, one might ask, lend themselves to historical treatment? Ideologies and abstract political concepts are some of the main examples that come to mind, not to mention the crucial area of false consciousness.

Mann (1972), in an incisive paper on the feasibility of treating empirically the notion of false consciousness, invokes the concept of manipulative socialization as a crucial phenomenon to account for the acceptance by the working class of a position in the social structure which is basically detrimental to their objective conditions. Through manipulative socialization, the working-class child confronts sets of social and political symbols which are not relevant to his experience and needs. The historical experience of the working class is typified by concrete, rather than abstract, symbols. And it is the latter that are needed, if the working-class child is to grow up to be able to articulate his aspirations in the context of a framework that is consonant with the ideology of the middle-class group (See also Claus Mueller, 1970). To quote Mann:

> Thus the most common form of manipulative socialization by the liberal democratic state does not seek to change values, but rather to perpetuate values that do not aid the working class to interpret the reality it actually experiences. These values merely deny the existence of a group and class conflict within the nation-state society and therefore are demonstrably false.[28]

The upshot of this process is that the working class adopts a pragmatic, accommodative view of the social order, rather than a position which is based either on the normative consensus or the conflict view of society. The success of this process of legitimation becomes more vivid if one's attention shifts to the historical domain. Similar to the incorporation of the bourgeois style of thought by the aristocracy at one time, working-class ideologies have all along been absorbed by the now dominant bourgeois style of thought (see Moore: 1969). This process of co-optation is best evident through examining the role of the trade union movement in industrial and post-industrial societies which is characterized by accommodation and instrumentalism. In other words, very few of most trade unions set out to transform social structure by doing away with economic inequalities, although the Quebec case might be considered an exception in a limited sense.

What makes the process of legitimation so successful is the absence of an explicit, articulated set of abstract political principles which could be assessed and critically examined. Working within the Marxian tradition, Raymond Williams (1973) sees in the notion of hegemony a useful dynamic concept which would account for variations and change *within* an epoch's styles of thought, such as in contemporary bourgeois society. The central features of the dominant culture are not its ideological imposition of specific notions, nor its conspiritorial nature, but rather its ability to tolerate residual or peripheral as well as oppositional styles of thought as long as they do not threaten or exceed the limits set forth by the dominant culture; if they do, they are attacked, transformed and finally incorporated into the dominant meanings and symbols of society. From the point of view of legitimation, socialization becomes a process of re-defining meanings and practices in society in accordance with a dominant cultural matrix. It is this which gives a hegemonic value system a supreme advantage over the orthodox Marxian notion of superstructure. In Williams' words:

The process of education; the process of a much wider social training within institutions like the family; the practical definitions and organization of work; the selective tradition at an intellectual and theoretical level: all these forces are involved in a continual making and re-making of an effective dominant culture, and on them, as experienced, as built into our living, its reality depends. If what we learn there were merely an imposed ideology, or if it were only the isolable meanings and practices of the ruling class, or of a section of the ruling class, which gets imposed on others, occupying merely the top of our minds, it would be—and one would be glad—a very much easier thing to overthrow.[29]

Research into specific aspects of political thought shows clearly the relevance of the historical argument. Nowhere is this more true than in the area of legitimation. We found in a study of English youth (Stradling and Zureik, 1973) that there is a widespread opposition to political change. Radicalism is usually thought to be class oriented in industrial societies, and yet less than half of this working-class group actually proposed social change which would directly favour the working class and 48 per cent of the middle-class fifteen to eighteen year-olds proposed some form of piecemeal reform. A further 18 per cent and 24 per cent, respectively, advocated no changes at all, feeling that conditions in Britain could not be improved upon.

It is logical to conclude from the foregoing discussion that the dominant institutions in the liberal democratic state are built on premises which are basically alien as far as the majority of the working class is concerned. According to Clark (1968), Canada lacked from the beginning and has never managed to develop a sense of national identity and political patriotism diffused on a mass basis. Rather, for Clark, patriotism ''was an expression of those monopolistic, religious or cultural interests identified with the imperial tie, or later with the Canadian Federal State.''[30] Thus, historically speaking, the Canadian middle class provided the backbone for an efficient government interlinked with the business and religious institutions, and it is these values that continue to dominate the ethnic structure of Canadian society. From John Porter's (1967) study of the social background of elites in Canada, it is safe to conclude that the hegemony of the dominant group has changed little in terms of broadening its cultural and socioeconomic composition.

Although systematic research along the above lines is needed to explain fully the process of legitimation in Canada, the findings of Pratt's* study demonstrate the role of manipulative socialization in the school system in transmitting a consensual view of society. Canadian society could provide useful grounds for examining the historical bases of legitimation in a society which, because of its multi-ethnic character, might pose interesting problems in explaining how the hegemony of the dominant white, Anglo-Saxon group is maintained.

Conclusion

We have attempted in this paper to outline what we consider to be key issues in political socialization research. Throughout, we have tried to present comparative evidence to demonstrate the generality of our argument. If the argument is in need of more substantiation, this in itself is an indication that more theoretical and empirical research is needed, in particular with reference to Canada.

Although we touched upon six separate issues in this paper, the core argument is basically simple, namely that political socialization research has suffered from a conservative bias on two main fronts. First, because of its ideologically conservative bent it was impossible to develop a theoretical framework which would be suitable to tackling serious social phenomena typifying the experience of youth in industrial societies such as alienation, class conflict and false consciousness. In other words, the processes of political legitimation in the face of contradictions in this capitalist system have been largely ignored. On the second front, this conservatism has manifested itself in a static view of man as a politically conforming being.

A set of related issues raised above, though by no means exclusive to political socialization research, is of a theoretical nature. They revolve around the causal link between values and behaviour, the elite mass dichotomy, the place of developmental-psychology in existing political socialization approaches, the relative importance of early socialization, notably family socialization, to explaining later behaviour. It would be presumptious to claim that we have resolved completely any of the central issues we raised, issues which have bedevilled the social scientist all along. Rather, we have attempted through illustrations and examples to demonstrate to the newcomer, too, as well as the practitioner in this field the nature of certain pitfalls which have plagued political socialization research.

Notes

[1] W.R. Schonfeld, "The Focus of Political Socialization Research: An Evaluation," *World Politics*, Vol. 23, No. 3 (1971), p. 556.

[2] Ibid., p. 573.

[3] Ibid., p. 575.

[4] F.I. Greenstein, "A Note on the Ambiguity of Political Socialization:

Definitions, Criticisms and Strategies of Inquiry," *Journal of Politics*, Vol. 32 (1970), p. 977.

[5]D. Searing *et al.*, "The Structuring Principle: Political Socialization and Belief Systems," *American Political Science Review*, Vol. 67 (1973), p. 415.

[6]H. Hirsch, *Poverty and Politicization* (New York: The Free Press, 1971), p. 10.

[7]L. Milbrath, *Political Participation; How and Why Do People Get Involved in Politics?* (Chicago: Rand McNally, 1965), p. 143.

[8]D. Marsh, "Political Socialization: The Implicit Assumptions Questioned," *British Journal of Political Science*, Vol. I (1971), p. 464.

[9]R.M. Merelman, "The Adolescence of Political Socialization," *Sociology of Education*, Vol. 45 (1972), p. 156.

[10]Searing, *et. al., op. cit.*, p. 429.

[11]R.W. Connell and M. Goot, "Science and Ideology in American 'Political Socialization Research,'" *Berkeley Journal of Sociology*, Vol. 17 (1972-73), p. 185.

[12]Ibid., p. 186.

[13]B. Barry, *Sociologists, Economists and Democracy* (London: Collier-Macmillan, Ltd., 1970), p. 96.

[14]T. Parsons, quoted by D. Lockwood, in P. Worsely *et al.*, eds., *Modern Sociology: Introductory Readings* (Harmondsworth: Penguin, 1971), p. 429.

[15]G.A. Almond, "A Functional Approach to Comparative Politics," in G.A. Almond and J.S. Coleman, eds., *The Politics of Developing Areas* (Princeton, N.J.: Princeton University Press, 1960), p. 27.

[16]Connell and Goot, *op. cit.*, p. 179.

[17]H. Zeigler and W. Peak, "The Political Functions of the Educational System," *Sociology of Education*, Vol. 43, No. 3 (1970), p. 120.

[18]D. Pratt, *The Social Role of School Textbooks in Canada*, Vol. 1, p. 110.

[19]Ibid., p. 122.

[20]D.M. Rafky, "Phenomenology and Socialization: Some Comments on the Assumptions Underlying Socialization Theory," *Sociological Analysis*, Vol. 32, No. 1 (1971), p. 11.

[21]Ibid., p. 14-15.

[22]D.C. Baker, "Political Socialization: Parameters and Predispositions," *Polity*, Vol. III, No. 4 (1971), p. 598.

[23]A. Cohen, "The Political Context of Childhood," Vol. 1, p. 165.

[24]P.R. Abramson, "Political Efficacy and Political Trust Among Black Schoolchildren: Two Explanations," *Journal of Politics*, Vol. 34 (1972), p. 1258.

[25]Ibid., p. 1260.

[26]R.W. Connell, *The Child's Construction of Politics* (Melbourne: Melbourne University Press, 1971), p. 230.

[27]R.W. Connell, "Political Socialization in the American Family," *Public Opinion Quarterly* (Fall, 1972), p. 330.

[28]M. Mann, "The Social Cohesion of Liberal Democracy," in M. Mankoff, ed., *The Poverty of Progress* (New York: Holt, Rinehart and Winston, 1972), p. 416.

[29]R. Williams, "Base and Superstructure in Marxist Cultural Theory," *New Left Review* (1973), p. 9.

[30]S.D. Clark, *The Developing Canadian Community* (Toronto, 1968), p. 234.

Bibliography

Abramson, Paul R. "Political Efficacy and Political Trust among Black School-children: Two Explanations," *Journal of Politics*, Vol. 34 (1972), p. 1243-1269.

Adelson, J. "The Political Imagination of the Young Adolescent," *Daedalus*, Vol. 100, No. 4 (Fall 1971), p. 1013-1050.

Adelson, J., Green, B. and O'Neil, R. "Growth of the Idea of Law in Adolescence," *Developmental Psychology*, Vol. 1, No. 4 (1969), p. 327-372.

Adelson, J. and O'Neil, R. "The Growth of Political Ideas in Adolescence: The Sense of Community," *Journal of Personality and Social Psychology*, Vol. 6, No. 2 (1966), p. 295-306.

Almond, G.A. and Verba S. *The Civic Culture: Political Attitudes and Democracy in Five Nations* (Boston: Little, Brown and Company, 1965).

Almond, G.A. "A Functional Approach to Comparative Politics," in G.A. Almond and James S. Coleman, eds., *The Politics of the Developing Areas* (Princeton, New Jersey: Princeton University Press, 1960), p. 3-58.

Anderson, I. *et al*. "Inside the Generations Gap: A Survey of Parents and Children," *Politics*, Vol. VII, No. 1 (1972), p. 31-36.

Baker, D.C. "Political Socialization: Parameters and Predispositions," *Polity*, Vol. III, No. 4 (1971), p. 586-600.

Barry, Brian. *Sociologists, Economists and Democracy* (London: Collier-Macmillan, Ltd., 1970).

Brooks, R.S. "The Self and Political Role: A Symbolic Interactionist Approach to Political Ideology," in J.G. Manis and B.N. Meltzer, eds., *Symbolic Interaction* (Boston: Allyn and Bacon, Inc., 2nd. ed., 1972), p. 462-471.

Budge, I. "Support for Nation and Government among English Children: A Comment," *British Journal of Political Science*, Vol. 1 (1971), p. 389-392.

Clark, S.D. *The Developing Canadian Community* (Toronto: University of Toronto Press, 1968).

Clarke, James and Kenski, Henry. Mimeographed research note, University of Arizona (1973).

Connell, R.W. and Goot, M. "Science and Ideology in American 'Political Socialization Research'," *Berkely Journal of Sociology*, Vol. 17 (1972-1973), p. 165-193.

Connell, R.W. "Political Socialization in the American Family," *Public Opinion Quarterly* (Fall, 1972), p. 323-333.

Connell, R.W. *The Child's Construction of Politics* (Melbourne: Melbourne University Press, 1971).

Converse, P.E. "Attitudes and Non-Attitudes: Continuation of a Dialogue," in E.R. Tufte, ed., *The Quantitative Analysis of Social Problems* (Menlo Park, California: Addison-Wesley, Pub. Company, 1971), p. 168-189.

Dawson, R.E. and Prewitt, K. *Political Socialization* (Boston: Little, Brown and Company, 1969).

Dennis, J. "Major Problems of Political Socialization Research," *Midwest Journal of Political Science*, Vol. 12 (1968), p. 85-114.

Dowse, R.E. and Hughes, J. "The Family, the School and the Political Socialization Process," *Sociology*, Vol. 5, No. 1 (1971), p. 21-45.

Dreitzel, H.P. "Introduction," in H.P. Dreitzel, ed., *Patterns of Communicative Behaviour* (New York: The Macmillan Company, 1970), p. vii-xxii.

Easton, David and Dennis, J. *Children in the Political System: Origins of Political Legitimacy* (New York: McGraw-Hill, 1969).

Eckstein, H. "Authority Relations and Governmental Performance," *Comparative Political Studies*, Vol. 1 (1969), p. 269-325.

Entwistle, Harold. *Political Education in a Democracy* (London: Routledge and Kegan Paul, Ltd., 1971).

Friedman, L.N., Gold, A.R. and Christie, R. "Dissecting the Generations Gap: Integenerational and Intrafamilial Similarities and Differences," *Public Opinion Quarterly* (Fall, 1972), p. 334-346.

Furby, R. "Political Socialization: The Need for a Cross-Cultural Approach," *International Journal of Psychology*, Vol. 6, No. 1 (1971), p. 229-303.

Greenstein, F.I. "A Note on the Ambiguity of 'Political Socialization': Definitions, Criticisms and Strategies of Inquiry," *Journal of Politics*, Vol. 32 (1970), p. 969-978.

Greenstein, F.I. *Children and Politics* (New Haven, Conn.: Yale University Press, 1965).

Greenstein, F.I. "Personality and Political Socialization: The Theories of Authoritarian and Democratic Character," *The Annals*, Vol. 361 (1965), p. 81-95.

Hess, R.D. and Torney, J. *The Development of Political Attitudes in Children* (Chicago: Aldine Press, 1967).

Hirsch, H. *Poverty and Politicization* (New York: The Free Press, 1971).

Hyman, H. *Political Socialization: A Study in the Psychology of Political Behaviour* (New York: The Free Press, 1969).

Jennings, M. Kent and Neimi, Richard. "The Transmission of Political Values from Parent to Child," *American Political Science Review*, Vol. 62 (1968), p. 169-184.

Jennings, M. Kent. "Pre-Adult Orientations to Multiple Systems of Government," *Midwest Journal of Political Science*, Vol. 11 (1967), p. 291-317.

Jones, F.E. and Lambert, W.E. "Attitudes towards Immigrants in a Canadian Community," *Public Opinion Quarterly*, Vol. 23 (1959), p. 537-546.

Kagan, Jerome and Moss, Howard H. *Birth to Maturity* (New York: John Wiley, 1962).

Kavanagh, Dennis, "Allegiance Among English Children: A Dissent," *British Journal of Political Science*, Vol. 2 (1971), p. 127-131.

Kolson, Kenneth C., and Green, Justin J., "Response Set Bias and Political Socialization Research," *Social Science Quarterly*, Vol. 51 (1970), p. 527-538.

Lambert, Allen T., "Generations and Change: Toward a Theory of Generations as a Force in Historical Process," *Youth and Society*, Vol. 4 (1972), pp. 21-45.

Luttbeg, N.R. "The Structure of Beliefs among Leaders and the Public," *Public Opinion Quarterly*, Vol. 32 (1968), p. 398-410.

Mann, M. "The Social Cohesion of Liberal Democracy," in Milton Mankoff, ed., *The Poverty of Progress* (New York: Holt, Rinehart and Winston, Inc., 1972), p. 399-419.

Young Englishmen: A Conflict Perspective," *Political Studies*, Vol. XXI,

Mannheim, Karl. *Ideology and Utopia* (London: Routledge and Kegan Paul, Ltd., 1960).

Marsh, D. "Beliefs about Democracy among English Adolescents: What Significance have They?," *British Journal of Political Science*, Vol. 2, Part 2 (1972), p. 255-259.

Marsh, D. "Political Socialization: The Implicit Assumptions Questioned," *British Journal of Political Science*. Vol. 1 (1971), p. 453-465.

Martinussen, W. "The Development of Civic Competence; Socialization or Task Generalization," *Acta Sociologica*, Vol. 15, No. 3 (1972), p. 213-227.

Merelman, R.M. "The Adolescence of Political Socialization," *Sociology of Education*, Vol. 45 (1972), p. 134-166.

Merelman, R.M. *The Role of Developmental Psychology in the Study of Political Socialization: Some Hypotheses and Some Data* (Paper delivered at the sixty-sixth annual meeting of the American Political Science Association, 1970).

Miliband, R. *The State in Capitalist Society* (London: Weidenfeld and Nicholson, 1969).

Milbrath, L. *Political Participation; How and Why do People Get Involved in Politics?* (Chicago: Rand McNally, 1965).

Moore, Barrington. *Social Origins of Dictatorship and Democracy* (Harmondsworth: Penguin Company, 1969).

Mueller, C. "Notes on the Repression of Communicative Behaviour," in H.P. Dreitzel, ed., *Patterns of Communicative Behaviour* (New York: The Macmillan Company, 1970), p. 101-113.

Parsons, T. quoted by D. Lockwood, in P. Worsely *et al.*, eds., *Modern Sociology: Introductory Readings* (Harmondsworth: Penguin, 1971), p. 428-438.

Piaget, Jean. *The Moral Development of the Child* (London: Routledge and Kegan Paul, Ltd., 1968).

Porter, J. *The Vertical Mosaic* (Toronto: University of Toronto Press, 1965).

Rafky, D.M. "Phenomenology and Socialization: Some Comments on the Assumptions Underlying Socialization Theory," *Sociological Analysis*, Vol. 32, No. 1 (1971), p. 7-20.

Rush, Gary. "The Radicalization of Middle Class Youth," *International Journal of Social Science*, Vol. 24, No. 2 (1972), p. 312-325.

Schonfeld, W.R. "The Focus of Political Socialization Research: An Evaluation," *World Politics*, Vol. 23, No. 3 (1971), p. 544-578.

Schuman, H. "Attitudes vs. Actions *Versus* Attitudes vs. Attitudes," *Public Opinion Quarterly* (Fall, 1972), p. 347-354.

Searing, Donald, Schwartz, Hoel J. and Lind, Alden E. "The Structuring Principle: Political Socialization and Belief Systems," *American Political Science Review*, Vol. 67 (1973), p. 415-432.

Steintrager, J. "Political Socialization and Political Theory," *Social Research*, Vol. 35 (1968), p. 111-129.

Steintz, Victoria, King, Prudence, Solomon, Ellen and Shapiro, Ellen. "Ideological Development in Working Class Youth," *Harvard Educational Review*, Vol. 43, No. 3 (1973), p. 333-361.

Stinchcombe, Arthur L., *Rebellion in a High School* (Quadrangle Books, Inc. 2nd ed., 1969), p. 49-102.

Stradling, R. and Zureik, E. "Emergence of Styles of Political Thought Among Young Englishmen: A Conflict Perspective," *Political Studies*, Vol. XXI,

No. 3 (1973), p. 285-300.

Tapper, T. *Young People and Society* (London: Faber and Faber, 1971).

Turner, R. *The Social Context of Ambition* (San Francisco: Chandler Publishing Company, 1964).

Weinstein, A.G. "Predicting Behaviour from Attitudes," *Public Opinion Quarterly* (Fall, 1972), p. 355-360.

Williams, Raymond. "Base and Superstructure in Marxist Cultural Theory," *New Left Review* (1973), p. 3-16.

Wrong, D.H. "The Oversocialized Conception of Man in Modern Sociology," *American Sociological Review*, Vol. 26 (1961), p. 183-193.

Zeigler, H. and Peak, W. "The Political Functions of the Educational System," *Sociology of Education*, Vol. 43, No. 3 (1970), p. 115-142.

Zureik, E. "Party Images and Partisanship among Young Englishmen," *British Journal of Sociology* (June, 1974).

I

Processes of Socialization: Internalization of Norms

THE main contribution of the developmentalist approach to studying thought development among young people has been its structuralist framework. The basic premise of this approach is that there are certain universal thought processes which emerge as a function of cognitive maturity, and that the unfolding of these processes is essential to understand if the moral development of the child is to be fully accounted for. In tracing the conception of peace among young Canadian, English and American children, Ehly examines the emergence of two main dimensions of peace: active/passive and personal/impersonal. Her findings show American children do develop faster in building an active involvement with peace, compared to Canadian and English children.

Although Ehly's findings confirm the presence of the developmental sequence noted by other researchers, the cross-national variations detected point to a need to incorporate the cultural dimension in applying the structuralist perspective.

In contrast to Ehly's paper, Davis, using a sample of British Columbia children, addresses himself to assessing the relative contribution of the school and family in accounting for the internalization of universalistic norms. His point of departure is Dreeben's work regarding the primary role of the school in inculcating norms of universalism. He finds, contrary to Dreeben's assertions, that among the children studied in a remote area of British Columbia, the home is the agent responsible for transmitting universalistic norms. As early as grade IV Davis finds that children have internalized these norms even though they have never undergone through formal schooling. If anything, Davis notes, the more the child spends time in a classroom setting, the lesser he becomes appreciative of universalistic norms.

2.

Images of Peace:
A Comparative Study
of Canadian, English,
and American Children*

Jennifer A. Ehly

> *I can think of three different meanings of peace: peace and quiet, peace in the world . . . and a piece of pie.*
>
> (Joe, 9 years, Edmonton)

AS Joe notes, peace is a complex subject. But it is one with which he has some familiarity, even at the age of nine. Realization that thinking about peace is not an adult preserve has stimulated a considerable amount of scholarly interest in recent years. In particular, four papers published in the *Journal of Peace Research* have contributed substantially to our understanding of children's ideas about peace and war (Cooper, 1965; Alvik, 1968; Rosell, 1968; Haavelsrud, 1970).

Cooper set the tone of the series by introducing a developmental approach to the research problem, looking to the stages of intellectual maturation posited by Piaget for a theoretical framework. His study of Manchester and Tokyo children was subsequently replicated and extended by researchers in several other locations—Oslo, Lund, and West Berlin. Their reports suggest interesting cross-cultural variations as well as similarities in children's peace concepts.

Perhaps the most striking difference between these sets of findings is in the thematic content of associations to the word peace. Cooper found his English subjects tended to think in personal passive terms, of inner peace or peace and quiet. This contrasted sharply with the Japanese eight-year-olds he studied, who associated peace almost entirely with sociable activity and friendship. Older Japanese children, however, increasingly equated peace with the absence of international conflict and referred to religious and secular symbols. Alvik's Norwegian sample was more inclined to "pacifist" responses in that at all age levels peace was associated overwhelmingly with respite from the processes and consequences of war—a finding repeated in Rosell's study. The latter's Swedish subjects also expressed a considerable

*This research was carried out with the financial support of the Canada Council.

amount of moral judgement on the subject. Haavelsrud, on the other hand, reported that although his younger West Germans thought of peace largely as the absence of war, this response was displaced by "coexistence" among the twelve-year-olds.

Alongside these intriguing thematic differences, there were at least two aspects common to the four discussions of peace concepts. First, with the single and apparently temporary exception of the younger Japanese group, all of these associations shared a predominantly passive or negative quality. Peace seemed to be defined as the absence of something else—be it noise or other threatening stimuli for the English children, or the suspension of conflict and war for the Scandinavians. Similarly, the coexistence responses of West German children suggested inactivity rather than co-operative interaction.

This lack of vigorous positive content was noted by each researcher in turn. Cooper concluded that the development of the peace concept lagged behind that of war and also fell short of children's general intellectual capabilities. Alvik presented more specific evidence along these lines by constructing separate indices for the abstract/concrete and active/passive aspects of war and peace concepts and by examining the relationship of all four indices to both age and a Piaget-style measure of logical development.

Rosell pointed out that a Swedish study of adult members of peace organizations indicated that they too had ideas of peace lacking in positive content. Perhaps, he suggested, there is an absence of emphasis on the positive aspects of peace in society as a whole, and this is simply reflected in the fact that children's mental ability to think of peace in more substantive terms is not put to use. Haavelsrud found peace to be a less "meaningful" concept for children than war as measured by the number of associations they could name in connection with these terms. The general consensus, therefore, seems to be that most of these children are acquiring passive concepts closer to what Galtung (1969) refers to as negative peace than to concepts with a positive dynamic content of their own.[1]

A second (and largely implicit) distinction shared by the four studies is that between personal-involved and impersonal-detached interpretations of peace. Cooper lamented the excessive personalism of the English children in their lack of a conception of peace as an international co-operative venture or even the small-group sociability of the younger Japanese. Concepts reported by the other three researchers were clearly more impersonal and internationalist in tenor. Respite from war or coexistence suggests a view of peace as something involving generals or heads of state at a great distance from the child's own situation. In another sense of personalism, however, peace as an internalized phenomenon of inner harmony or calm and peace as an international "foreign affair" share a basic quality of detachment or non-involvement. In this vein Alvik (1968) concluded his paper with a call for more personalistic methods of teaching about peace and conflict resolution in order that such subjects be recognized by children as relevant to their own lives and interpretable in terms of familiar experiences.

Thus, three major conclusions can be drawn from this group of studies:

1. Peace concepts vary considerably in thematic emphasis from one political culture to another.
2. Most children studied conceive of peace in passive, negative terms rather than as a phenomenon with its own dynamic and positive content.
3. Impersonal detachment appears to characterize these children's peace concepts to a greater degree than does personal involvement.

For those who value active citizen participation in the task of imagining and creating a peaceful world, these findings are not very encouraging. It may be asking too much of small children either to have or to articulate their visions of a future-perfect society (for this is essentially what is required of a peace concept with a positive, vigorous content—that is, a view of peace not merely as the elimination of war but as a political prescription for a just solution to the problems which cause war). It may be asking even more for a child to feel directly involved in issues of such global portent. In effect what is entailed by this involvement is an awareness of what Boulding calls citizenship in the "total earth" (1964); Chardin, the "Sense of the Species" (1959). As Rosell has pointed out, many adults have only the vaguest mental pictures of what a peaceful world would be like and equally vague opinions as to what measures would have to be taken to reorganize life so that major conflicts need not arise. Similarly, it is the unusual adult who does not feel that these are matters best left to leaders and experts to deal with in some remote conference room or battlefield.

In fact what is most interesting about the four studies just reviewed is that some children, although a minority, *did* have such far-reaching views. Differences between these children and the majority of others offer a fascinating area for further study. The research which is reported below takes the previous findings as an initial basis of comparison for three new sets of data, looks more explicitly at the dimensions indicated, and extends the discussion to some additional aspects of children's peace images.

Research Sample and Methodology

The four preceding research projects differed considerably in sampling characteristics, data-gathering instruments, methodologies, and coding procedures—thereby making direct quantitative comparison of their findings very problematic. However, they did illustrate the potential value of a cross-national design in future investigations of this type, as well as the possible cross-cutting influences of such variables as sex, socio-economic status, and age.

Accordingly, research was conducted during the 1969-70 school year with a total of 548 children in three locations: Lancaster, England (189); Edmonton, Canada (191); and north-suburban Chicago, U.S.A. (168).[2] Each subsample was divided approximately evenly between girls and boys in grades three to five (Junior two to four in Lancaster) with an age range of from eight to eleven years.[3]

By including children from three different schools in each location, an attempt was made to obtain balanced socio-economic distribution.[4] But in this respect the three subsamples do differ to some extent. As Table 1 indicates, there are fewer children of working-class backgrounds in the Chicago sample. Also, each of the Edmonton schools tended to be more economically homogeneous than did schools in the other locations, an added factor which may well serve to reinforce differences along class lines within the Edmonton group. Thus while the three subsamples can be considered roughly comparable, these caveats should be kept in mind.

Data were obtained primarily by means of tape-recorded individual interviews, with additional material provided by pictures of peace which a random half of the children were asked to draw in class.[5]

Peace Themes

Children in this study were asked, "What is peace? What do you think of when you hear that word?"[6] Since the thematic coding suggestions made by Cooper seemed to fit their responses very well, and since these categories were also employed by Alvik, they have been used again here. They are as follows:

1. *Inactivity* quiet, absence of stimuli, peace of mind
2. *Respite* cessation of hostilities, defeat or victory, an end to war or interpersonal conflict
3. *Sociable Activity* friendliness and co-operation on a person to person basis
4. *Reconciliation* positive measures to heal a present conflict or prevent further conflict between nations or people

TABLE 1

Socio-economic Distribution of the Sample

Location	School	WC*	MC
Lancaster (N=189)	A (N=63)	70%	30%
	B (N=65)	66	34
	C (N=61)	62	38
Edmonton (N=191)	A (N=62)	89	11
	B (N=66)	89	11
	C (N=63)	5	95
Chicago (N=168)	A (N=66)	67	33
	B (N=58)	45	55
	C (N=44)	7	93

* WC = working class/MC = middle class

TABLE 2

Percent Frequency of Peace Themes

	Inactivity	Respite	Soc. Activ.	Reconcil.
Lancaster	34.9%	33.1%	13.7%	18.3%
Edmonton	21.8	43.6	10.1	24.5
Chicago	13.0	37.3	17.4	32.3
Total sample	23.5	38.2	13.5	24.8

$$(\text{chi}^2 \text{ prob.} \leq .001)$$

As Table 2 illustrates, the distribution of these responses between subsamples does indeed seem to reaffirm that peace themes receive varying degrees of emphasis in different locations. In the interests of cross-sample comparison, a summary of the modal categories reported in all five studies is given in Table 3.

TABLE 3

Modal Peace Themes Reported in Five Studies

(Cooper) Manchester ....inactivity
(Cooper) Tokyo ....sociable activity
(Alvik) Olso ....respite
(Rosell) Lund ....respite/moral judgement*
(Haavelsrud) W. Berlin ....respite/coexistence
(Ehly) Lancaster ....inactivity/respite
(Ehly) Edmonton ....respite
(Ehly) Chicago ....respite/reconciliation

* *For comparative purposes, Rosell's two categories "Absence of War Consequences" and "Absence of War Processes" are combined here as Respite.*

Just as in Cooper's Manchester sample, the Lancaster children are much more inclined to think of peace as inactivity. The Edmonton responses are strikingly similar to those of children in Oslo, both clearly favouring the respite category at all ages. Among older children in the Edmonton and Lancaster groups (as well as in Alvik's Oslo sample), peace is increasingly seen in terms of the reconciliation of nations and people instead of just the cessation of hostilities. In Chicago, however, the more inclusive reconciliation theme is highly popular even among the eight-year-olds. Older children in the latter location increasingly cite sociable activity.

Since the only subsample distribution of the three presented here which changes significantly over the age span studied is that of Lancaster,[7] shifts due to an increase in age seem relatively minor. In Lancaster, inactivity responses decline sharply among older children in favour of the other three categories. When socio-economic status is controlled, a more complex pattern can be seen. In the working-class group even the eldest Lancaster children continue to think of peace largely as inactivity, and also to a considerable extent as sociable activity, whereas respite and reconciliation dominate the responses of those of the same age from middle-class homes. A tendency to relatively more inactivity responses among poorer children is found in the Edmonton and Chicago subsamples as well, although it is not as pronounced in these locations.[8]

Sex-related differences also appear to be a factor in the choice of peace themes. In the sample as a whole, girls are much more inclined to think of peace as inactivity than are boys, who tend to cite reconciliation and respite instead.[9] Within the subsamples, however, this variation is most noticeable among the Lancaster children, particularly the working-class group, and to a lesser extent among the Edmontonians generally.[10] No theme differences on the basis of sex appear in the Chicago sample.

Thus, while inter-location differences are clear, the Chicago responses do not seem to relate significantly to any of the three cross-cutting variables considered; Edmonton peace themes differ to some extent on the basis of sex; and those in Lancaster appear to be influenced considerably by the interactive effects of age, socio-economic status, and sex.

When the pictures of peace are considered as an additional source of data, the sociable activity theme, somewhat neglected in the verbal responses, is found to be the most popular of all. There remain strong locational differences along much the same lines as the verbal responses though, with inactivity (somebody dozing contentedly in a hammock, for example) most commonly drawn by Lancaster children, respite by the Edmontonians, and reconciliation by the Chicagoans.[11]

Differences on the basis of sex are also evident in the peace pictures. Boys most often draw respite. This is not surprising since by adding two weary generals shaking hands in one corner, the subject gives them the opportunity to display their considerable artistic skill at drawing tanks, planes, and soldiers. The girls display an equally strong preference for drawing subjects of most interest to them, such as everyday family scenes, flowers, houses, and happy children.[12] These differences follow the same pattern as do the verbal responses, but in this case a similar trend is found in the Chicago pictures as well.

The Active/Passive Dimension

In order to take a closer look at the first of the two dimensions referred to earlier, the children's descriptions of peace were recoded explicitly according to their passive or active content. Recoding was found necessary because although those coded as inactivity or respite tended to be passive and sociable activity and reconciliation more active, there were many examples of varying degrees of activity within each theme category.

Passive responses received the value 1, slightly active, 2, and active responses were coded 3.[13] On the assumption that these approximated equidistant positions on the underlying continuum, mean scores provide a rough indication of the active content of various groups for comparative purposes. The low grand mean for the total sample, 1.61 (or about halfway between passive and slightly active), lends support to the finding of general passivity which characterized children's peace concepts in previous research.

FIGURE 1

Mean Scores on the Active/Passive Dimension of the Peace Concept

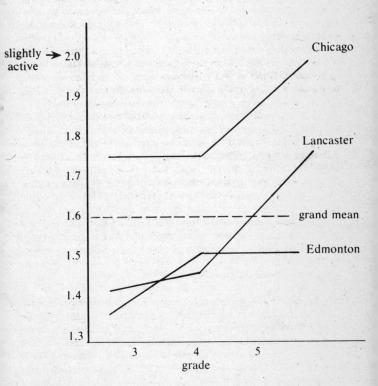

In examining the means of various subgroups, some interesting variations can be seen. Figure 1 indicates that of the three locational subsamples, the Edmonton and Lancaster scores are the lowest or most passive and those of the Chicagoans are higher. However, while scores in Chicago and Lancaster increase sharply over the age span studied, those in Edmonton remain comparatively low. There is some tendency for more activity over time in the Edmonton responses as well, but even the grade five group have scores well below the grand mean.

Alvik also reported increases with age in the active/positive aspects of peace concepts. Among his subjects, who were of about the same age range as the present sample, the maturing child seemed to be more aware of peace as a positive process and less inclined to define it in terms of the absence of harmful stimuli. This change of emphasis may be the result of the child's increasing confidence and ability to understand the environment in general. Such a thesis is lent support by Castaneda *et al.*, (1956) who adapted the Manifest Anxiety Scale for use with children and found younger children and girls to be more anxious and lacking in confidence.

Even though the *Journal of Peace Research* studies failed to find sex-related differences in the peace concept itself, both Alvik and Rosell do report differences in terms of active participation and interest in these subjects. They demonstrate that boys make more use of available sources of information about war and peace—a finding similar to that of many reviewed by Hyman (1959). In addition, it is a truism in the child development literature that activity levels and aggressive behaviour as a rule are higher among boys (for example, see Johnson and Medinnus, 1969). Assuming that these findings about overt behaviour may be paralleled in the content of children's verbal responses, girls were expected here to have more passive peace concepts.

The present data seem to confirm this expectation, for in all locations girls' scores on the activity dimension are lower. This difference is most evident in Lancaster, again particularly within the working class, and in the middle-class portion of the Edmonton sample. No social-class based variations appear in the Chicago data, but girls' scores tend to be slightly lower there as well.[14] Thus, socio-economic class, sex, and age are all important factors influencing the action content of Lancaster peace concepts, while only the first two of these affect Edmonton scores appreciably. Chicagoans' scores are found to be relatively more active as early as grade three and become increasingly so, with some tendency toward passivity in girls' peace concepts in that location also.

Action depicted in the peace pictures also varies considerably according to the artist's sex. In Edmonton and Chicago, middle-class girls are especially likely to draw passive pictures, whereas working-class girls' pictures are most passive in Lancaster.[15] But in both socio-economic groups in each of the three locations, the trend is consistently in the direction of more active peace drawings among boys.[16]

Changes with age are unclear on the basis of the pictorial data. One reason for this is that older children drew more peace symbols —subjects more amenable to coding along concrete/abstract lines. Interestingly, the symbols chosen by the children vary distinctly between locations. Edmonton and Chicago drawings often contain hippies, protest marches, and the peace symbol ⊕ ; these very rarely appear in Lancaster pictures, which feature poppies instead. Cooper noted that his older Japanese children sometimes cited religious symbols or doves of peace in their verbal associations. One common symbolic representation of peace found in all locations of the present study is the traditional "Indian and Cowboy Smoking the Peace Pipe." Perhaps this is a tribute of sorts to the international influence of the western movie. The connotations about peace images implied in these different symbols offer an intriguing subject for speculation, but an impossible one for an adult researcher to assess adequately without more information from children themselves as to just what such symbols mean to them.

The Personal/Impersonal Dimension

One of the difficulties inherent in trying to delineate the personal and impersonal aspects of children's peace concepts is to relate such a dimension to Piaget's notion of egocentrism. All of the four earlier researchers were interested in distinguishing immature concepts from mature ones. One way of doing so is to link up changes in the content of children's responses about peace with changes in their general mental development.

Piaget contends that the years from eight to twelve encompass a major turning point in the development of reasoning, from what he calls a stage of "concrete operations" to one of "formal operations." When a child is capable of formal operations he can ". . . connect assumptions—propositions . . . in which one does not necessarily believe, but which one admits in order to see what consequences they will lead to."[17] At the stage of concrete operations, however, Piaget argues that such hypothetical-deductive thought is not yet possible, and instead reasoning is grounded in the direct observation of phenomena.

Almy describes the changes that can be expected in children's thinking with this development:

Along one dimension the person has moved from a completely subjective view of the world, to one that is increasingly objective.

On another dimension, the concrete-abstract, he has moved from a "world of things present to a world of things possible."[18]

According to Piaget, egocentrism is characteristic of the earlier stage in this developmental process, when the child takes his own immediate perception as absolute and is ". . . ignorant of objective relations in favour of subjective relations."[19] Increasing maturity replaces this egocentrism with sociocentrism. The child gains an increased understanding of reciprocal relationships and is able to imagine the viewpoint of others. By then it is possible to perceive the pattern of events more holistically and objectively, in terms of causes and effects and alternative courses of action.

Piaget and Weil applied these concepts to children's developing perceptions of geopolitical units (1951). They found that increasing age brought knowledge of ever larger and more distant places, moving outward from the child in a series of concentric circles. But along with this development, the child grew more aware of how to relate himself and his immediate environment to the larger picture and vice versa.[20]

Personalism is used here simply to mean the interpretation of phenomena in terms that relate to one's own situation and involve oneself. In this sense personalism does not equate with egocentrism, as it does not necessarily mean that a child who responds in this way is "ignorant of objective relations." In fact it may require quite a sophisticated knowledge of cause and effect in a broad context to see that "being kind to my sister" or "sharing my things" have any connection whatever to that which adults call peace. On the other hand, an equally mature child might well conclude, along with many adults, that war and peace are things which more important people look after somewhere else and which have very little real connection with oneself.

Personalism, it is argued here, is a matter of political interpretation and not something which necessarily relates to the general development process. A child with a personalistic view of peace has a feeling of direct involvement in it; a child with an impersonalistic peace concept feels that peace is something remote and detached from himself.

From this perspective many of what Cooper has called personal definitions of peace, such as quiet or stillness, are considered here as impersonal—since often they do not really involve the child at all. For example, one of the Lancaster subjects defined peace as a "street with no children." The classic pictorial expression of a detached peace concept found here shows a rabbit sitting on a hill and looking at the sunset. Another type of impersonal response includes people but is entirely divorced from the child's situation:

A general and a general getting together to have a talk. Probably one army has just a few men left . . . and they sign a treaty.

(Edmonton, 8)

Figure 2 presents the distribution of verbal peace definitions on the personal/impersonal dimension. Coding has again been done on the basis of a trichotomy, with impersonal responses coded as 1, slightly personal or mixed as 2, and personal as 3.

As this figure demonstrates, there are distinct differences, according to location and age, in children's feelings of personal involvement in peace. The Chicagoans have the highest or most personal scores, but the difference between the three subsamples, highly significant at the grade three level, decreases with age. By grade five the Chicago children continue to have the most personalistic peace descriptions, but the other two groups are not far behind. If personalism were synonymous with Piaget's egocentrism, one would have expected a decrease in these scores over time rather than the general increases reported in Figure 2. The grand mean for the total sample on this dimension is 2.08, or moderately personal. It would seem that the impersonal tone of some theme categories disguises a fair amount of personal involvement in peace, at least among the children studied here.

The largest increase in score due to age is found in the Lancaster sample, but here again a closer inspection of the data reveals that there is an interesting interaction with the socio-economic variable. Working-class children show a strong inclination to more personal peace concepts as they grow older whereas those of the middle class become even more impersonal and detached over the years eight to eleven. In Edmonton also, there is a stronger tendency to personalistic responses among poorer children as they grow older, but there the trend in both socio-economic groups is in the same direction of increasing involvement in the peace descriptions.[21] No consistent changes with age, or differences on the basis of socio-economic class are found in the Chicago sample. There, personalism scores are high as early as grade three, decline temporarily in grade four, and rise again to about the same level in grade five.

Sex-related differences on this dimension are mixed. There is some tendency for Edmonton and Lancaster boys to conceive of peace in more personal terms than do girls in these locations. As in previous cases, this is most pronounced in the Lancaster working-class and the Edmonton middle-class groups.[22] Such a finding is in contrast to what might be expected on the basis of past political socialization research, where it is often reported that girls are more personalistic and home-centred and boys more interested in the wider environment (see Green-

FIGURE 2

Mean Scores on the Personal/Impersonal
Dimension of the Peace Concept

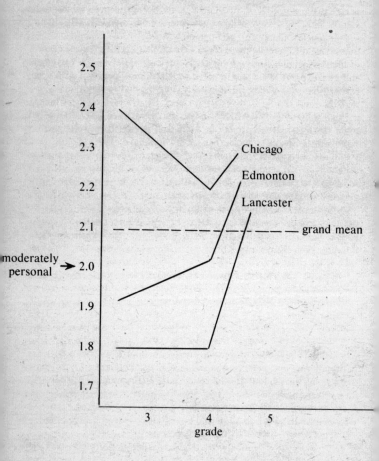

stein, 1961; Hess and Torney, 1967). Most of this type of research has been done with American subjects, however, and the present data point to the possibility of quite different patterns of sex-role learning, relating to this subject area, between locations and within social classes. Chicago girls in the present study did indeed have slightly more personalistic descriptions of peace than did Chicago boys, as well as significantly higher scores than their sisters in the other two locations.

It appears, therefore, that all the variables considered here interact to produce differential effects, both as to the strength and the direction of their association with the amount of personal involvement in peace children express. This would seem to support the contention stated earlier, that such a dimension is not connected in any inevitable way with the general process of child development or maturation. Cooper's regret that his older English subjects did not tend to conceive of peace in more international terms may thus be more a reflection of his own political leanings than an appropriate application of Piagetian theory.

When the peace pictures are coded on the basis of a similar trichotomy, their content is seen to be highly personal (with a grand mean of 2.40). Here the popular sociable activity theme lends itself to personal interpretations, particularly within the Chicago sample.

Generally speaking, the responses demonstrate a higher degree of personal involvement in peace than theme categories such as respite and reconciliation suggest. More often than not, children found ways to interpret such themes in terms which relate to their own lives:

> Peace? . . . That's like when my brother and I stop kicking each other and decide to take turns with the basketball after school. Or maybe we'd go to a game together . . . or help each other with homework.
>
> (Chicago, 10)

To this point the discussion has been based solely on peace definitions or concepts. Some of the variations found in these concepts may be based on language habits, which, although interesting in themselves, perhaps mask underlying similarities. The next sections focus on two additional aspects of the peace image in an attempt to see which differences are really basic and which are more superficial.

The Peace-Building Process

Rosell notes that some children define peace as a process, while others describe it as a state of stillness. Differences found earlier on the active/passive dimension may well decrease in importance if those who choose to define peace as an end state have very vigorous ideas about how that end state is reached. Views concerning the peace-building process have been probed here by means of two questions: "Is peace something that just happens by itself, or do we have to work to build it? How do we get peace?"

The children's responses have been coded into five categories, which can be considered a rough active/passive continuum, beginning with the most passive or negative responses (peace happens by itself, or, only God can make peace) through to those most active and positive (peace is built by changing the world to a place where there is no need for conflict). Children coded in this fifth and last category think in terms of long-range cause and effect and the relationship of parts to the whole:

> People get together. Scientists and other people get together and they plan it . . . work together . . . play together. . . . And they don't have wars going on. They put their minds together and they do terrific things. Like if we could put all our minds together and all our money, we could probably stop pollution on the earth. We could do a lot of things that people thought we could never do.
>
> (Chicago, 10)

The activity prescribed by those coded in the fourth category, however, relates only to putting a physical stop to ongoing conflict rather than finding ways to prevent or justly resolve such conflict:

> Get some volunteers and stop 'em from fighting.
>
> (Lancaster, 8)

In this respect the last two categories reflect the thinking characteristic of Piaget's stages of concrete and reciprocal reasoning respectively.

Age distributions and total frequencies by location are given in Figure 3. In terms of total frequencies, the most obvious difference is the greater inclination of Lancaster children to think that peace just happens by itself. This response is less frequent among the Edmontonians and almost non-existent in Chicago. The age graphs at the top of the Figure show that the most active category (5) dominates the Edmonton and Chicago graphs at an early age.

Apparently the passivity of Lancaster children's peace concepts extends to their ideas of the peace-building process as well. This is not the case for the Edmontonians, however, who, despite the sustained passivity of their peace descriptions, clearly have active and positive ideas about what must be done to reach such a peaceful state. Perhaps the most important conclusion to be drawn from these findings is not

FIGURE 3

Distribution of Peace Process Responses
by Grade and Location

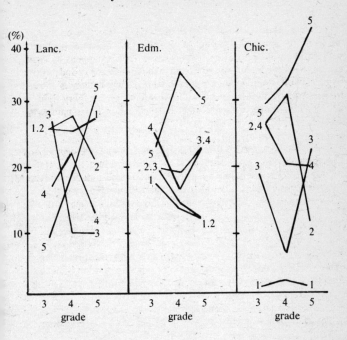

How do we get peace?
1. happens by itself; God does it
2. must be built; don't know how
3. by not doing bad things
4. by stopping ongoing conflict
5. by creating a world in which
   conflict does not arise.

Total Frequencies (%)

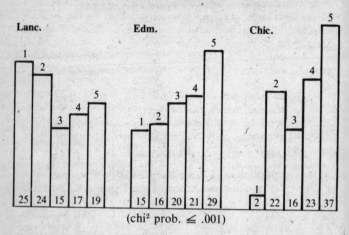

(chi² prob. ≤ .001)

the different content of the responses so much as the earlier age at which active, positive ideas about peace-building develop among American and Canadian children studied here. Ultimately development seems to be heading in the same direction in all three locations; the major difference is one of timing.

The tendency for girls to have more passive peace concepts is repeated in their process responses. They emphasize the first three categories while boys favour the last two. Again, this is most evident in the Edmonton middle-class and Lancaster working-class sub-samples.[23]

With these exceptions, it is noteworthy that the most positive, active conception of the peace-building process is predominant over time, even though the favourite nominal peace description was the less active "respite." These children seem to have highly developed ideas about obtaining peace through communication and problem-solving, even if they do not usually define the end product in those terms.

Peace Responsibility

Another component of the peace image, and one that extends the personal/impersonal dimension one step further, is the notion of responsibility. Even though a child may describe peace as something of direct relevance to his own life, it does not necessarily follow that he feels included in the effort to attain or sustain it. Responsibility is closely tied up with ideas about authority and efficacy (who *should* do something and who is *able* to do it), and these two are almost impossible to separate in children's responses.[24] Data on the question of responsibility, therefore, must be accepted as a blend of children's ideas about the desirable and the possible.

Responses to the interview question, "Whose job is it to get peace?" were coded in one of the following four categories:

1. nobody's job, or, God's job
2. leaders: queens, presidents, generals . . .
3. special groups: armies, men, "the good guys" . . .
4. everybody, including you and me

FIGURE 4

**Distribution of Peace Responsibility Responses
by Location Percent Total Frequencies**

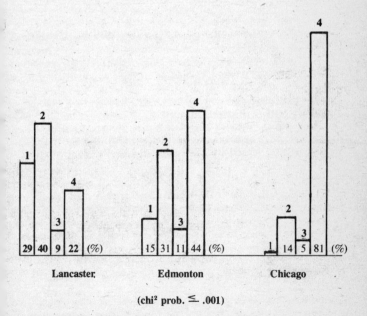

29	40	9	22	(%)		15	31	11	44	(%)		1	14	5	81	(%)

Lancaster   Edmonton   Chicago

(chi^2 prob. $\leq$ .001)

As Figure 4 makes clear, it is the Chicagoans who are most inclined to feel it is incumbent upon everyone, including themselves, to help work towards a peaceful state. Most Lancaster children, on the other hand, judge this to be a job for leaders, or perhaps God, and Edmontonians appear to be squarely in the middle of these two positions.

Variations in these responses according to age are not large, but those which occur reflect changes in the personal/impersonal dimension discussed above. Within both the Edmonton and Chicago samples, more stress is placed on the ''everybody'' category by older children. In Lancaster, a slight tendency in this same direction in the working-class group offers an interesting contrast to older middle-class children's markedly increasing emphasis on the responsibility of leadership.[25] As with the concepts themselves, growing feelings of personal involvement in peace seem to be limited to poorer Lancaster children, while their richer fellows become even more detached from this phenomenon as they grow older.

Sex-related differences as to responsibility for peace are negligible in Edmonton and Chicago, and in Lancaster are limited to somewhat more ''nobody'' responses among girls. Socio-economic class bears a direct relationship to this issue only in Edmonton, where wealthier children are most inclined to say that peace is everybody's job.[26]

In general, variations on the basis of location outweigh any cross-cutting influences produced by the other variables considered here. Again, this would seem to argue the case that an involved/detached dimension is dependent upon political learning rather than developmental necessity.

When the two additional aspects of peace images, process and responsibility, are directly cross-tabulated with their respective concept dimensions, their interrelationships can be assessed more closely.

TABLE 4

Gamma Coefficients of Association Between the Two Concept Dimensions and Related Aspects of the Peace Image

	Lanc.	Edm.	Chic.
active/passive concepts and ideas about process	.50***	.23*	.34**
personal/impersonal concepts and ideas about responsibility	.29**	-.12	.36**

| * prob. $\leq$ .05 | ** prob. $\leq$ .01 | *** prob. $\leq$ .001 |

Judging from the gamma coefficients reported in Table 4, the Lancaster and Chicago responses represent two fairly cohesive peace images, the former more passive and impersonal in content, and the latter active and personally involved. Edmontonians' responses do not seem to hang together as coherently. In their case, active ideas about process are to some degree predictable from the action content of peace concepts, but there is even a slight negative relationship between describing peace as something close to home and feeling personally responsible for helping to secure it.

In absolute terms, none of the gammas reported in Table 4 are spectacularly high. This suggests caution in making deductions about other image-components from children's definitions or descriptions of peace.

Summary of Findings

On the basis of the data presented in this paper, it is possible to trace the outlines of distinctly different peace images held by the three samples of children studied. The largest of these differences apparently are the result of varying patterns of socialization in the national cultures. The American children included here have more vigorous, personalistic definitions of peace and view the peace-building process as entailing long-range problem-solving and the prevention of conflict. They feel everyone is responsible for obtaining peace and seem confident they will be able to make some contribution themselves.

The English children, in contrast, define peace along more passive, impersonal lines and commonly view the process of obtaining peace as something beyond human effort—which either happens by itself or is willed by God. Accordingly, the responsibility for trying to get peace is seen in rather exclusive terms, as a task either for God or leaders, and most English children in this sample do not envisage an active role for themselves in such an undertaking.

The Canadians' peace concepts tend to be similar to the English version, that is, passive and impersonal. When the issues of process and responsibility are also considered, however, Edmonton children's views are closer to the active, egalitarian model but remain significantly different from both other groups.

In general, the changes which occur in these images as the children grow older are found to be in the direction of the American pattern. The major exception to this is the increasing detachment of the English middle-class group, who are more inclined as they grow older to define peace as something remote from their own lives and to see the responsibility for obtaining peace as resting on the shoulders of the elite. On the basis of these divergent trends, it has been argued that such a personal/impersonal dimension is a result of political training, and not inherent in the overall process of maturation. It is interesting that the views of poorer English children appear to be heading in the opposite, personalistic, direction. In the Canadian sample quite a different selective socialization process seems to be operating, for here both socioeconomic groups increasingly feel that peace affects them in a personal manner, but poorer children are more likely to forfeit to leaders the responsibility for contributing to the peace-building process.

Active/passive aspects of peace images appear to be closer to a genuinely developmental dimension. The direction of change along these lines is basically the same in all the groups studied and roughly parallels the changes in the development of children's reasoning ability that are posited by Piaget. Definitions of peace become more dynamic and positive in content, and the process of obtaining peace is increasingly seen in a system-oriented sense as including the prevention as well as the resolution of conflict.

But the timing of this sequence differs considerably. The American children studied acquire such views a good deal earlier; in effect, they have what looks to be a one to two-year head start. Several explanations can be suggested for their accelerated pace of development. First, the values given emphasis in their political culture may play a part. American political life is often characterized as placing high value on active, egalitarian citizen participation, while Britons are commonly described as more reserved and deferent to political authority (Lipset, 1963 and 1967; Litt, 1965; Almond and Verba, 1963; Rose, 1964; Clark, 1968). Almond and Verba, for example, sum up such differences with their finding that a citizen-orientation is given emphasis in the United States, in contrast to a subject-orientation which receives relatively more stress in Britain. Such sweeping categorizations have been overdrawn and oversimplified in the past, but in the most general sense of political style they may be a factor here.[27] Presumably Canadian political life inherits something from both of these cultures.

Another possible explanation may lie in different sets of experiences. It is understandable that the issue of peace may be more salient to those children who cannot remember a time when their country was not embroiled in the Vietnam war, who are constantly exposed to a barrage of discussion on this topic, and who have likely witnessed anti-war protests and known or heard of people who were personally caught up in the conflict. If historical events such as this are responsible for accelerating the development of American children's peace concepts, the influence may be only temporary, or alternatively may leave a lasting generational impression.

Leaving aside for the moment the differential effects of such broad factors as political culture and generational experience, if development proceeds at an uneven pace within each locational subsample, it may be appropriate to talk of what Piaget calls décalage, or a lag-effect.[28] Décalage occurs when thought in a particular subject-area is not so mature as children's general reasoning ability would allow, or when a certain group of children seem to lag behind others of the same age and stage of mental development. Such a concept may be applicable to the girls in this study whose ideas are lacking in the vigour and complexity of the boys' responses. This is particularly the case in Lancaster and Edmonton, and the relative lack of such sex-based differences in the Chicago sample argues against any explanation grounded in biology. If such differences are the result of social training, this early manifestation of female political passivity should be a cause for concern to those who value equal participation in political life.

On what could be described as the naive assumption that citizens' attitudes have a major effect on governmental peace policy (or at least the hope that proceeding on this assumption might help produce a self-fulfilling prophecy), two value-laden suggestions are offered on the basis of the findings presented here:

1. that more research be undertaken to establish how certain groups—such as girls or poorer children in Edmonton, for example—are acquiring more passive or alienated ideas about peace, with a view to eventually equalizing the learning of active, participant orientations.
2. that children as young as eleven or twelve are ready to explore alternative models of global political futures. Perhaps exposure to the existence of various routes to a peaceful existence, and encouragement to create their own, might lead to peace images with a more coherent positive content among future global citizens.

Notes

[1]Such distinctions are not limited to children's thought. For a lively discussion of peace researchers' various definitions of their subject, see Boulding (1970).

[2]Clearly, no claim can be made for generalizing from data from such limited subsamples to the populations of the nations or even the subnational regions involved. At best they can be considered as indicative of what children in these particular urban areas feel about the issues presented here.

[3]Due to the sequencing of the research schedule, which began with Lancas-

ter and proceeded to Edmonton and then Chicago, the average age of the American sample is three months older than the Lancaster group.

[4]The occupational classification (of the subjects' fathers) suggested by Kahan and his associates has been used here (Kahan *et al.*, 1966).

[5]The other half of the children were asked to draw war. In addition, all of the subjects in this research participated in simulation games, which generated further data not presented here. For a more extensive discussion of some of the material included in this paper, as well as information on the children's ideas about conflict and war, see the author's Ph.D. dissertation.

[6]Note that this combined both an associational question and a definitional question. Other researchers used one or the other alternative. Rosell asked both types separately and presented two different graphs on war concepts. The fact that his two sets of data were somewhat different seemed to justify the use of both questions in this case in order to maximize the richness of children's responses.

[7]chi^2 prob. $\leq$ .01 (Lancaster, total).

[8]Only those statistics which reach probability levels of .05 or less will be reported here.

[9]chi^2 prob. $\leq$ 001 (total sample).

[10]chi^2 prob. $\leq$ .01 (Lancaster, WC);
  chi^2 prob. $\leq$ .05 (Lancaster, MC);
  chi^2 prob. $\leq$ .05 (Edmonton, total).

[11]chi^2 prob. $\leq$ .001 (total sample, N=56).

[12]Conversely, when asked to draw war, girls often adapted these same themes by adding tears and stab wounds to family members.

[13]Alvik took a somewhat different approach to the one used here, since he assigned each child in his sample two peace scores: one on the passive aspects of peace and another on the active aspects. A child could score highly on both indices as they were made up of different items (Alvik, 1967, 74-76). The assumption made in the present case is that activity and passivity belong at opposite ends of a single continuum, such that more of one implies less of the other. The same is assumed for the personal/impersonal dimension. All of the coding of taped interviews was done by the researcher. As a check on reliability, a random sample of interviews was redone by a second coder. The two sets of results were compared on the most stringent basis; that is, an identical coding decision was counted as an agreement and all others were considered disagreement. A reliability score was computed for each dependent variable separately (as they required varying amounts of subjective judgement), and in no case did the agreement scores fall before 83 percent.

[14]gamma=.56, prob. $\leq$ .001 (Lancaster, WC);
  gamma=.51, prob. $\leq$ .01 (Edmonton, MC).

[15]gamma=.56, prob. $\leq$ .001 (Lancaster, WC);
  gamma=.60, prob. $\leq$ .01 (Edmonton, MC);
  gamma=.66, prob. $\leq$ .001 (Chicago, MC).

[16]The tendency for sex-related differences to be emphasized in the Lancaster working-class sample may in some part explain why Cooper does not report differences on this basis in his Manchester group, as his sample was composed largely of middle-class children.

[17]J. Piaget, *Judgement and Reasoning in the Child* (New Jersey: Littlefield, Adams and Co., 1928), p. 250-251.

[18]M. Almy, "New Views on Intellectual Development in Early Childhood Education," in A. Passow and R. Leeper, eds., *Intellectual Development: Another Look* (Washington: Association for Supervision and Curriculum Development, 1964), p. 14.

[19]J. Piaget, op. cit., p. 228.

[20]The difficulties inherent in applying Piaget's theory of a "concentric circle" spatial-political learning sequence to children in other locations have been demonstrated by several researchers (Jahoda, 1963; Miller, 1970; Ehly, 1972). In broad outline, however, the developmental pattern suggested by Piaget seems to hold true across cultures: children first learn about their immediate surroundings or town, later of their nation or country, and still later about foreign countries.

[21]gamma=.39, prob. $\leq$ .01 (Lancaster, WC);
    gamma=.24, prob. $\leq$ .05 (Edmonton, MC).

[22]chi^2 prob. $\leq$ .05 (Lancaster, WC);
    chi^2 prob. $\leq$ .05 (Edmondon, MC).

[23]chi^2 prob. $\leq$ .05 (Lancaster, WC);
    chi^2 prob. $\leq$ .001 (Edmonton, MC).

[24]Easton and Dennis (1967:26) make the same point: ". . . a young child is not likely to respond differently whether he is asked: *should* ordinary people have a say in what the government does? or *do* ordinary people have such a say?"

[25]chi^2 prob. $\leq$ .05 (Chicago, total);
    chi^2 prob. $\leq$ .05 (Lancaster, MC);
    chi^{2}prob. $\leq$ .05 (Edmonton, total).

[26]chi^2 prob. $\leq$ .05 (Edmonton, total).

[27]For a recent study offering an empirical challenge to the "English-Deference Hypothesis," see Erickson (1972).

[28]A useful explanation of this concept is given in Flavell (1963, 23) as quoted in Alvik's article. Alvik discusses décalage at some length, and Rosell makes note of it also.

Bibliography

Almond, G. and Verba, S. *The Civic Culture: Political Attitudes and Democracy in Five Nations* (Boston: Little, Brown and Co., 1963).

Almy, M. "New Views on Intellectual Development in Early Childhood Education," in A. Passow and R. Leeper, eds., *Intellectual Development: Another Look* (Washington: Association for Supervision and Curriculum Development, 1964).

Alvik, T. *The Development of Views on Conflict, War and Peace Among School Children: Some Theoretical Considerations and an Empirical Study* Part II, Appendix. Avdeling til Pedagogisk (Embetseksamen: Universitet i Oslo, 1967).

Alvik, T. "The Development of Views on Conflict, War and Peace Among School Children," *The Journal of Peace Research* (1968), p. 171-195.

Boulding, K. *The Meaning of the Twentieth Century: The Great Transition* (New York: Harper and Row, 1964).

Boulding, K. "The Philosophy of Peace Research" in *Proceedings of the International Peace Research Association: Third Conference* (Assen: Van Gorcum and Co., 1970).

Castaneda, A. *et al.* "The Children's Version of the Manifest Anxiety Scale," *Child Development* (1956), p. 317-326.

de Chardin, P. *The Future of Man* (New York: Harper and Row, 1959).

Clark, S. *The Developing Canadian Community* (Toronto: University of Toronto Press, 1968).

Cooper, P. "The Development of the Concept of War," *Journal of Peace Research* (1965), p. 1-17.

Easton, D. and Dennis, J. "The Child's Acquisition of Regime Norms: Political Efficacy," *American Political Science Review* (1967), p. 25-38.

Ehly, J. "Images of War and Peace: A Cross-National Study of Children's Orientations to Conflict and Cooperation in the Global System" (Unpublished Ph.D. dissertation, Northwestern University: Evanston, 1972).

Ehly, J. "Children's Developing Spatial-Political Concepts: A Replication of the Jahoda Study in an American Setting," (Unpublished paper, 1972).

Erickson, L. "Youth and Political Deference in England," (Paper presented at the annual meeting of the Canadian Political Science Association, Montreal, 1972).

Flavell, J. *The Developmental Psychology of Jean Piaget* (Princeton: Van Norstrand, 1963).

Galtung, J. "On the Future of the International System" in R. Jungk and J. Galtung, eds., *Mankind 2000* (Oslo: Universitetsforlaget, 1969).

Greenstein, F. "Sex-Related Political Differences in Childhood," *Journal of Politics* (1961), p. 353-371.

Haavelsrud, M. "Views on War and Peace Among Students in West Berlin Public Schools," *Journal of Peace Research* (1970), p. 99-120.

Hess, R. and Torney, J. *The Development of Political Attitudes in Children* (Chicago: Aldine, 1967).

Hyman, H. *Political Socialization: A Study in the Psychology of Political Behavior* (New York: The Free Press, 1959).

Jahoda, G. "The Development of Children's Ideas About Country and Nationality, Part I: The Conceptual Framework," *British Journal of Educational Psychology* (1963), p. 47-60.

Johnson, R. and Medinnus, G. *Child Psychology: Behavior and Development*, 2nd edition (New York: John Wiley and Sons, 1969).

Kahan, M. *et al.* "On the Analytical Division of Social Class," *British Journal of Sociology* (1966), p. 122-132.

Lipset, S. "The Value Patterns of Democracy: A Case Study in Comparative Analysis," *American Sociological Review* (1963), p. 515-531.

Lipset, S. *The First New Nation* (Garden City: Doubleday and Co., 1967).

Litt, E. "Education and Political Enlightenment in America," *Annals of the American Academy of Political and Social Science* (1965), p. 32-39.

Miller, J. "The Development of Children's Ideas About Other Countries" (Unpublished Ph.D. dissertation, Northwestern University: Evanston, 1970).

Piaget, J. *Judgement and Reasoning in the Child* (New Jersey: Littlefield, Adams and Co., 1928).

Piaget, J. and Weil, A. "The Development in Children of the Idea of the Homeland and Relations with Other Countries," *International Social Science Bulletin* (1951), p. 561-578.

Rose, R. *Politics in England* (Boston: Little, Brown and Co., 1964).

Rosell, L. "Children's Views of War and Peace," *Journal of Peace Research* (1968), p. 268-276.

3.

Learning the Norm of Universalism: the Effect of School Attendance[1]

John E. Davis

And although other agencies of socialization undoubtedly contribute to the learning of norms, the school more than others at the same stages of the life cycle, probably makes a greater impact than they do, on learning the norm of . . . universalism.[2]

TRADITIONALLY, schools have been assigned an important role in the socialization of children and many studies have documented ways by which schooling has consciously developed children's predispositions toward definite kinds of behaviour.

Not all behaviour is consciously inculcated, however. Evidence also suggests that the unique structural properties of a socialization setting, that is, features of the social organization of the setting, cause the unconscious internalization of a certain pattern of attitudes which differ in their nature from setting to setting.

Both particularistic and universalistic attitudes may be learned unconsciously as a result of children's participation in the experiences provided by structural features of two important socializing agencies, the home and the school. There has been some contention as to which of these agencies plays the most important role in fostering an acceptance of the norm of universalism, and it is to this question that this paper is addressed.

Universalism—Particularism

As conceived by Parsons (1962), the terms universalism and particularism are considered to be dichotomous and are part of a larger set of five pattern variables which provide the total system of alternative actions open to an individual. In his interpretation of Parsons' concept of universalism the American sociologist Dreeben (1968) places primary importance upon the concept of categorization, and views learning the norm of universalism as equivalent to learning to accept being treated, under certain conditions, as a member of a category.

> The relevant distinction here is whether individuals are treated in terms of their membership in categories or as special cases. In one respect or another an individual can always be viewed as a member of one or more categories, universalistically; he is viewed particularistically if, considering his similarity to others in the same category, he still receives special treatment.[3]

The process by which norms such as universalism are learned is the subject of much of the literature included in the general topic of socialization. Many theories have been developed to explain the process by which socialization occurs. Dreeben's basic assumptions are as follows.

1. Tasks, constraints, and opportunities available within social setting vary with the structural properties of those settings.
2. Individuals who participate in those tasks, constraints, and opportunities derive principles of conduct (norms) based on their experience in coping with them.
3. The content of the variables varies with the setting.
4. The family and the school each possesses peculiar structural characteristics from which emerge normative outcomes in the children participating in them.[4]

Substantial support for these assumptions may be found in sociological literature but, on the other hand, Gerwitz (1969) documents almost three hundred research studies to support his contention that attitudes also may be learned through such features of environment-organism interaction as stimuli, responses, and their interchanges.

Dreeben's assumptions incorporate some of these beliefs for he sees that children, as a result of their experiences with authority figures in one setting, will transfer their modes of interaction with them to other authority figures in the political field. However, he interjects the authority figures of the school between those of the home and those of the political world, inasmuch as he sees features of the social organization of schools are more like those of the political world than are those of families. Consequently, he is led to conjecture that, at least with respect to children's learning of the norm of universalism, schools, rather than families, make the greatest impact.

The Argument

The argument of this paper follows from the conjecture stated above. If formal schooling fosters an acceptance of the norm of universalism, it should be possible to assess the effect of various amounts of schooling upon children's acceptance of the norm. Because it is possible, however, that the norm may be learned in other socialization settings, especially in the family, an examination of both family life and schooling is made in the following paragraphs.[5]

Family Life.

In his consideration of family life Dreeben notes the following points. First of all, he follows the proposal made by Goode (1963) that family members are mutually supportive because they are kin and are bound by ties of affection. Consequently, he sees that in this unique type of relationship, individuals' value orientations tend to be particularistic. Secondly, he notes that children in the family are most commonly of varying ages and on that basis alone are accorded particularistic treatment. Finally, he observes that children's pre-school experience in the family is weighted heavily on the side of special treatment and parental consideration of the whole child. Thus in terms of the full range of each child's personal characteristics, Dreeben concludes that the family setting is conducive to the particularistic rather than the universalistic treatment of each child, leaving children little opportunity to learn the norm of universalism.

Schooling.

Like the family, the school represents adult authority of society. Unlike those of the family, however, its authority figures usually are not related to the children, and in this respect its structure more closely parallels that of the political system than does that of the family. Because of this fact, certain writers (Dreeben, 1968; Haller and Thorson, 1968) contend that attitudes learned in the school setting will likely be generalized into the political setting more easily than they would be from an institution whose structure was less similar to that of the political system.

A brief examination of the way that children in public schools appear to learn the norm of universalism would seem to be in order. Dreeben equates categorization with universalism and sees the public school as establishing well-marked membership categories through three processes, all of which take place in a public context. These are: (1) the assignment to pupils of similar tasks; (2) the formation of classes on the basis of age which makes possible the categorization of tasks and sanctions; and (3) the system of yearly promotions which helps pupils realize that a different set of circumstances is associated with each grade as, for example, a new curriculum and teacher. The public nature of these processes is to be emphasized.

One aspect of school structure which Dreeben does not mention, but which is emphasized by Haller and Thorson (1968) is that teachers often act particularistically in an endeavour to establish a degree of rapport between themselves and their pupils, believing that this creates an environment which is more conducive to learning. At the same time, they agree with Dreeben that the exercise of universalistic norms is essential in order to maintain control over large numbers of children. McCandles (1969) claims that schools are often grossly unfair to their pupils. He levies charges that discrimination, both subtle and obvious, is practised against lower-class, minority group, non-conforming and borderline ability youngsters.

Consequently, the school situation may be seen as one in which discriminating or particularistic as well as universalistic practices are common. Thus, the structure of the school setting bears a certain resemblance to that of the family. It would seem more reasonable, therefore, to conjecture, unlike Dreeben, that both families and schools may contribute to the acceptance of particularistic and universalistic norms, rather than to ascribe the learning of a single different norm to any one institution.

The Research

For children to accept the norm of universalism, Dreeben argues, they must participate in the tasks and constraints of situations governed by the exercise of universalistic norms. He argues further that such situations are not likely to be found in the home but are present in the social organization of schools. The three areas investigated by this study are specifically related to Dreeben's argument since they are concerned with the effects of the recency and length of school attendance upon children's acceptance of universalism.

The sample of children selected for this study were those enrolled in correspondence courses prepared by the British Columbia Department of Education for grades four to eight. This group exhibited the following characteristics: (1) its members were prevented from attending school only because of such geographic factors as distance or the nature of the terrain; (2) their contact with the formal structure of the school ranged from zero to eight years; (3) the recency of that contact ranged from zero to seven years; (4) the sample (See Table 1) was composed of both boys and girls; and (5) since the lowest grade level was grade four, each child should have been able to answer a questionnaire without assistance. Such children seemed to be ideally suited for testing hypotheses concerned with the effects of length and recency of school attendance upon their acceptance of universalism.

TABLE 1
THE SAMPLE

	Younger Ages 8-12	Older Ages 13-16
BOYS	36	55
GIRLS	32	32

Selection of the Variables

Dreeben argues that normative outcomes emerge as a result of pupils' experiences in participating in the sequential nature of situations which are characteristic of schools. Furthermore, he sees school attendance as one part of the whole developmental sequence commonly known as socialization and one which, independent of other parts of that sequence, makes the greatest contribution to children's acceptance of the norm of universalism. Moreover, he suggests that there is a cumulative effect in its acceptance in that children at higher grades will have internalized the norm to a greater degree than will have children in lower grades. Since Dreeben talks only of children who have had school experience, the phrase "children at higher grades" has been interpreted as meaning children who have had more years of formal schooling. Recognizing that the effect of higher grades may in reality be attributable to an increased level of cognitive development, it was necessary in this study to control for age as well as for years of past schooling.

The choice of "length of schooling" as the first independent variable follows from a consideration of Dreeben's arguments. It should be noted, however, that his hypothesis has been challenged by Haller and Thorson (1968) who contend on the basis of empirical evidence that children internalize the norm of universalism at an early age.

Haller and Thorson as well as Dreeben assume that children learn norms by participating in the tasks, constraints, and opportunities peculiar to the structural properties of the social setting within which they find themselves and act according to them. Consequently, it seemed necessary to determine the recency of a child's schooling, for a child who attended school for only a short while a few years ago may not be so strongly oriented towards universalistic norms as another child who attended school for a similar length of time but at a more recent date. This would be especially true if, following Dreeben's argument, the child were now participating in a social setting whose structural properties were not conducive to learning the norm of universalism. "Recency of schooling" was considered, therefore, as a second independent variable.

Finally, it was necessary to include an intervening variable between the two major independent variables stated above and the extent to which children accept the norm of universalism. Dreeben's hypothesis states that the structure of schools is such that children not only learn the norm of universalism, but also come to perceive that teachers should act universalistically. This perception of teachers' actions is then generalized onto other non-family authority figures. Consequently, this study sought to determine whether children's acceptance of the norm of universalism is influenced by the extent to which they perceive non-family authority figures as acting universalistically.

It should be noted that many different factors have been proven or considered by other authors to be important in the political socialization process. However, when one refocuses on the facets of universalism as interpreted by Dreeben, it is apparent that certain variables deserve consideration. For the purpose of this study, those variables selected all relate to situations in which an authority figure has the opportunity to interact with children particularistically or universalistically, to environmental measures, or to biological attributes of the children themselves which might influence their perceptions of authority figures and their own acceptance of universalistic norms.

The theoretical context from which the problem emerges may be expressed with greater clarity in the visual form of a general causal model, shown in Figure 1.

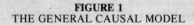

FIGURE 1
THE GENERAL CAUSAL MODEL

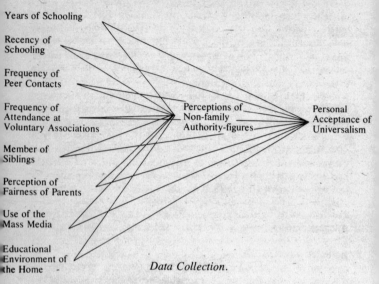

Data Collection.

To gather data, a two-part questionnaire and a series of interviews were used. The first part of the questionnaire was composed of items forming two scales. One scale was designed to measure children's perception of the universalistic action of non-family authority figures. A sample item reads:

> A boss in a factory would try hard to make sure that his friends got the best jobs there.

The second scale was designed to measure children's personal acceptance of the norm of universalism. A sample item from this scale is:

> If I were marking a test that my best friend had written and I saw that he needed just one more mark in order to pass the test, I would find a way to give him that extra mark.

Responses to these questions were indicated on a five-point scale ranging from "agree very much" to "disagree very much." The other part of the questionnaire solicited personal information from each child.

When the questionnaires had been returned, three sets of interviews were conducted. The first of these, with the markers who corrected the lessons submitted by the correspondence pupils, endeavoured to determine what features of correspondence education might inculcate universalistic norms in students. There did not appear to be any such features. The second set of interviews, held with one or more parents of fifteen families whose children had completed questionnaires, sought to discover the extent of particularistic and universalistic tasks, situations, and attitudes met by children within their day to day family situations and routines. The final set of interviews, held with the children from these families, was directed toward discovering reasons for the attitudes expressed by the children on their questionnaire returns.

The interviews revealed a definite pattern of life common to most of the families visited which might have gone undetected had only the questionnaire data been used. In the discussion which follows, this apparent way of life assumes considerable importance in explaining the learning of universalistic norms by children in the family setting.

Analysis and Discussion

Both the interview and questionnaire data showed that most of the children of the sample, including those who had never attended schools, made more universalistic than particularistic responses to the questionnaire items. Because the implication seems to be that factors other than schooling can be responsible for children's internalization of universalistic norms, it may be relevant at this point to introduce some information about the family life of the children surveyed by this study.

Isolated Families

Most of the families surveyed by this study were involved in ranching, fishing, lumbering and lighthouse keeping, or a combination of those jobs. For many families clearing the land was a major task which occupied at least part of the energy and time of every physically capable member of the family. Even in one well-to-do family where a private income ensured a high standard of living, the wife and three children regularly spent time on the land picking up the sticks and stones left behind after the bulldozer had completed the major job of removing the trees and boulders which prevented the cultivation of the fields. At the same time, it was noted that the boys invariably spent more time working out-of-doors while girls were expected to assist with inside chores.

None of the families interviewed was able to earn a living completely from the land. In most cases, the father had a weekday job away from home, often in town, which meant that the daily chores and other necessary jobs had to be undertaken by the wife and children who were left at home. Each of them had one or more definite tasks to do. Nor was the assignment of jobs a feature only of the most isolated families. It was true of practically every family returning a questionnaire, regardless of the family's proximity to town or of the age of the respondents.

The fact that these isolated children were members of work-oriented families and had particular jobs to do assumes special relevance in this study, for although there were some age-adapted tasks in each family, there were also certain broad sanctions applied to insure that all children, irrespective of age, conformed to the basic rules regulating the actions of every member of the family. Eighty-six per cent of those returning questionnaires indicated that they were aaare of universalistic rules, usually made in the interests of safety, which governed the behaviour of all children in the family. Most children saw the assignment of age-adapted tasks as being quite fair. Only eleven per cent of the children stated that they thought that the assignment of these tasks was unfair. It would seem, then, that the children of isolated families share many common experiences which lead to the internalization of universalistic norms. Children of urban families tested during a pilot study in the early stages of this research also were aware of the exercise of universalistic rules in their homes.

That one parent usually worked in a mill in town is also important to this study, for it means that the family, although isolated, still maintained some contact with the technological society of the town. Children of such workers were asked if their parents ever brought home tales of particularistic treatment from their employers. There were none.

The questionnaire and interview data revealed the rather interesting fact that a large majority of the families were first-generation pioneers on their present homesites as opposed to being second-generation families reared on them. The parents, then, of practically every isolated child had received, at some time or other, a certain amount of formal education in schools. In the school setting, if we may accept the arguments proposed by Dreeben and by Haller and Thorson, they should have learned universalistic norms. Also, these families, even in isolation, still maintained contact with society, and therefore might be expected, with varying degrees of intensity, to act according to the universalistic norms they had learned in their own childhood. Since this research indicates that children at as low a level as that of grade four accept universalistic norms, even though they have never participated in the public process of formal schooling wherein universalistic norms are supposedly inculcated, the role of the family in transmitting these norms assumes new importance.

Statistical analysis of the data showed that age and sex were powerful determinants of socialization patterns, and for subsequent analyses each sex group was dichotomized in terms of age, the age of thirteen being taken as the dividing point within groups.

In order to clarify the issues investigated by this study, the three problems are restated as follows:

1. Are recency and amount of school attendance the most important variables affecting the extent to which children perceive non-family authority figures as acting universalistically?
2. Are recency and amount of school attendance the most important variables affecting the extent to which children accept the norm of universalism?
3. Is the extent to which children accept the norm of universalism influenced by the extent to which they perceive non-family authority figures as acting universalistically?

Detailed causal analysis of the data carried out during the course of the study and reported elsewhere (Davis, 1971) shows that only for younger boys does the length of schooling variable exercise a strong positive effect upon their perceptions of the universalistic actions of non-family authority figures. Although this may be a statistical artifact, it may also reflect the severity of socialization demands made upon young boys in their early school years by teachers who are predominately female and who reward universalistic behaviour. Ironically, this study suggests that the teachers themselves, in their own actions, are often perceived as acting particularistically.[6]

When attention is focused upon the contribution of years of schooling to children's acceptance of universalism, two findings emerge. First, the effects of this variable are significant only for boys, and only for younger boys does recency of schooling exercise a strong positive effect. For both boys' groups, years of schooling exercises negative effects upon their acceptance of universalism. These findings suggest that there is insufficient justification for believing that both recency and length of school attendance are the most powerful variables in the causal model developed for this research. Thus, the first two questions posed by this study must be answered negatively.

When the attempt is then made to determine the factors that do affect children's perceptions and acceptance of universalism, the centre of attention shifts from the school to the home. Two major conclusions develop. First of all, the particularistic allocation of sanctions by teachers as perceived by students may force compliance to the universalistic rules of the school, but as children grow older, these demands are often seen as unfair. This perception, coupled with the cynical and sophisticated outlook on life which is typical of adolescents, leads students to believe that schools are characterized by the exercise of particularistic norms. The second conclusion leads to a consideration of the home where, contrary to some speculation, an element of universalism is present and where the authority figures enforcing the rules are also seen as acting universalistically. This idea is elaborated upon in a later paragraph.

The third problem of this study was concerned with discovering if children's perception of the universalistic actions of non-family authority figures influenced the extent to which those children accept the norm of universalism. The effects of the authority variable as compared with those of other independent variables are strong, especially for girls.

The models for boys provide excellent examples of the effect of authority and also provide evidence of two aspects of school structure. In the first instance, years of schooling exercises a strong, negative, direct effect upon younger boys' acceptance of universalism. Yet the same variable's indirect effects, influenced by perceptions of non-family authority figures, are even more strongly positive. In a similar fashion the direct effects of schooling for older boys are also negative, but the indirect effects through authority figures are positive.

Thus, it may be seen that perceptions do indeed influence the extent to which children personally accept the norm of universalism. At the same time, the data substantiate the argument that both particularistic and universalistic norms may govern many school situations. As was suggested earlier, however, the possibility should not be overlooked that, especially for children who have only limited contacts with non-family authority figures, perceptions of the universalistic action of parental authority figures may be the precursors of children's perceptions of non-family authority figures.

Conclusion and Implications

In the attempt to assess the effect of schooling upon children's perceptions of the universalistic action of non-family authority figures and upon those children's personal acceptance of the norm of universalism, two general conclusions have been reached. To begin with, the pattern of socialization seems to vary across age and sex groups, a finding which supports the conclusions reached by socialization studies which have investigated other aspects of attitude formation. In this study, the general effect of age seems to be one of growing sophistication toward the general application of universalistic norms and an increasing awareness of their situationally specific nature.

The dominant role of the home in socializing children into accepting the norms of particularism and universalism receives a new emphasis, particularly in task-oriented family groups such as those studied by this research. This study documents proof that children are aware of universalistic rules which govern family life, and in the family setting the same bonds of kinship seen by Goode (1963) as fostering the development of particularistic norms also seem to create an atmosphere conducive to the acceptance of universalism. Nor is there any particular reason to believe that these findings apply only to isolated children. Although in urban families a powerful task orientation may be missing, it is still reasonable to suppose that the family might play a dominant and influential role, especially with younger children.[7]

Paralleling the development of both particularistic and universalistic norms in the family is the school where, the evidence from this study shows, children feel that certain broad universalistic rules should and, in many cases, do govern specific situations but also where they often see teachers as behaving particularistically. Consequently, although the school may make a meaningful contribution to the development of universalistic norms, its role also extends to developing an awareness of particularism.

The acceptance of the norm of universalism by a substantial component of the population has been seen (Dreeben, 1968) as being necessary for the effective continuance of a democratic political system. This study, in endeavouring to discover the effect of school attendance upon children's learning of the norm, showed that universalism is learned early in life and that families, rather than schools, probably make the greatest contribution to its learning. This is especially true in isolated areas, but the evidence suggests that even should schooling be lacking in urban areas, other agencies of socialization would likely fulfill the same socializing role quite satisfactorily. Thus, if a democratic political system does indeed require that a substantial number of its citizens accept the norm of universalism, it seems reasonable to believe that acceptance, initially inculcated in the family setting, can be reinforced by socializing agents other than schools.

Notes

[1]For a more comprehensive account of this study, including a detailed statistical analysis, readers are referred to the bibliographic entry under Davis (1971).

[2]R. Dreeben, *On What is Learned in School* (Reading, Mass.: Addison-Wesley, 1968), p. 144.

[3]Ibid., p. 75.

[4]Ibid., p. 44.

[5]The study from which this paper is drawn also investigates the effects of other agents of socialization such as the mass media and the peer group. These effects are not reported here.

[6]Of all the adults rated by children on a particularistic-universalistic continuum, teachers were perceived as acting most particularistically.

[7]The one major difference between the isolated families of this study and other families is that of distance from town. This is to be expected since one criterion for participation in this study was that children live at least twenty miles from a school, thus making them eligible for correspondence lessons. This distance, although possibly precluding school attendance, rarely prevented families from participating in the usual social and economic activities associated with town life.

Bibliography

Bandura, A. and Walters, R.H. *Social Learning and Personality Development* (New York: Holt, Rinehart and Winston, 1963).

Bloom, B.S. *Stability and Change in Human Characteristics* (New York: Wiley, 1964).

Coleman, J.S. *The Adolescent Society* (New York: The Free Press, 1961).

Coleman, J.S. *Equality of Educational Opportunity* (Washington: U. S. Government Printing Office, 1966).

Coleman, J.S. *Harvard Graduate School of Education Association Bulletin*, XXII (1967).

Davis, J.E. "The Political Socialization of Children in Remote Areas of Canada" (Unpublished Ph.D. dissertation, University of Toronto, 1971).

Dreeben, R. *On What is Learned in School* (Reading, Mass.: Addison-Wesley, 1968).

Elder, G.H. and Bowerman, C.E. "Family Structure and Child-rearing Patterns: The Effect of Family Size and Sex Composition," *American Sociological Review*, Vol. XXVIII (1963), p. 891-905.

Gerwitz, J.L. "Mechanisms of Social Learning: Some Roles of Stimulation and Behavior in Early Human Development," in David A. Goslin, ed., *Handbook of Socialization Theory and Research* (Chicago: Rand McNally, 1969).

Goode, W.J. *The Family* (Englewood Cliffs, N.J.: Prentice Hall, Inc., 1964).

Haller, E.J. and Thorson, S.J. "The Political Socialization of Children and the Structure of the Elementary School" (Paper presented at the meeting of the American Educational Research Association, Chicago, Illinois, February, 1968).

Hess, R.D. and Torney, J.V. *The Development of Political Attitudes in Children* (Chicago: Aldine, 1967).

Kohlberg, L. "Development of Moral Character and Moral Ideology," in M.L. Hoffman and L.W. Hoffman, eds., *Review of Child Development Research*, Vol. 1 (New York: Russell Sage Foundation, 1964), p. 383-432.

Kohn, A. and Fiedler, F.E. "Age and Sex Differences in the Perception of Persons," *Sociometry*, Vol. XXIV (1961), p. 157-163.

Maccoby, E.E. "Effects of Mass Media," in M.L. Hoffman and L.W. Hoffman, eds., *Review of Child Development Research*, Vol. 1 (New York: Russell Sage Foundation, 1964).

McCandles, B.R. "Childhood Socialization," in David A. Goslin, ed., *Handbook in Socialization Theory and Research* (Chicago: Rand McNally, 1969).

Mead, G.H. *Mind, Self and Society* (Chicago: University of Chicago Press, 1934).

Mussen, P.H. "Early Sex Role Development," in David A. Goslin, ed., *Handbook of Socialization Theory and Research* (Chicago: Rand McNally, 1969).

Parsons, T. *The Social System* (Glencoe, Ill.: The Free Press, 1964, 1951).

Parsons, T. "The School Class as a Social System: Some of its Functions in American Society," *Harvard Educational Review*, Vol. XXIX (1969), p. 297-318.

Parsons, T. and Shils, E., eds. *Toward a General Theory of Action* (Cambridge, Mass.: Harvard University Press, 1962).

Piaget, J. *The Moral Judgment of the Child* (Glencoe, Ill.: The Free Press, 1948, 1932).

Riesman, D., Denny, R., and Glazer, N. *The Lonely Crowd* (New Haven: Yale University Press, 1953).

Simpson, R.L. "The School, the Peer Group and Adolescent Development," *Journal of Educational Sociology*, Vol. XXXII (1958), p. 37-41.

II

Agents of Socialization: The Textbook

THE influence of school textbooks on shaping the political values of young people has been documented in more than one case study in the United States, with the repeated conclusion that history and civics textbooks act primarily to reinforce and transmit the dominant ideology. The two papers which follow further confirm the legitimating role of the schools in both French- and English Canada. Although Pratt deals with a sample of civic textbooks used in Ontario schools, more than one-third of these books are used in other parts of Canada. Ross analyses the contents of teachers' manuals in Quebec.

Pratt's findings are of particular significance to students of Canadian society. Contrary to the officially espoused ideology of pluralism, what emerges from Pratt's findings is a homogenous image of Canadian society which is biased in favour of the middle-class, Anglo-Saxon group. This has political and social ramifications. Socially, it portrays a negative image of the various ethnic groups which fall outside the two main chartered groups. Politically, the textbooks in question convey a picture of Canadian society in which class cleavages are absent, and in which consensus and middle-class ethos abound.

Ross's perspective is a socio-historical one. He shows that, between 1853 and 1948, the pedagogy textbooks used in the Normal Schools and teachers' colleges of Quebec placed a heavy official emphasis on the goal of maintaining a cultural and ideological consensus in a society which was becoming increasingly diversified as a result of urbanisation and industrialisation. Since 1948, however, and more particularly since 1960, this traditional view of the social order (and of education as a means to maintaining that order) has been replaced by an image of Quebec as a technologically advanced, future-oriented society in which the school is officially perceived as a "dynamic agent of social and economic progress." Such an ideological volte-face offers a valuable commentary on the role of the educational system as a purveyor of changing official images of Canadian society. Paradoxically, it is Ross's opinion that the current emphasis in Quebec on modernisation and progress has created a necessity for a new exploration of her socio-cultural heritage and core-values.

4.

The Social Role of School Textbooks in Canada

David Pratt

Textbooks and the School Context

PUBLIC schools exist primarily for the purpose of socializing the young. The child's basic political and social orientation is established during his years in elementary school; thereafter his ideology may change in complexity, but rarely in its general direction (Sullivan, Byrne, and Stager, 1970). From these and similar findings, such researchers as Hess and Torney (1967) have concluded that "the public school appears to be the most important and effective instrument of political socialization," but, as critics have pointed out, this conclusion does not necessarily follow (Sears, 1968). The actual effect of the school as compared to the effects on attitudinal development of such other socializing agencies as the family, the media, and the peer group has yet to be exactly determined. And while a continuity of attitudinal development in children is apparent, more research is needed before it can be known to what extent adult behaviour is determined by attitudes developed in early life. This cautious approach to the role of the school, however, does not affect the initial premise: that what distinguishes the school from other socializers is that it is the agency through which society makes its most deliberate attempt to structure socialization.

The school socializes in many ways. Haller and Thorson have argued that the group-teaching pattern that prevails in schools develops in children ideas of universalism and equality before the law (1970). The hierarchy of power in a school and the sex distribution of teachers at different grade and authority levels provide important sex and political models for children and adolescents. Grading and streaming practices not only determine a student's academic cohorts, but also influence his choice of peers outside the classroom. Sports and extra-curricular activities provide quasi-formal socializing experiences. Even apparently trivial policies are capable of having important affective results. The arrangement of desks in a classroom reflects certain conceptions of human relationships. The choice of norm-referenced over criterion-referenced grading implies a belief in the relationship between competition and achievement. The effect of such elements will vary with such factors as the size of the school and its social and economic setting.

But society makes its most conscious attempt at developing students' attitudes and beliefs through the school curriculum. Curriculum guidelines issued by provincial Departments of Education endeavour to outline the knowledges, skills, and values which should be inculcated, and the experiences to which students should be exposed in the classroom. Such guidelines, however, can do no more than give general directions, which will be interpreted variously by different schools and different teachers. The degree of influence over the curriculum as it affects the student is in inverse relation to distance from the classroom. In Western educational systems, accordingly, the classroom teacher is normally the most important modifier of the curriculum, his or her influence, however, being subject to three potential constraints.

The first constraint is a powerful inspectorate, which enforces adherence to a single interpretation of the official curriculum. This constraint exists in few present-day Canadian jurisdictions. The second is a system of external examinations, such as prevails in England and prevailed in Ontario for grade thirteen until 1967, which obliges teachers to follow a common curriculum. The third constraint on the teacher's curricular autonomy is the limitation of his or her choice of textbooks to an officially authorized list. This constraint is the only one of the three that currently prevails in all provinces of Canada.

Hodgetts' study of the teaching of Canadian studies in 847 Canadian classrooms in 1966-1967 clearly demonstrated that teachers of history and civics allow the content of the textbook to determine to a great extent the content of instruction. Hodgetts' researchers found that in studying controversial issues:

> Eighty-nine percent of the classes we observed unquestioningly followed the gray, consensus version of the textbook. . . . In twenty-five percent of the Canadian history classes we visited, the students were engaged in learning and recording in their notebooks . . . the "ready made verdicts of the textbooks". . . . The lowest category in our scale of methods was reserved for classes in which . . . the content was obviously a mere recitation of the prescribed textbook. Twenty-one iercent of all classes included in our survey fell into this lowest category.[1]

To the influence of the teacher over the content of instruction, then, must be added the influence of those who write, edit, and authorize textbooks. While the textbook influences students indirectly, by influencing instruction, it also has the potential to affect students' attitudes directly. It has long been established that written communications can affect the attitudes of readers (Tannenbaum, 1953; Watts, 1967). It has further been shown that school children's attitudes toward social issues, and especially toward minority groups, can be influenced by certain kinds of textbook and other reading material (Fisher, 1968; Lichter and Johnson, 1969). There are a number of reasons why this should be so.

For many children, textbooks constitute the bulk of the reading material that they encounter, particularly throughout the formative elementary grades. Moreover, the textbook is not simply *any* book; it is an *official* book, authorized by the government, promoted by the school, acknowledged by the teacher. Textbooks, particularly those in such social studies as history, civics, and geography, will provide students with their first introduction to many social issues. For some social and cultural questions, the influence of the textbook may remain decisive. Only in the later years of their schooling do students reach the Piagetian stage of formal operational thought, at which a mature critical attitude toward what is read may emerge (Hallam, 1967; Sullivan, 1967). When this biologically-determined uncritical attitude toward textbooks is reinforced by institutional policy, the potential influence of a textbook becomes immense. Furthermore, research on the dogmatic and authoritarian personality has indicated that students who make high scores on scales on authoritarianism tend to treat teachers and textbooks as sources of ultimate truth (Gladstein, 1960); this tendency, one suspects, applies to some extent to the majority of students, especially in elementary school.

The attitudinal content of school textbooks is therefore a matter of interest. There is now a growing body of knowledge concerning the attitudes and ideologies propounded in school textbooks. This chapter focuses attention on the attitudes expressed in textbooks toward questions of social and political diversity, culture conflict, and cultural pluralism.

Attitudes in Canadian textbooks

Treatment of cultural differences in textbooks has been a subject of research in Europe and North America since the early part of the century. The European work, largely conducted under the aegis of such organizations as the League of Nations, the Council of Europe, and UNESCO, has tended to concentrate on treatment of other nations in history and geography textbooks. The postwar influx of non-white immigrants into Britain has resulted in attention being paid more recently in that country to the racial attitudes of textbooks. In the United States, where most of the work has been done within universities, studies of textbook treatment of the American Negro have predominated, with more recent work on treatment of Indians and other ethnic minorities. The amount of textbook analysis completed in Canada has been relatively small, and it has concentrated mainly on treatment of French Canadians and Indians; nevertheless, the accumulated evidence is now sufficient to allow some general conclusions to be drawn concerning evaluative treatment of various social and cultural issues in Canadian textbooks.

Two limitations need to be borne in mind in the ensuing discussion of Canadian textbooks. First, most of the textbook analysis in Canada has used Ontario texts for its data. However, it is probably legitimate to generalize from these findings to Canadian textbooks as a whole. More than one-third of Canadian school pupils are found in the public and separate schools of Ontario. Many of the texts used in Ontario are also used in other provinces (Pratt, 1969). The official list of textbooks authorized for use in Ontario schools includes both English texts and French texts written by French Canadian authors and intended for students in francophone or bilingual schools in Ontario. Finally, the findings of studies of textbook treatment of most social issues have been remarkably consistent across different provinces, and, for that matter, throughout the English-speaking world. A second limitation on the textbook studies is in terms of subject. Research has shown that evaluative treatment of social and cultural topics is largely found in social studies texts, especially history. Where the subject of the texts studied in the research cited in the following pages is indicated as social studies, this term is used to comprehend history, geography, civics, economics, politics, sociology, and law as they are taught at the pre-university level.

Treatment of Racial Groups.

Non-white racial groups receive relatively little attention in Canadian textbooks, but as a function of the history of Canada, the Canadian Indian is the non-white group most visible in social studies textbooks, and references to this group probably outnumber those to all other non-white racial groups. This is particularly the case in the later elementary grades, where the history of Canada is a common subject of study. The nature of the treatment this group receives in textbooks is now fairly well established.

In 1963 Leduc, Belanger, and Juneau completed a study of history texts used in Protestant and Catholic elementary schools in Quebec. The study was the first in Canada to use quantitative techniques for textbook analysis, employing a word-count of the favourable terms applied to different groups. The study indicated that while the English and French texts differed reciprocally in their treatment of English and French Canadians, they concurred in the small number of favourable terms they applied to Indians. In the following year, the Indian and Métis Conference of Manitoba studied the textbooks used in that province and reported that the texts were contemptuous of Indian religious beliefs, concentrated on Indian faults but ignored Indian virtues, glossed over the negative results of the white man's impact, ignored Indian contributions to Canada's development, and represented drinking, gambling, and fighting as specifically Indian habits. During the next few years, this particular subject became a popular area of study: research was conducted by federal and provincial departments, by community organizations and individuals. The reports of the Royal Commission on Bilingualism and Biculturalism and the Ontario Committee on Aims and Objectives of Education (1968) commented on the inadequate treatment of Indians in school texts. The federal Department of Indian Affairs conducted its own study of textbooks used in its schools (usually those used in the province in which the schools were located) and reported a lack of information on Indian contributions to Canadian culture, use of pejorative terms to describe Indians, stereotyping, anachronism, lack of balance, and inappropriate illustrations. According to this study, "the history books in general use in Quebec would appear to require a complete review."[2] The press and television became interested in the subject (*Globe Mail*, 1967; *Telegram*, 1968; *Toronto Daily Star*, 1968; CHCH Television, 1969), particularly after the Ontario Human Rights Commission, following numerous complaints it had received concerning textbooks, commissioned a major study of the treatment of minorities in Ontario textbooks. This study by McDiarmid and Pratt (1971) of 143 Ontario social studies textbooks, and a subsequent study of sixty-nine history textbooks by Pratt (1971), reviewed treatment of various racial, ethnic, religious, and political minorities and out-groups. A technique was developed for analysis, using the ratio of favourable to unfavourable evaluative terms, which made it possible to plot the evaluative treatment of subjects in a text as points on an interval scale. Figure 1 shows the mean positions of French Canadians, Arabs, Indians, and Negroes in Ontario history textbooks authorized for 1968-1969 (Pratt, 1971). The scale indicates that whereas approximately four out of every five evaluative terms applied to French Canadians in the texts were favourable, only one out of every three terms applied to Indians and Negroes was favourable. A frequency count was made of the evaluative terms

FIGURE 1

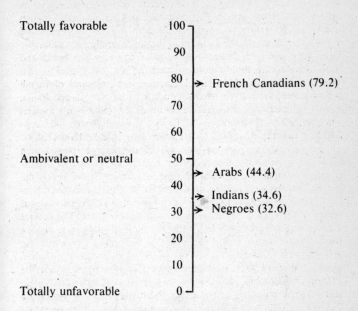

Location of Four Groups on A Favourable-Unfavourable Continuum in Ontario History Textbooks

applied to the four groups. Table 1 shows the percentage of all evaluative references to each group accounted for by each of the ten terms most frequently applied to the group. The high frequency of the word "savage" associated with Indians is due to the tendency of texts to use this word as a synonym for Indian, particularly in the case of French textbooks ("sauvage"). The illustrations in social studies textbooks were also analysed, the main results of the analysis being shown in Table 2. As the table indicates, the stereotype of Indians which prevails normally shows them half naked or in native dress, with feathers in their hair, and frequently in some aggressive posture.

These studies also provided clear evidence of the tendency of textbooks to ignore important aspects of the history of non-white racial groups as well as their contemporary situation, and to minimize interracial conflict except where the non-white race could be unequivocally cast in the role of aggressor. Thus it was discovered that the extermina-

TABLE 1

Arabs	%	Fr. Canadians	%	Indians	%	Negroes	%
great	3.9	great	4.2	savage	10.1	friendly	9.2
cruel	2.1	brave	3.9	friendly	6.1	unfriendly	5.0
feuding	2.1	courageous	3.6	massacre	4.9	savage	4.2
kind	2.1	skillful	3.3	skillful	4.0	faithful	3.4
pagan	2.1	heroic	2.7	hostile	3.8	kind	3.4
brilliant	1.6	determined	2.0	fierce	3.1	fierce	2.9
dictator	1.6	proud	1.7	great	2.3	primitive	2.6
fierce	1.6	devoted	1.6	murder	2.1	murder	2.4
friendly	1.6	famous	1.6	unfriendly	1.7	violent	2.4
resentful	1.6	daring	1.4	thief	1.6	backward	2.4

**Relative Frequency of Application of 10 Terms
Most Frequently Applied to 4 Groups in 69 Ontario History Textbooks**

tion of the Beothuk Indians of Newfoundland and the status of the
modern Canadian Indian were both largely ignored by texts; the history
of the American Negro was characterized by blandness and superficial-
ity where it was not ignored altogether; treatment of the Japanese
Canadians in the Second World War was rarely discussed in textbooks
dealing with the period; and the racial policies of the Nazis were
omitted or glossed over in a manner that was surprising even to
hardened textbook analysts. Less surprising was the finding that the

TABLE 2

	White Canadians	Asians	American Indians	Africans
	%	%	%	%
Clothing				
Naked, halfnaked	0	11	42	39
Native costume	0	66	53	41
Western dress	100	23	5	20
Aggression				
Fighting	0	2	12	2
Weapon in hand	6	5	20	13
Nonagressive	94	93	68	85
Decoration				
Feathers			86	
No Feathers			14	

**Depiction of Four Groups
in Illustrations in Ontario Social Studies Textbooks**

treatment of the concept of race was marked by omission, confusion, inaccuracy, and outright ignorance in nearly all textbooks. Of the thirty-four history and geography textbooks which the researchers expected to treat this topic, only four were classified as "good," the best two of these being French geography texts published in Paris.

A few quotations from textbooks may serve to summarize the issue of treatment of racial groups:

Champlain spent the winter with the Hurons, living in a long house swarming with Indians, mice, fleas, and lice. (Creighton (1962) p. 77)

The Jesuits fought bravely against the rude beliefs of the Indians. It was hard to make them understand the white man's God. Gentleness and kindness were signs of weakness to the savages. (Chatterton, Holmes, and Kuska (1966), p. 112)

Slaves on the southern plantations were seldom badly treated. It was in their master's interest to keep them healthy and content to work in the tobacco fields. (Tait (1960), p. 338)

In Britain, before the war, there was hardly any coloured population and therefore no problem. Of late, however, immigrants have
begun to pour into Britain from Jamaica and elsewhere in the West
Indies. They were used to a low standard of living and soon turned
several areas of London and other cities into coloured slums.
(Ricker, Saywell, and Rose (1960), p. 373)

The nations of the West have all outstripped the other world,
which economically, politically, and socially, stopped centuries
ago. . . . The ruling aristocracy in their luxury must bear a large
part of the blame for the poverty, sloth, and backwardness of
much of the Asian continent. . . . In many ways Asia must blame
herself for her backwardness. (Innis (1965), p. 24)

The results of the survey of Ontario social studies textbooks were
published in a book entitled *Teaching Prejudice*, which provoked
considerable comment in the press and in the Provincial Legislature.
The Minister of Education countered by citing evidence from his
Department's own study of textbooks, the results of which, however,
were not published at that time.

Treatment of ethnic groups.

Studies of treatment of ethnic groups have concentrated largely on the
relative treatment of English and French Canadians. As early as 1945, a
committee of the Canada and Newfoundland Education Association
discovered that two histories were being taught in Canada: in French
schools, a history that focused on the glories of New France and saw the
post-conquest history of Canada largely as the struggle for "la survivance"; in English schools, a political and constitutional history of
English Canada, with French Canada providing occasional local colour
(Committee for the Study of Canadian history Textbooks, 1945). These
findings were confirmed by a succession of studies (Quebec: Royal
Commission of Inquiry on Education in the Province of Quebec, 1965;
Sevigny, 1966; Wilson, 1966), and both French- and English-
Canadian historians have deplored the chauvinistic nature of history-
teaching in French and English Canada (Adair, 1943; Brunet, 1954,
1968). The Royal Commission on Bilingualism and Biculturalism
summarized the results of a study conducted for it by Trudel and Jain
with the comment that, "After studying Canadian history from a
textbook, a student may well conclude that only French- and English-
speaking Canadians count for anything—and that only the attitudes and
actions of his own language group can be justified."[3]

It is to be expected that authors approaching Canadian history from different cultural perspectives will produce essentially different histories. But despite the attention it has received, it seems probable that the French-English issue is more fairly treated in Canadian text-books than most other subjects in the area of intercultural relations. The research of Leduc, Belanger, and Juneau showed that French texts reserve their praise largely for French Canadians, and English texts largely for English Canadians; other than that study, there is a lack of quantitative comparative evidence on treatment of English Canadians in English and French texts. But the findings that emerge from study of treatment of French Canadians in English and French texts used in Ontario suggest that the difference is not between favourable and unfavourable treatment, but between favourable and very favourable. A comparison by Pratt of evaluative terms used to describe French Canadians in twenty-six English texts and seven French texts used in Ontario showed that an average of seventy-seven per cent of the terms were favourable in the English texts and eighty-seven per cent in the French texts (difference significant at .05) (1969, 131). Of the eleven "critical issues" whose treatment was studied by McDiarmid and Pratt, the two issues in English-French relations (the expulsion of the Acadians and the Conscription crisis in World War I) were the most adequately dealt with in Ontario social studies texts. The major criticism to be made of treatment of French Canadians in English texts is not of negative treatment but, as Table 1 suggests, of an unconvincing stereotype.

White ethnic groups other than English and French Canadians are accorded little space in Canadian textbooks. The nineteenth-century immigrants to Canada are admired because "they were hardy peasants and were not afraid of work" (Peart & Shaffter, 1961), and because "they stuck it out to become respected and valuable Canadian citizens" (Hodgetts, 1960). They were a "problem" only insofar as they were slow to assimilate: "they would have become Canadian more quickly if they had associated with English-speaking Canadians from the first" (Garland, 1961). The definition of a Canadian in Anglo-Saxon terms precludes recognition of the contribution of immigrants in adding a dimension to the Canadian ethnic mosaic. The cosmopolitan influence of the million non-British European immigrants to Canada since 1945 is similarly overlooked, as is the entire question of economic exploitation of immigrant groups.

In sum, the ethnic model of Canadian society conveyed in the texts is a far cry from a position of cultural pluralism, and if it does not exactly fit the melting-pot metaphor, then the appropriate image is perhaps that of a double-boiler.

Treatment of religious groups.

Where religious issues arise, Canadian textbooks normally adopt a Christian viewpoint. "David and Susan Go to Church" in the second-grade social studies text (Holmes, 1958); "Your father puts money on the collection plate at church each Sunday morning" in the history book (Deyell, 1958). Some French texts adopt an avowedly confessional point of view. "On a big sheet of paper," instructs an exercise in an elementary history text written by two religious, "write in large letters the invocation: Holy Canadian Martyrs, pray for us" (Charles and Léon, 1960). A number of such texts express their regrets over the Reformation, while one categorizes the Spanish Civil War as "essentially a war of religion between Catholicism and Communism" (Brault, 1965).

McDiarmid and Pratt compared the treatment of Christians, Jews, and Moslems in Ontario social studies texts, and found that treatment of all three was favourable, with Christians and Jews significantly more favourably treated than Moslems. Christians were typically "devoted," "zealous," and "martyrs"; Jews "great," "faithful," and "just"; while Moslems were "infidels" and "fanatics," but also "great," "devout," and "tolerant." While the development of Christianity is a major theme of history textbooks up to the Reformation, other religions rarely obtain more than a two- or three-page synopsis.

Treatment of social classes.

It is a truism that a middle-class stereotype prevails in school textbooks. It would be unrealistic to expect that the school, a middle-class institution par excellence, should reinforce any but middle-class mores. Studies by Sobel (1954) and Meyers (1968) provided empirical evidence of the class bias in American textbooks, but little research has been done into this aspect of Canadian texts. Poverty, unemployment, and economic disparity rarely feature in textbook accounts of the contemporary Canadian scene. Hard work, respectability, ambition, and the deferment of gratification are seen as the means to success, which is measured in terms of property and financial affluence. This much is revealed by a superficial reading of the texts. The study conducted for the Ontario Human Rights Commission reviewed the treatment in Ontario history texts of the Canadian labour movement; the findings throw some light on the class assumptions of textbook writers. Textbook accounts of strikes usually associate them with violence and bloodshed, without indicating which parties were responsible (McDiarmid and Pratt, 1971). The labour relations policies of governments and corporations in the 1920's are praised; the practices of Henry Ford in this area are cited by one text as "typical of a new concern by businessmen for their employees' welfare" (Nicholson, Boyd, Rannie, and Hobbs, 1962). Treatment of the Winnipeg General Strike, the watershed of Canadian union history, is marked by inaccuracy and hostile insinuation—Woodsworth, Dixon, and Heaps, on trial for seditious conspiracy, "put up such a brilliant defence that they were acquitted" (Hodgetts, 1960). There tend to be few references to the Canadian labour movement since 1920, but McDiarmid and Pratt cite the following passage from an intermediate level textbook as indicative of a patrician approach to the subject:

> The appearance of an organization like the Canadian Labour Congress, with a membership of well over one million workers, and the recent exposure of criminal leadership in some of the American unions, raises the question of whether trade unions are in danger of becoming too strong. Many Canadians feel that new laws are required to control the unions, while others advocate that they should be forced to sever their connection with the American labour movement. Whatever the outcome of these suggestions may be, it is certainly true that the workmen of Canada should be more determined than ever before to elect trade-union officials capable of wielding their power with a deep sense of responsibility to society as a whole as well as for the benefit of their own members. Otherwise, there is the danger that an overly aggressive, irresponsible labour movement could kill the goose that lays the golden egg.[4]

It is, however, significant that within the past few years two well-balanced texts specifically on the Winnipeg General Strike have been authorized for use in Ontario in secondary school history courses (Balawyder, 1967; Magder, 1969).

Treatment of political groups.

The political viewpoint espoused by textbooks is of major interest because of the role of the school in political socialization; yet of all aspects of textbooks, this has been among the least studied.

Canadian school textbooks identify "democracy" with the North American way of life. Democracy, however, is never defined; rather, it is used as a synonym for a general political good. A middle-of-the-road political position is usually promoted implicitly and occasionally made explicit. In one Ontario text, for example, a cartoon illustrates the caption, "Moderates who stand near the centre are usually those who think over a problem calmly and carefully" (Deyell, 1958).

It is impossible to say whether the generally cautious treatment of political topics in Canadian texts is voluntary on the part of authors or the result of pressure from publishers or governments. Such pressure has been known to exist elsewhere. In Mississippi, a Senate Education Committee recommended in 1940 that civics texts for Negro schools be void of references to voting, elections, civic responsibility, or democracy (Bierstedt, 1955). The writer has been unable to verify the legend that in the 1940's a committee was appointed by the Department of Education in British Columbia to comb school textbooks for references to the C.C.F. and to expunge them. What is obvious from a reading of the textbooks is the contrast between the lack of critical discussion of North American political institutions and the no-holds-barred treatment of Communist countries. "The problem of peace: The Soviet menace" is a chapter heading in a Grade 10 history text (Ricker, Saywell, and Rose, 1960). A textbook authorized for use in the Ontario World Politics programme, and written by a Canadian political scientist, reads like a primer for the Cold War: "Chapter 6: The Iron Fist—Nazism and Fascism . . . Chapter 7: The Iron Mind—Communism" (Fox, 1965). One text, published in 1954, but still authorized for use in Ontario in 1971-1972, includes a cartoon depicting election day in the Soviet Union, complete with bus labelled "Salt Mine Special"—"A special bus for ungrateful comrades who do not vote for George" (Brown, Careless, Craig, and Ray, 1954).

While texts expatiate on the "spying, secret arrests, torture, Siberian exile, forced labour camps, and individual and mass executions" (Ricker, Saywell and Rose, 1960) in the Soviet Union, treatment of right-wing totalitarian states receives rather cursory coverage. McDiarmid and Pratt found that of nineteen Ontario textbooks dealing with twentieth-century history, eight did not mention Nazi treatment of minorities, and none was rated higher than "fair" in their discussion of this topic.

In order to determine more exactly the political complexion of Canadian textbooks, an analysis was conducted by the writer* on six textbooks authorized for the study of history at the intermediate level (Grades 7-10) in Ontario for 1971-1972. The six texts were the following:

1. Brown, Careless, Craig, and Ray. *Canada and the World*. 1954.
2. Hodgetts. *Decisive Decades*. 1960.
3. Lambert. *The Twentieth Century*. 1960.
4. Ricker, Saywell, and Rose. *The Modern Era*. 1960.
5. Peart and Schaffter. *The Winds of Change*. 1961.

6. Nicholson, Boyd, Rannie, and Hobbs. *Three Nations*. 1962, Revised 1969.

The sample represented all the English-language texts for that level that dealt with the twentieth-century history of North America and Europe. The study aimed to assess the relative treatment of various political individuals and groups from the political "left," "centre," and "right." Three hypotheses were proposed: 1) that the textbooks would favour the political right over the political left; 2) that the textbooks would favour the political centre over the political extremes; and 3) that the political viewpoints of history textbooks and of history teachers would be similar. The instrument used to analyse the texts was ECO Analysis. This is a quantitative content analysis technique which has been described fully elsewhere (Pratt, 1971a); it produces a "Coefficient of Evaluation" representing the percentage of the value judgements expressed about a subject in a source which are favourable. Thus a Coefficient of zero indicates a totally unfavourable affective treatment of a subject, and a Coefficient of 100 totally favourable.

A minimum of ten evaluative assertions concerning a subject is necessary to calculate the Coefficient of Evaluation. As five of the twenty-six subjects originally chosen (Duplessis, Anarchists, Castro, Franco, Chiang Kai-Shek) received less than ten evaluative references, these subjects were not included in the analysis. The Coefficients achieved by the other subjects are shown in Table 3.

The unit of analysis in the study was the six textbooks as a whole. To determine whether grouping of the results in this way obscured differences among the texts, scores were determined for each subject in each text, where sufficient references could be found. The Coefficients for those subjects for which Coefficients could be determined in four or more texts are shown in Table 4, which reveals a high degree of consistency among the texts.

Having determined the evaluation of the political subjects in the texts, the next stage was to investigate the relationship between evaluation of the subjects and their location on the political spectrum. The ranking of the twenty-one subjects on the left-wing-right-wing continuum is largely self-evident, but to avoid the unreliability of a single judgement, practising history teachers were asked to rate each subject on a scale of 0 (extreme left) to 100 (extreme right). The teachers (N = 35, median age = 30.7 years, median teaching experience = 5.5 years) were engaged in an in-service training programme at Queen's University during the summer of 1972. Table 5 shows the median judgements of the thirty-five teachers regarding political location of the subjects, compared to the evaluation of the subjects in the textbooks. Correlation

TABLE 3

Rank	Subject	Coefficient of Evaluation	N of Evaluative References
1	Sir John A. MacDonald	95.2	21
2	J. S. Woodsworth	88.0	25
3	President Herbert Hoover	70.6	34
4	President Woodrow Wilson	69.9	113
5	President Franklin D. Roosevelt	69.9	83
6	Sir Wilfrid Laurier	67.7	89
7	Sir Robert Borden	57.8	45
8	C.C.F.-N.D.P.	50.0	18
9	Karl Marx	45.0	27
10	Socialists	33.9	59
11	Nicolai Lenin	33.3	30
12	John Foster Dulles	31.3	13
13	Richard B. Bennett	30.0	20
14	Bolsheviks	27.0	36
15	Communists	24.5	380
16	Benito Mussolini	24.1	108
17	Fascists	21.8	78
18	Nazis	21.4	143
19	Adolf Hitler	18.8	307
20	Ku Klux Klan	10.3	29
21	Senator Joseph McCarthy	4.3	46

**Evaluation of 21 Political Subjects
in 6 History Textbooks**

TABLE 4

Subject	Text					
	Canada & the World	Decisive Decades	The 20th Century	The Modern Era	The Winds of Change	Three Nations
	1	2	3	4	5	6
Wilson	—	64.7	60.0	86.7	73.1	70.0
Roosevelt	—	76.0	66.7	68.8	66.7	—
Laurier	—	65.4	—	76.2	65.2	70.0
Communists	19.3	22.6	34.0	30.8	25.5	18.2
Mussolini	—	29.4	19.0	23.1	25.0	26.7
Fascists	12.5	31.7	8.3	—	46.2	—
Nazis	—	23.4	4.5	11.8	37.5	20.0
Hitler	14.3	17.5	22.0	14.0	19.3	20.0

Evaluation of 8 Political Subjects
in 6 History Textbooks

of the two sets of scores yielded a correlation coefficient of -.320. The first hypothesis was therefore not sustained. Instead of favouring the right-wing subjects, the texts showed a slight and not statistically significant tendency to evaluate right-wing subjects less favourably than left-wing subjects. (No immediate relationship between political orientation and age was established for the teachers. The correlation between teacher age and evaluation score accorded by teachers to Socialists was .075).

TABLE 5

Subject	Coefficient in Texts	Evaluative Rank in Texts	Right-left score by teachers	Right-left rank by teachers
MacDonald	95.2	1	60.7	11
Woodsworth	88.0	2	35.5	16
Hoover	70.6	3	70.9	8
Wilson	69.9	4	55.2	12
Roosevelt	69.9	5	50.5	14
Laurier	67.7	6	52.0	13
Borden	57.8	7	70.7	9
CCF-NDP	50.0	8	32.5	17
Marx	45.0	9	10.2	21
Socialists	33.9	10	35.6	15
Lenin	33.3	11	10.9	18
Dulles	31.3	12	78.0	7
Bennett	30.0	13	62.5	10
Bolsheviks	27.0	14	10.8	20
Communists	24.5	15	10.9	18
Mussolini	24.1	16	85.8	6
Fascists	21.8	17	90.3	3
Nazis	21.4	18	90.6	1
Hitler	18.8	19	90.4	2
Ku Klux Klan	10.3	20	90.1	4
McCarthy	4.3	21	88.0	5

**Evaluation of Political Subjects by Texts
Compared to Location on Political Spectrum**

An "index of extremeness" was next derived by measuring the distance of the median "right-left score" as judged by teachers from the theoretical mid-point of fifty. This data is summarized in Table 6. The observed correlation between the columns in Table 6 was -.772 (sig. at .01). The second hypothesis was therefore sustained: the evaluation of political subjects in textbooks is related to the distance of the subject from the political centre.

Finally, a comparison was made between evaluation of political subjects by the textbooks and by history teachers. The history teachers mentioned above were asked to rate each subject on a scale of 0-100, representing their evaluative opinion of each subject. The order of this and the previous question were scrambled to counteract the reaction of one question with the other. Subsequent discussion with the teachers revealed that some of the thirty-six teachers completing the questionnaire misinterpreted the instructions to "evaluate the subjects" as being intended to elicit their opinion as to how interesting the topics were as school subjects. Favourable evaluation of both Communists and Hitler (at sixty or over) was taken as *prima facie* evidence of this misinterpretation. Eleven papers were rejected for this reason, leaving a sample of twenty-five (median age 30.5, median years experience 5.5). The median evaluations of the political subjects by this group is shown in Table 7. The similarities in rank, and in some cases in score, between the textbooks and the teachers are remarkable, and amongst other things further validate the instrument used in text analysis. Only three subjects are evaluated much differently by teachers than by texts; textbooks evaluate Hoover more favourably than do teachers, while teachers are more favourably inclined toward Socialists and Lenin than are texts. The observed correlation between the scores in Table 7 was .797 (sig. at .01). The third hypothesis was thus sustained: the political viewpoints of teachers and textbooks reinforce one another.

A final indication of the nature of the value judgements of political subjects by textbooks was provided by a frequency count of the evaluative terms used in texts about political subjects. The five or six terms most frequently used in evaluative assertions concerning six of the subjects are shown in Table 8. It should be borne in mind that terms such as "just" and "idealist" in the list comprehend such words as "justice" and "ideals" or "idealism" in the sources. The table illustrates the somewhat stereotyped and repetitive treatment of political extremes by textbooks.

Conclusions and Implications

The content analysis studies show that Canadian school textbooks do

TABLE 6

Subject	Coefficient in Texts	Evaluative Rank in Texts	Extremeness Index	Extremeness Rank
MacDonald	95.2	1	10.7	18
Woodsworth	88.0	2	14.5	15
Hoover	70.6	3	20.9	12
Wilson	69.9	4	5.2	19
Roosevelt	69.9	5	0.5	21
Laurier	67.7	6	2.0	20
Borden	57.8	7	20.7	13
CCF-NDP	50.0	8	17.5	14
Marx	45.0	9	39.8	5
Socialists	33.9	10	14.4	16
Lenin	33.3	11	39.1	7
Dulles	31.3	12	28.0	11
Bennett	30.0	13	12.5	17
Bolsheviks	27.0	14	39.2	6
Communists	24.5	15	39.1	7
Mussolini	24.1	16	35.8	10
Fascists	21.8	17	40.3	3
Nazis	21.4	18	40.6	1
Hitler	18.8	19	40.4	2
Ku Klux Klan	10.3	20	40.1	4
McCarthy	4.3	21	38.0	9

**Political Extremeness and
Evaluation of Political Subjects by Texts**

TABLE 7

Subject	Coefficient in Texts	Evaluative Rank in Texts	Evaluation by teachers	Evaluative rank by teachers
MacDonald	95.2	1	74.9	1
Woodsworth	88.0	2	60.0	5
Hoover	70.6	3	35.0	13
Wilson	69.9	4	69.9	4
Roosevelt	69.9	5	70.3	3
Laurier	67.7	6	70.4	2
Borden	57.8	7	49.8	10
CCF-NDP	50.0	8	50.3	9
Marx	45.0	9	59.6	8
Socialists	33.9	10	60.0	5
Lenin	33.3	11	60.0	5
Dulles	31.3	12	35.0	13
Bennett	30.0	13	45.0	11
Bolsheviks	27.0	14	40.0	12
Communists	24.5	15	30.2	15
Mussolini	24.1	16	19.6	16
Fascists	21.8	17	14.8	17
Nazis	21.4	18	10.4	19
Hitler	18.8	19	10.2	20
Ku Klux Klan	10.3	20	0.4	21
McCarthy	4.3	21	14.0	18

**Evaluation of Political Subjects
by Textbooks and by Teachers**

TABLE 8

Wilson	%	Laurier	%	Communists	%
just	7.1	eloquent	5.6	dictatorship	8.2
idealist	5.3	great	4.5	threat	3.9
peace	5.3	bitter	4.5	strong	3.4
failure	5.3	determined	3.4	fear	3.2
freedom	3.5	remarkable	3.4	force	2.6
great	3.5				

Mussolini	%	Nazis	%	Hitler	%
dictatorship	27.8	aggressive	7.0	dictatorship	8.8
aggressive	4.6	tyranny	6.3	aggressive	5.2
threat	3.7	menace	3.5	threat	4.2
ruthless	2.8	dictatorship	3.5	force	2.6
failure	2.8	threat	2.8	ruthless	2.3
glory	2.8			strong	2.3

**Relative Frequency of Application of Terms
Most Frequently Applied to 6 Subjects in 6 History Textbooks**

not represent or support a culturally pluralist model of society. They do support a consensus, non-controversial, conventional view of society. A number of reasons may be suggested for this.

School textbook authors themselves represent a narrow segment of the population. Much more source analysis is needed in this area, but the general delineation is clear. Authors are typically successful teachers in their thirties or forties who have risen in the administrative hierarchy of the schools to Department Head, Principal, or teachers' college instructor. Often a university academic is included as co-author or consultant, but textbook authors are not as a rule academics. The books are written ten or twenty years after the authors' academic training. The similarity of treatment of topics among different textbooks suggests use of common secondary sources rather than original research. Almost inevitably, these middle-class, middle-aged, middle-income, middle-status authors share common social and political ideologies: they are middle Canada.

The centripetal tendency of the authors' output is compounded by the existence of official authorization committees. A textbook that fails to obtain authorization may not even pay for the cost of its publication; but a text which achieves authorization and retains it for a decade or more can reap enormous profits. It is therefore in the interest of publishing houses to ensure that textbook content is acceptable to authorizing committees, and this common sieve through which textbooks pass probably serves to eliminate expressions of divergent opinion on social issues.

A further conformist pressure subsists in the nature of the textbook itself. If a text is designed as a compendium or condensation of knowledge in a social area, sometimes compressing the history of three centuries or the geography of a dozen countries into three hundred pages, then it is most likely that the text will concentrate on common features and ignore diversity. In consequence of these factors, the advantages of authorities providing a choice of alternative textbooks and encouraging teachers to use multiple textbooks for a given grade level and subject are illusory.

Conformity goes hand in hand with blandness. Culture conflict is not a serious issue in many textbooks. Where it exists, it is recorded in terms of savage natives who unsuccessfully opposed the inexorable march of progress, represented by the white man. Deliberate pains are taken to minimize well-known episodes of conflict. The Canadian Indian perpetrates, but is rarely the object, of massacres; he simply fades quietly out of the textbooks in the later nineteenth century. Life was rosy in the ante-bellum South, except for the "extremists known as Abolitionists" (Rogers and Harris, 1967). Joe Hill, Sacco and Vanzetti, Norman Bethune, and the Rosenbergs do not appear in school texts. Little or no coverage is given to movements suggesting alternative patterns of social organization. The labour and civil rights movements are seen only as the struggle of certain groups to become more, not less, typically North American. The Canadian Bill of Rights, a barely-enforcible showpiece statute, is invariably cited in civics textbooks; mention of enforcible Provincial legislation against discrimination is conspicuous by its absence.

In sum, the school textbook introduces students to a unitary view of society. Official pronouncements in favour of cultural pluralism find no counterpart in Canadian school textbooks. Social and ideological divergence provide occasional interesting episodes and anecdotes, but are not considered part of the mainstream of Canadian life. Canada is viewed as a white, Christian, homogenous, middle-class country where liberal democracy and free enterprise have combined to produce the ideal society. That society may not remain static, but may be transformed, does not concern the textbooks, for none of the subjects taught in school consider the future a legitimate part of their subject matter. Students whose aspirations and opinions differ from this monolithic model are likely to be considered, and to consider themselves, misfits.

But there are signs of the beginning of change. The academic writing of Canadian history is itself changing, so that the history of Canada is no longer written as the view from the Commons' press gallery. Mealing's criticism of Canadian historians, issued in 1965,

> Our shortcoming has been to ignore rather than to deny the class structure of society. . . . The greater number of historians have taken their agenda from dead politicians[5]

has since become less valid. It would be unlikely that one of Canada's leading historians could today, as Creighton did in 1957, publish a "history of Canada" that made no mention of the Winnipeg General Strike. Admittedly a time-lag of about two decades exists between the leading edge of academic thought and school textbooks. But textbooks authorized for use in Ontario in the last two years include at least ten texts on Canadian Indians, and several on such topics as immigration, student unrest, Americanization, Progressivism and Socialism, and particular episodes of culture conflict such as the Conscription crises, the Riel affair, and the Acadian deportation. The great majority of these texts are collections of readings, which increases the diversity of viewpoints represented. (On the other hand, some of them perpetuate the deficiencies of the traditional textbook; in one reader on Canadian Indians (Sheffe, 1970), made up almost entirely of newspaper articles, less than a quarter of the items are actually written by Indians.) New courses of study, such as the Ontario programmes in World Religions, Man, Science, and Technology, and People and Politics, provide a vehicle, and in fact call for, a close look at questions of cultural diversity and social dissent. In the long run, these changes may have little effect on students' attitudes, partly because it is easier to change texts and programmes than to change teachers, and partly because students' social beliefs are largely determined in the elementary school, where little change in textbooks and programmes is evident.

We return, therefore, to the original proposition of this paper, that the school reflects society, and reflects most accurately the stratum of society which controls education by providing the civil servants, Board members, and teachers whose decisions largely determine the nature of schooling. If society changes radically enough to alter the complexion of this middle stratum, then schools and textbooks will alter with it, as educational decision-makers begin to co-opt as teachers, administrators, or textbook authors, individuals who at present would be classified as dissenters, and this in turn will socialize school children into varied or different social ideologies. Such changes are already visible on a minute scale. On any major scale, they remain in the distant future.

Notes

[1]A.B. Hodgetts, *What Culture? What Heritage? A Study of Civic Education in Canada* (Toronto: Ontario Institute for Studies in Education, 1968), p. 24, 26-27, 45.

[2]Canada. Department of Indian Affairs and Northern Development, *Report on Textbooks* (n.d. Received February 1969), p. 7.

[3]Canada. Royal Commission on Bilingualism and Biculturalism. *Report*, Vol. 2. Education (Ottawa: Queen's Printer, 1968), p. 282.

[4]Hodgetts, *op. cit.*, p. 537.

[5]S. R. Mealing, "The Concept of Social Class and the Interpretation of Canadian History," *Canadian Historical Review*, Vol. 46 (1965), p. 202.

Bibliography

Adair, E.R. "The Canadian Contribution to Historical Science," *Culture*, Vol. 4 (1943), p. 63-83.

Balawyder, A. *The Winnipeg General Strike* (Toronto: Copp Clark, 1967).

Bierstedt, R. "The Writers of Textbooks," in L. J. Cronbach *et al.*, *Text Materials in Modern Education* (Urbana, Ill.: University of Illinois Press, 1955), p. 96-128.

Brault, L. *Le Canada au XXe siècle* (Toronto: Nelson, 1965).

Brown, G.W., Careless, J.M.S., Craig, G.M., and Ray, E. *Canada and the World* (Toronto: Dent, 1954).

Brunet, M. "Histoire et Historiens," in M. Brunet, *Canadians et Canadiens* (Montreal: Fides, 1954), p. 32-46.

Brunet, M. "La Recherche et l'Enseignment de l'Histoire," in M. Brunet, *Quebec-Canada Anglais: Deux itineraires, un affrontement* (Montreal: Editions H.M.H., 1968), p. 43-58.

Canada. Department of Indian Affairs and Northern Development. *Report on Textbooks*. Mimeographed (n.d. Received February 1969).

Canada. Dominion Bureau of Statistics. *Canada Yearbook 1971* (Ottawa: Queen's Printer, 1971).

Canada. Royal Commission on Bilingualism and Biculturalism. *Report*, Vol. 2. *Education* (Ottawa: Queen's Printer, 1968).

Charles, Frère, and Léon, Frère. *La nouvelle France* (Toronto: Nelson, 1960).

Chatterton, W.G., Holmes, M.W., and Kuska, A. *New World Social Studies* (Toronto: Holt, Rinehart, Winston, 1966).

CHCH Television, Hamilton, Ontario. Programme on the Treatment of Indians in School Textbooks (First broadcast 18 February 1969. C. Screen Gems, Toronto).

Committee for the Study of Canadian History Textbooks. "Report," *Canadian Education*, Vol. 1 (1945), p. 2-34.

Creighton, D. *Dominion of the North: A History of Canada*. Rev. ed. (Toronto: MacMillan, 1957).

Creighton, L.B. *Canada: The Struggle for Empire*. Rev. ed. (Toronto: Dent, 1962).

Deyell, E. *Canada: A New Land* (Toronto: Gage, 1958).

Deyell, E. *Canada: The New Nation* (Toronto: Gage, 1958).

Fisher, F.L. "Influences of Reading and Discussion on the Attitudes of Fifth Graders towards American Indians," *Journal of Educational Research*, Vol. 62 (1968), p. 130-134.

Fox, P. *Battlefront: The Fight for Liberty* (Toronto: Holt, Rinehart, Winston, 1965).

Garland, A. *Canada, Our Country: Part 2* (Toronto: MacMillan, 1961).

Gladstein, G.A. "Study Behavior of Gifted Stereotyped and Nonstereotyped College Students" *Personnel Guidance Journal*, Vol. 38 (1960), p. 470-474.

The Globe and Mail. "Human rights: Insulting references sought in textbooks," (November 28, 1967).

Hallam, R.N. "Logical Thinking in History," *Educational Review*, Vol. 19 (1967), p. 182-202.

Haller, E.J. and Thorson, S.J. "The Political Socialization of Children and the Structure of the Elementary School," *Interchange*, Vol. 1, No. 3 (1970), p. 45-55.

Hess, R.D. and Torney, J.V. *The Development of Political Attitudes in Children* (Chicago: Aldine, 1967).

Hodgetts, A.B. *Decisive Decades* (Toronto: Nelson, 1960).

Hodgetts, A.B. *What Culture? What Heritage? A Study of Civic Education in Canada* (Toronto: Ontario Institute for Studies in Education, 1968).

Holmes, M.W. *We live in Greenwood Village* (Toronto: Dent, 1958).

Indian and Métis Conference, Committee of the Community Welfare Planning Countil. *Survey of Canadian History Textbooks: Submission to the Curriculum Revision Committee, Manitoba Department of Education*. Mimeographed (Winnipeg, 1964).

Innis, H. *History of Civilization*. Rev. ed. (Toronto: McGraw Hill, 1965).

Lambert, R.S. *The Twentieth Century* (Toronto: Grant, 1960).

Leduc, A., Belanger, P.W., and Juneau, A. *Les Manuels d' histoire du Canada*. Mimeographed (Quebec City: Laval University, 1963).

Lichter, J.H., and Johnson, D.W. "Changes in Attitude of White Elementary School Students after Use of Multiethnic Readers," *Journal of Educational Psychology*, Vol. 60 (1969), p. 148-152.

Magder, B. *The Winnipeg General Strike: Management-Labour Relations* (Toronto: MacLean-Hunter, 1969).

McDiarmid, G.L. and Pratt, D. *Teaching Prejudice* (Toronto: Ontario Institute for Studies in Education, 1971).

Mealing, S.R. "The Concept of Social Class and the Interpretation of Canadian History," *Canadian Historical Review*, Vol. 46 (1965), p. 201-218.

Meyers, H.W. "An Analysis of Selected Elementary Textbooks to Determine the Extent of Expression of Certain Social Class Values," *Dissertation Abstracts*, Vol. 28 (1968), p. 4537-A.

Nicholson, G.W.L., Boyd, H.H., Rannie, R.J., and Hobbs, A.E. *Three Nations* (Toronto: McClelland and Stewart, 1962).

Ontario. Provincial Committee on Aims and Objectives of Education in the Schools of Ontario. *Living and Learning: Report* (Toronto: Ontario Department of Education, 1968).

Peart, H.W. and Schaffter, J. *The Winds of Change* (Toronto: Ryerson, 1961).

Pratt, D. "An Instrument for Measuring Evaluative Assertions concerning Minority Groups and Its Application in an Analysis of History Textbooks Approved for Ontario Schools" (Unpublished Ph.D. dissertation, University of Toronto, 1969).

Pratt, D. "Value Judgments in Textbooks: The Coefficient of Evaluation as a Quantitative Measure," *Interchange*, Vol. 2, No. 3 (1971), p. 1-14.

Pratt, D. *How to find and measure bias in textbooks* (Englewood Cliffs, N.J.: Educational Technology Press, 1971).

Quebec: Royal Commission of Inquiry on Education in the Province of Quebec. *Report*. Vol. 3. *L'Administration de l'enseignment* (Quebec City, 1965).

Ricker, J.C., Saywell, J.T., and Rose, E.E. *The Modern Era* (Toronto: Clarke Irwin, 1960).

Rogers, S.J. and Harris, D.F. *Nation of the North* (Toronto: Clarke Irwin, 1967).

Sears, D.O. Review of *The Development of Political Attitudes in Children* by R.D. Hess and J.V. Torney, *Harvard Education Review*, Vol. 38 (1968), p. 571-577.

Sevigny, R. "Analyze de contenu de manuels d'histoire du Canada" (Unpublished M.A. thesis, Université Laval, Quebec City, 1966).

Sheffe, N. *Issues for the Seventies: Canada's Indians* (Toronto: McGraw-Hill, 1970).

Sobel, M.J. "An Analysis of Social Studies Textbooks in regard to their Treatment of Four Areas of Human Relations," *Dissertation Abstracts*, Vol. 14 (1954), p. 950.

Sullivan, E.V. *Piaget and the School Curriculum: A Critical Appraisal*. (Toronto: Ontario Institute for Studies in Education, 1967).

Sullivan, E.V., Byrne, N., and Stager, M. "The Development of Canadian Students' Political Conceptions," *Interchange*, Vol. 1, No. 3 (1970), p. 56-67.

Tait, G.E. *Fair Domain* (Toronto: Ryerson, 1960).

Tannenbaum, P.H. "Attitudes Towards Source and Concept as Factors in Attitude Change through Communications," *Dissertation Abstracts*, Vol. 13 (1953), p. 1288.

The Telegram. "Bias as history," (Editorial, Dec. 13, 1968), p. 6.

The Toronto Daily Star. "Tell it the way it was," (Editorial, Oct. 15, 1968), p. 6.

Watts, W.A. "Relative Persistence of Opinion Change Induced by Active compared to Passive Participation," *Journal of Personality and Social Psychology*, Vol. 5 (1967), p. 4-15.

Wilson, R.D. "An Inquiry into the Interpretation of Canadian History in the Elementary and Secondary School Textbooks of English and French Canada," (Unpublished M.A. thesis, McGill University, 1966).

5.

Evolution de l'idéologie scolaire officielle dans les manuels de pédagogie québecois*

Vincent Ross

English Abstract

THIS text, an abridged and updated version of an earlier monograph, presents an analysis of the thematic structure of the educational ideology formulated in the five successive general textbooks on pedagogy that were approved for official use in the Normal Schools of Quebec's educational system between 1853 and 1948. The concept of ideology used here specifies the five following levels: 1) the supporting group, or source; 2) the intended ideological "audience"; 3) the "action programme," or model; 4) the "normative premises" or explicit value orientations; and 5) the definition of the situation. A second phase of analysis attempted to determine, over time, those thematic elements which were: 1) preserved; 2) modified or introduced; 3) normatively challenged or rejected; and 4) abandoned. In the last section, a brief overview is presented of the more recent trends in Quebec's official educational ideology since 1948, with special reference to the ideology of school reform in the 1960's. A general interpretation emerges: the official doctrine evolved historically from an ideology of preservation of a rural, agriculturally-based traditional community through "last-ditch" attempts to preserve the unity of the traditional value structure against the growing pluralism of a society which was becoming *de facto* industrialized, urbanized, and technology-instrumented; the present

*A modified version of this paper by Vincent Ross originally appeared in *Recherches Sociographiques*, Vol. 10, Nos. 2-3 (1969), published by Les Presses de l' Université Laval. This paper is reproduced with their permission.

prevailing ideology now explicitly recognizes, and even welcomes, this state of modernity but reveals a marked uncertainty about its own sociocentric value orientations.

NOUS étudierons ici le système d'éducation du Québec à travers la doctrine idéologique dont s'est servie l'organisation scolaire pour fonder son action depuis le milieu du XIXe siècle. Le contenu idéologique des manuels de pédagogie officiellement en usage dans les écoles normales a servi à justifier périodiquement l'action du système d'enseignement en fonction des valeurs dominantes et en fonction de représentations particulières de la société québécoise.

Le matériel soumis à l'analyse est constitué de cinq manuels, depuis celui de 1853 jusqu'à celui de 1948 encore en usage au moment de la rédaction de cette étude.[1] Si l'on ne considère que le seul contenu proprement idéologique de ces manuels, notre matériel se présente comme une série de reformulations successives (1853, 1865, 1901, 1924 et 1948) de l'idéologie scolaire autorisée concernant l'enseignement public du niveau primaire et du niveau secondaire et transmis institutionnellement aux futurs enseignants durant leur formation dans les écoles normales. Les deux premiers manuels (ceux de Valade et de Langevin) sont inclus dans la période d'existence politique du Bas-Canada d'avant la Confédération; les trois autres (celui de Rouleau, Ahern et Magnan, celui de Mgr Ross et celui de Vinette) ont été publiés sous le régime constitutionnel de la province de Québec.

Perspectives théoriques et modèle d'analyse

On peut considérer les idéologies au moins sous deux angles. D'une part, en tant que représentations culturelles manifestes impliquées concrètement dans le fonctionnement et les transformations des structures sociales, elles peuvent être analysées dans leur fonction d'adaptation aux changements socio-historiques. L'idéologie apparaîtra alors comme une technique particulière utilisée par les pouvoirs sociaux pour adapter les justifications de leurs stratégies plus ou moins implicites à une conjoncture historique donnée (F. Dumont, 1963a, 158)[2].

La seconde perspective d'analyse consiste à aborder l'idéologie dans sa structure interne, comme système de pensée, dans sa fonction de représentation et de justification de l'action par rapport à un contexte socio-historique. L'idéologie est alors analysée dans la structure et les transformations internes qu'elle manifeste à travers sa propre histoire. Dans cette perspective, qui est ici adoptée, Fernand Dumont a défini les idéologies comme ''des schémas explicites constituant, pour les fins de l'action à poursuivre, des définitions solidaires de la situation et des groupes qui y sont engagés'' (1963b, 48)[3].

Niveau synchronique

Cette définition nous semble permettre d'expliciter cinq niveaux d'analyse de la structure idéologique.

1. *Le définiteur idéologique* (ou ''groupe idéologique,'' ou ''groupe de support'' de l'idéologie) est le groupe qui définit et propose le schéma justificateur; il fait donc partie des pouvoirs sociaux parmi lesquels il occupe une position stratégique plus ou moins avantageuse.

2. *Le destinataire* de l'idéologie est constitué par l'''auditoire'' (plus ou moins particularisé, plus ou moins explicitement défini) visé par l'argumentation justifiant le modèle d'action défini. Le destinataire se compose de tous ceux que le groupe idéologique cherche à mettre d'accord sur la justification de son action et sur sa définition de la situation.

3. *Le modèle d'action* est défini par l'ensemble des schémas d'action impliqués dans une justification.

4. *Les prémisses* (ou ''sources'') idéologiques sont les ''conceptions générales,'' les ''évidences fondamentales,'' les valeurs ou les ''finalités désirables'' considérées comme étant de sagesse commune, et au nom desquelles s'énoncent les normes explicites (les ''principes'' ou règles) justifiant le programme d'action et contestant les groupes idéologiques divergents (dans leurs propres modèles d'action et prémisses).

5. *Les représentations de la situation* sont les ''éléments'' de la situation socio-historique qui sont visés explicitement comme conditions ou objets (immédiats ou lointains) des modèles d'action définis.

La justification consiste à poser comme nécessaire la double relation qui articule le modèle d'action, d'une part sur les prémisses idéologiques et, d'autre part, sur les représentations de la situation. En d'autres termes, justifier un modèle d'action c'est le définir comme dépendant normativement des prémisses invoquées et des exigences de la situation décrite (compatibles à la fois ou séparément).

Cette articulation du raisonnement normatif sur des définitions de situations (qui ne sauraient, par ailleurs, être que précaires et provisoires) fait que l'idéologie est un mode de pensée fondamentalement syncrétique et donc à remanier périodiquement en fonction de l'évolution historique du consensus social perçu par l'idéologue.

L'analyse comparative et les transformations diachroniques de l'idéologie

La fonction de cette seconde phase de l'analyse sera de dégager d'une façon un peu précise la direction des transformations décelables, d'un manuel au suivant, dans la série chronologique des documents.

Dans la perspective où nous situons notre étude, il ne s'agira pas d'analyser l'adaptation idéologique dans le cadre d'une sociologie de la société globale où le fonctionnement de l'idéologie aurait à s'articuler par rapport aux autres niveaux de la structure sociale. Nous abordons ici l'idéologie uniquement comme représentation culturelle explicite. C'est pourquoi nous parlerons de 'modifications' plutôt que d'ajustements' ou d' adaptations': il faudra en effet opérer la lecture de ces modifications strictement à l'intérieur de la structure du phénomène idéologique lui-même.

Une approche comme celle de Gérald Fortin (qui intègre après coup les résultats d'une analyse limitée, comme la nôtre, à la structure interne de l'idéologie) offre des indications importantes pour cette étape de notre modèle d'analyse:

> Ces ajustements se traduisent ordinairement par un changement dans l'accent placé sur les différents éléments. Ils peuvent aussi se traduire par l'incorporation de nouveaux éléments compatibles ou rendus compatibles avec la structure existante. L'analyse des caractéristiques des nouveaux éléments au moment de l'incorporation est utile non seulement par rapport à l'étude des mécanismes de la pensée idéologique mais aussi par rapport à l'étude de la structure et du contenu d'une idéologie particulière (1963, 224).

Concrètement, il s'agira d'une technique d'analyse comparative dont la fonction sera de déterminer, en ordonnant les cinq formulations successives de l'idéologie scolaire officielle, quels sont les éléments explicites (aux cinq niveaux définis pour l'analyse synchronique) qui, dans le temps, sont:

1. *conservés* (maintenus; réaffirmés);
2. *modifiés ou introduits* (élargissement des définitions);
3. *contestés ou rejetés* (condamnés, refusés);
4. *abandonnés* ('refoulés' dans l'implicite; 'retirés').

On pourra ainsi caractériser les principales tendances dans la transformation de l'idéologie aux divers niveaux de sa structure.

La Structure idéologique des cinq manuels de pédagogie

L'idéologie formulée dans chacun des manuels sera très brièvement décrite dans cette section, qui résume les résultats de la première étape du modèle d'analyse. Les citations directes tirées du matériel n'auront ici qu'une valeur illustrative, et un grand nombre d'analyses détaillées seront omises.

Le manuel de F.-X. Valade (1853)

L'intention centrale de ce manuel apparaît comme éminemment pratique et 'concrète'; son contenu idéologique est très peu dense et nettement circonscrit dans les pages du texte. Le manuel de Valade est le seul parmi les cinq où l'on trouve si peu de justifications de la situation dans le corps même du volume. C'est moins un manuel de pédagogie proprement dit qu'un résumé serré de toutes les matières que les instituteurs auront à enseigner. Les seuls passages proprement idéologiques se trouvent dans la brève *Introduction* de Valade lui-même et dans la *Recommandation* du Surintendant de l'Education, le Dr J.-B. Meilleur.

Les destinataires de l'idéologie sont, d'une part, "tous ceux que préoccupe l'éducation," et d'autre part les instituteurs eux-mêmes.

Le modèle d'action de l'instituteur se présente d'emblée comme l'analogue d'une mission divine, articulée sur un schéma providentialiste: "L'instituteur a un noble devoir à remplir, car il est chargé d'un véritable sacerdoce: celui de former aux vertus morales et civiles, l'enfant qui lui est donné" (IV).

L'éducateur (destinataire de l'idéologie) a pour tâche de former les enfants (objet immédiat) ou la "jeunesse" à des vertus; ces vertus sont la sobriété, l'amour du travail et le "travail éclairé"; ce travail "éclairé" répond à son tour, de quelque manière, à des "besoins" de la société (objet lointain du modèle d'action scolaire).

Il n'est donc pas étonnant que dans le prolongement de ce modèle d'action éducative, la société apparaisse sous l'angle des métiers et des professions et renvoie à une crise de la structure des occupations:

> Les professions libérales, écrit Meilleur, sont généralement plus que remplies de sujets, souvent médiocres, qui passent dans l'oisiveté . . . un temps précieux que le manque d'ouvrage ne leur permet pas d'utiliser, soit pour leur bien personnel, soit pour celui de la société; tandis que des branches d'industrie honnête sont presque désertes, et que des emplois honorables sont dédaignés, dont cependant l'exercice serait très utile aux individus et à la

société, si nos jeunes gens s'y adonnaient davantage. Nous devons donc disposer les enfants de bonne heure, et les préparer promptement, mais aussi solidement, à ces divers genres d'occupation profitable, en leur donnant le goût du travail, et une instruction adaptée aux besoins et aux circonstances du pays. Ce sont des artisans, des industriels, des agriculteurs instruits qui nous manquent dans le Bas-Canada, et on ne saurait trop faire d'efforts et de sacrifices pour en augmenter le nombre, au moyen de nos écoles (VIII).

Il résume ensuite globalement les exigences de la situation, en signalant cette disparité de base:

Les professions libérales souffrent du trop plein et les mécaniques du trop peu de leurs membres respectifs; double mal, auquel il devient urgent d'apporter un remède prompt et efficace. L'intérêt moral et matériel de la société le demande (VIII).

La solution consiste donc à proposer des "maximes" compatibles avec ce qui est conçu comme étant les "véritables intérêts" dans la situation; or c'est précisément ce que l'idéologie propose déjà par ailleurs, sous la forme explicite de "vertus" propices à un travail efficace dans la société.

Cette idéologie est une sorte de compromis entre une justification du modèle d'action par les vertus traditionnelles d'une part et, d'autre part, les critères d'une pensée qu'on pourrait caractériser comme "technicienne". Notre dernière citation illustre admirablement cet aspect structurel de l'idéologie:

Les habitants Canadiens, écrit Valade[4], sont en général frugaux et industrieux; leurs terres ont un bel aspect, malgré que, pour la plupart, elles soient épuisées. Tout ce qui manque à l'agriculteur du Bas-Canada, c'est un bon système. Un tel système, pour être valable, doit posséder les qualités suivantes, savoir:

1. Il doit être économique, et ne pas requérir plus de capitaux que le système actuel, ou plutôt l'absence actuelle de tout système ne requiert. . . .
2. Il doit ramener la fertilité du sol où elle a été détruite, et la conserver ensuite avec les propres moyens de la terre. . . .
3. Il doit être simple et d'une application facile.
4. Enfin, et par dessus tout, il doit se recommander par le mérite de l'expérience et du succès obtenu (258).

Cette idéologie apparaît donc finalement comme une tentative pour montrer la compatibilité immédiate, dans une situation sociale historiquement définie, entre les "vertus" de la sagesse commune et les exigences concrètes (professionnelles et économiques) de la société, par le moyen d'une action éducative sur la jeunesse dans un système scolaire uniformisé. "On saura faire aller de pair, affirme le Dr Meilleur, l'éducation et l'instruction pratique dans nos écoles" (IX).

Le manuel de l'abbé Jean Langevin (1865)

La situation sociale représentée dans ce manuel apparaît d'emblée comme précaire pour l'institution support de l'idéologie scolaire. Dans un appendice de trente-six pages à la fin du volume (intitulé: "Aperçu historique des progrès de l'Instruction dans le Bas-Canada"), l'auteur en vient à décrire les célèbres résistances populaires qui avaient été opposées à l'instruction primaire dans les écoles locales durant la décade précédente: la "guerre des éteignoirs". Cet appendice, qui apparaît d'abord comme une sorte de hors-d'oeuvre sans rapport direct avec le contenu des chapitres sur le maître ou sur les matières d'enseignement, fournit cependant une définition globale de la situation de l'éducation dans la société de l'époque.

Par définition, cette situation sera difficile pour les destinataires aussi bien que pour le Bureau d'éducation pour le Bas-Canada, dont l'auteur se déclare solidaire. Et c'est d'abord pour les maîtres que la situation sera difficile puisque leur rôle d'éducateurs les impliquera personnellement dans les conflits entre groupes.

L'auteur construit alors un véritable "type idéal" du maître et de ses fonctions sociales et religieuses, dont l'accomplissement importe beaucoup "aux enfants, aux parents, aux paroisses, à la société, enfin, à la religion" (6). L'insistance sur l'importance de ses fonctions, sur ses "qualités physiques, intellectuelles et morales", sur les "marques" de sa "vocation spéciale" (9), tout contribue à définir un personnage compatible avec les exigences d'action dans une situation hostile à l'école.

A ce niveau, le modèle d'action du maître consisterait donc à être, dans son milieu paroissial et dans son école, l'illustration quotidienne d'un modèle idéal de comportement, défini par des vertus précises et par de minutieuses prescriptions concernant ses principaux secteurs d'activités visibles. Ces prescriptions très nombreuses, dont nous donnerons deux exemples de formulation plus générale, concernent aussi bien la conduite publique que la conduite privée de l'instituteur. Comme chrétien et comme "fonctionnaire public", il doit être en "accord parfait" avec l'autorité religieuse et "respectueusement soumis" à l'autorité scolaire.

Le statut social du maître est donc une position intermédiaire entre les autorités ecclésiastiques, scolaires et civiles d'une part, et les parents d'autre part. Envers les parents, l'instituteur doit manifester des ''égards'' et des ''politesses'', mais aussi une ''noble indépendance''. Il doit aussi s'interdire la ''compagnie des gens inférieurs à sa condition'' (363).

Dans sa conduite publique, il ''doit tenir par-dessus tout à jouir de l'estime générale de la paroisse où il enseigne''.

> Que l'instituteur se tienne éloigné de tous les partis qui peuvent exister dans la localité; s'il avait l'imprudence de se mêler une seule fois à ces divisions toujours regrettables, il s'aliénerait à jamais les esprits d'un grand nombre, et créerait contre lui des préjugés ineffaçables (338).

Le modèle d'action a pour fonction de critiquer les éléments de la situation et de rejeter ceux qui sont incompatibles avec les éléments définis comme acceptables et désirables selon les normes dominantes. Ces éléments ''acceptables'' profilent la représentation d'une société rurale traditionnelle, moralement guidée par le clergé catholique; une société d'economie agricole autarcique où la femme est un personnage stabilisateur nécessaire à cause de son rôle central dans la formation des générations montantes. L'image de la situation incorpore l'existence des classes sociales urbaines et des milieux sociaux non agricoles, mais à la condition que leur équilibre ne se déplace pas au désavantage de la civilisation rurale traditionnelle—qui, elle, doit se développer, notamment par la colonisation. La religion est par ailleurs le suprême bien et le sens dernier de la vie, ce qui justifie la position et le pouvoir le l'Eglise dans la société.

La seule ''branche'' d'éducation qui doit être totalement homogène est le domaine religieux et moral; l'école ''neutre'' est donc condamnée.

C'est ensuite la nation elle-même qui est visée par l'action scolaire:

> D'ailleurs dans le temps où nous vivons, l'instruction est si généralement répandue, qu'un peuple qui la néglige, ne peut éviter d'être en état d'humiliante infériorité. Pour nous particulièrement, Canadiens[5], qui sommes environnés de gens possédant tous un certain degré d'instruction, il est indispensable de la répandre parmi nous, si nous voulons marcher de pair avec eux (48).

L'éducation doit se différencier selon la position sociale future des enfants dans les divers milieux:

> Reconnaissons encore que le degré d'instruction doit varier suivant les différentes classes de la société. Il ne faut pas du tout les mêmes connaissances aux jeunes gens qui se destinent à l'état ecclésiastique ou aux professions libérales, et à ceux qui doivent devenir des artisans; à ceux qui embrasseront une carrière industrielle ou commerciale, et à ceux qui auront à se livrer à l'agriculture (89).

De même, l'enseignement de l'anglais marquera la différence ville-campagne: ''dans les campagnes, il est à peine utile que dans quelques localités importantes, et pour les garçons seulement'' (162-63).

L'accent mis sur l'enseignement de l'agriculture fournit un autre exemple d'articulation du modèle d'action scolaire sur les normes traditionnelles et sur la représentation de la situation:

> Oui, détournons-les de l'envie d'abandonner le séjour paisible et moral des champs pour les dangers et les séductions des villes; . . . enfin, prêchons-leur sur tous les tons l'importance vitale pour les Canadiens Français [sic] de s'emparer des terres vacantes et d'y fonder de nouvelles paroisses. Faisons-leur envisager cette colonisation de nos terres incultes comme une entreprise patriotique, comme une question de vie ou de mort pour notre race. Sachons leur faire aimer les moeurs si douces de l'homme des champs: . . . la nourriture, l'habillement, la satisfaction de tous leurs besoins, qu'ils peuvent trouver si aisément dans la maison paternelle, plutôt que de recourir aux importations souvent ruineuses. Que nos élèves aient donc le luxe en horreur, qu'ils le regardent comme un des grands ennemis de la prospérité de notre peuple (192-93).

Le manuel, devant le problème des innovations techniques en agriculture, devait réduire l'incompatibilité (au niveau général des principes) entre les normes traditionnelles et les normes de ''progrès''. L'idéologie conseille donc à l'instituteur de travailler ''à déraciner chez eux les préjugés nuisibles au progrès'' (193), dans un passage où le syncrétisme de l'argumentation est particulièrement évident:

> Surtout ne paraissez pas vouloir critiquer la conduite de vos élèves; mais dites tout cela sous forme de conseils, et citez des exemples à l'appui de vos avancés. . . . donnez-les comme le fruit

de l'expérience des plus habiles cultivateurs; faites-leur com-
prendre que, si la prudence conseille de ne pas adopter sans
examen toutes les innovations, le bon sens veut de même que l'on
ne s'attache pas aveuglement à la routine, uniquement parce que
c'était la coutume de nos pères, et qu'on ne rejette pas les amélio-
rations réelles que le temps a amenées dans la culture de la terre
(193).

La femme, enfin, est un personnage social qui symbolise très
profondément la sécurité et la survivance de la nation; elles ne doivent
pas quitter la campagne pour la ville en prenant pour époux "un homme
d'une condition qu'elles s'imagineront être audessus de la leur''. Nous
avons déjà vu que l'enseignement de l'anglais ne devait pas les toucher
(de crainte qu'elles n'épousent des anglophones, sans doute).

Le manuel de l'abbé Th.-G. Rouleau,
J.-C. Magnan et J. Ahern (1901)

La page titre de ce manuel identifie formellement les destinataires (les
futurs instituteurs) aussi bien que l'institution support de l'idéologie: le
manuel est "publié à la demande du Bureau central des examinateurs
catholiques de la province de Québec''.

La religion occupe, dans la structure de cette idéologie, une
position nouvelle par rapport à sa fonction dans les deux premiers
manuels. En plus d'affirmer (comme c'était le cas dans les deux
formulations antérieures) le ''rôle premier'' et l'importance suprême
de cette matière parmi les autres branches du programme, les auteurs de
ce manuel en font un instrument normatif qui sert à justifier systématiquement tous les éléments majeurs du modèle d'action.

L'enseignement de l'histoire prend également ici un rôle normatif
qui était moins central dans les manuels précédents, et c'est encore la
religion qui sert de norme transcendante pour en orienter le sens:

On doit enseigner l'histoire pour préparer les enfants à la vie, et
dans un pays comme le nôtre, régi par une monarchie con-
stitutionnelle dans laquelle le peuple joue un grand rôle,
l'enseignement de l'histoire comporte une responsabilité considérable. Il faut que l'élève y discerne et y puise les principes
rationnels et chrétiens qui le guideront comme citoyen, électeur ou
député. . . . Pour former le coeur des enfants le maître doit exposer
les faits historiques à la lumière de la foi et de la raison pour les
nations chrétiennes et suivant les données de la loi naturelle s'il
s'agit de nations infidèles. Il habituera ainsi les élèves aux notions
du juste et de l'injuste, leur inculquera l'amour de la vertu, la

répulsion pour le vice. . . . Que le maître chrétien n'oublie pas que Jésus-Christ est le centre de l'histoire. Tous les peuples, de gré ou de force, délibérément ou insciemment, par leur hostilité ou leur soumission, ont concouru ou concourent, diversement mais inévitablement, à l'établissement du règne de Jésus-Christ à qui toutes les nations ont été données en héritage (219).

L'orientation de la formation des élèves se différencie suivant les milieux sociaux. L'idéologie justifie ainsi le modèle de "bifurcation des programmes".

Notre population étant surtout agricole, ce serait rendre un service éminent au pays que d'inspirer aux enfants de la campagne l'estime et le goût de l'état de leurs pères et de leur faire sentir combien il est honorable et heureux. L'instituteur s'attachera donc à faire aimer l'agriculture et la vie des champs, à combattre la routine et à faire naître le désir d'étudier les bonnes méthodes de culture. Dans les centres industriels et commerciaux, il s'appliquera surtout à faire connaître aux enfants ce qui se rapporte à l'industrie et au commerce. Former les enfants des centres agricoles de la même manière que la population des centres industriels et commerciaux, c'est favoriser une agglomération excessive dans les villes et dépeupler les campagnes. Le pays a déjà trop souffert de cette erreur de jugement (235).

La ville est donc une sorte de 'mal nécessaire', une enclave étrangère dans la société rurale; on tolère cette enclave, à la condition qu'elle demeure cloisonnée et que la communication de sa culture et de ses valeurs—du moins via l'école—ne s'étende pas jusqu'à contaminer les caractères les plus désirables de la société rurale que représente l'idéologie:

Que le maître mette en relief sa supériorité sous le rapport de la dignité humaine, de la paix, de l'honorabilité; les ressources diverses que peuvent y trouver les hommes laborieux et intelligents qui, rompant avec la routine et les méthodes surannées, se tiennent au courant de la chimie agricole, de la mécanique industrielle, du commerce local et international; les avantages qu'elle présente au point de vue religieux et social, ainsi que les qualités et les vertus requises pour qu'on y trouve le bonheur et l'indépendance (235-36).

C'est l'histoire qui fournit ici la source culturelle des vertus requises pour perpétuer, par l'action éducative, ce genre de vie traditionnel; l'idéologie est progressiste quant aux techniques agricoles mais traditionnaliste en vertus.

Le manuel de Mgr F.-X. Ross (1924)

Les axes structurels majeurs de cette quatrième formulation de l'idéologie scolaire officielle s'articulent selon la logique suivante. L'action scolaire de l'institutrice est justifiée, d'une manière globale, par la prémisse suprême d'une mission divine. Cette mission est déléguée simultanément à l'Eglise, aux parents et à l'Etat, qui, à leur tour, confient à l'institutrice l'objet immédiat visé par sa tâche: l'enfant. Cette structure formelle de délégation détermine, entre l'institutrice et les trois sources institutionnelles de sa mission, des rapports de comportement déterminés.

Les visées lointaines du modèle d'action par rapport aux réalités sociales s'articulent toutes en un schéma commun: créer une "mentalité" chez les élèves, les inclinant à poursuivre un "idéal" correspondant au "plan divin". C'est donc le noyau transcendant des normes religieuses qui domine tout l'appareil des justifications plus empiriques. Chaque "segment" du modèle d'action s'articule sur des représentations normatives de la situation, mais il est ultimement rapporté, par ailleurs, aux normes religieuses (volonté divine, Providence, confessionnalité, etc.).

"L'idéal, dit l'auteur, c'est le degré de perfection ou de beauté qui convient à chaque être dans le plan divin" (90). Il va de soi que l'idéologie contestera tout ce qui, dans sa représentation de la situation sociale, sera conçu comme incompatible avec cet idéal:

> Tout dans nos moeurs actuelles semble conspirer pour dépraver le goût des enfants, exalter leur imagination. Les caricatures des journaux jaunes, leurs faits divers dégoûtants, les vues cinématographiques, les romans à sensation, les modes ridicules, disproportionnées et démoralisantes, les monstrueux Teddy Bears qui suivent le bébé jour et nuit: voilà autant de causes de corruption du goût, de l'esprit et du coeur. . . . Il est du devoir de l'institutrice de s'entretenir dans une grande horreur de toutes ces infections et d'inspirer le même sentiment à ses élèves" (71-72).

A cette représentation de la culture urbaine naissante (incorporée ici pour la première fois dans les images de la situation), l'idéologie oppose ses propres modèles, les idéaux de la culture qui doit être transmise aux enfants.

Les deux grands pôles autour desquels s'organise la représentation de la situation sont la nation et la société rurale, toutes deux garanties par les normes religieuses.

L'enseignement du français est un autre moyen, avec l'enseignement de l'histoire, de préserver à la fois les valeurs nationales et religieuses des séductions d'une autre culture:

> Chargée de toute la pensée catholique et pénétrée de tout l'idéal de l'âme ancestrale, la langue française est un préservatif contre l'infiltration hérétique et matérialiste du verbe étranger qui fait sonner àses oreilles une autre foi et d'autres aspirations (170).

Le texte suivant est un exemple remarquable de l'idéologie nationaliste religieuse de l'époque, autant par le style que par le contenu:

> C'est la civilisation chrétienne que voulaient les découvreurs, qu'ont implantée les fondateurs, les organisateurs, les apôtres de toute catégorie, et qu'ont fécondée les martyrs. C'est par le dévouement sacrifié, l'héroïsme, l'esprit religieux, l'endurance et l'attachement au sol, qu'ils fondèrent cette oeuvre et qu'ils l'embellirent de tout ce que l'âme française reflète d'idéal, de politesse, de gaieté franche et d'esprit hospitalier.
>
> Ce rôle, il le continue après la conquête. Séparé violemment de la mère-patrie, il fait revivre dans un milieu où il est apparemment noyé, l'âme qu'il a reçue d'elle. Malgré mille obstacles, il garde sa foi, sa langue, son idéal, ses traditions. Uni à son clergé, il multiplie sur ce continent les clochers de ses églises, ses maisons religieuses, ses institutions de charité, ses écoles, ses collèges, ses maisons d'enseignement supérieur, monuments qui attestent sa vitalité croissante. . . . Coloniser et évangéliser restent, aujourd'hui comme autrefois, le lot principal de sa race: "la croix et la charrue" demeurent ses outils préférés.
>
> Tenir toujours vivace le flambeau de l'idéal au milieu des races plus vouées par tempérament aux choses matérielles, entretenir la culture classique, le goût de l'art, la flamme de l'apostolat: voilà le rôle que la providence semble lui assigner et qu'il remplira tant que, fidèle à ses traditions, il restera digne de sa mission providentielle (323).

L'enseignement donné aux garçons et aux filles ne doit pas être le même. Le rôle de la femme est tel que sa formation doit être "pratique" et centrée sur "le travail manuel de l'intérieur", si elle veut "rendre un foyer attrayant et heureux" (356). Elle ne doit pas se faire de fausses idées sur la condition des hautes classes urbaines: "La dame ou la demoiselle n'est pas la personne richement habillée qui ne sait rien faire; c'est celle qui, ne rougissant pas de son rang, sait remplir avec perfection et dignité les obligations que lui impose sa condition" (356). Il va de soi que, suivant ces conseils, la femme rurale ne quittera pas la campagne.

Somme toute, l'idéologie adopte une position de compromis, qui consiste à conserver l'équilibre rural-urbain dans un cloisonnement favorable à la campagne plutôt que de condamner totalement le milieu urbain comme tel ou de chercher à l'éliminer de sa représentation de la société.

Le manuel de Roland Vinette (1948)

Non seulement cette dernière reformulation de l'idéologie scolaire officielle comporte-t-elle des éléments nouveaux par rapport aux manuels précédents, mais la structure de son argumentation normative manifeste des articulations plus nombreuses et plus intégrées. Pour élaborer sa doctrine, l'auteur en définit l'exigence sous la forme d'une "loi fondamentale" de la pédagogie:

Toute pédagogie repose sur une philosophie de l'homme et de la vie et tout pédagogue agit sous l'inspiration plus ou moins consciente de cette philosophie (28).

L'auteur propose donc les trois propriétés d'une philosophie catholique de l'homme et de la vie, qui rejette explicitement les doctrines concurrentes:

Par son théocentrisme et son ecclésiocentrisme, la philosophie catholique de l'homme et de la vie est exempte de l'erreur fondamentale commune à la plupart des autres philosophies; par son universalisme, elle est exempte des erreurs particulières à chacune. Elle est une façon unique de concevoir l'homme et la vie. De cette conception unique naîtra une pédagogie unique (41).

Le souci d'articuler systématiquement toutes les normes de l'appareil de justification sur une "fin suprême" unique est déjà un indice de la difficulté de définir les termes du consensus social dans le contexte d'une situation nouvelle. D'où cette construction remarquable d'une doctrine très finement articulée.

Par son théocentrisme et son ecclésiocentrisme, la pédagogie (le modèle d'action) proposée par le manuel est justifiée globalement par son inclusion dans un contexte confessionnel.

Voici donc la hiérarchie des fins de l'éducation dans l'ordre d'intention, selon le résumé de l'auteur:

a: *La fin suprême de l'éducation*. Pour le chrétien, la fin dernière de l'homme c'est la possession de Dieu dans l'éternité. En conséquence, toute la vie du chrétien doit être ordonnée à cette vie éternelle et toute son éducation doit être, en définitive, une préparation à cette vie.

b: *Les fins intermédiaires de l'éducation*. La fin ultime n'est pas atteinte immédiatement, ni directement, mais après et par la vie temporelle qui a été donnée à l'homme pour mériter l'autre. L'éducation doit donc préparer l'homme à sa vie temporelle. Comme celle-ci est complexe, l'éducation doit préparer l'homme aux différents aspects de la vie. Il y aura donc autant de fins intermédiaires à poursuivre en éducation qu'il y a de vies différentes auxquelles il faut préparer l'homme.

1. *L'éducation sociale* qui consiste dans la préparation de l'enfant à la vie en société.

2. *L'éducation familiale* qui consiste dans la préparation de l'enfant à la vie familiale.

3. *L'éducation professionnelle* qui consiste dans la préparation de l'enfant à l'exercice d'une profession, d'un métier, ou d'une fonction.

4. *L'éducation civique* qui consiste dans la préparation de l'enfant à sa vie de citoyen.

5. *L'éducation nationale* qui consiste dans la préparation de l'enfant à la vie nationale.

6. *L'éducation humanitaire* qui consiste dans la préparation de l'enfant à sa vie de citoyen de l'humanité.

Ces différents aspects de la vie exigent tous des connaissances et des habitudes particulières. C'est le but de ces différentes éducations de faire acquérir les unes et de développer les autres.

c. *Les fins immédiates de l'éducation*. L'enfant ne sera préparé à vivre ces vies comme elles doivent être vécues que s'il a développé toutes ses puissances, toutes ses facultés. La fin immédiate de l'éducation sera donc de perfectionner l'enfant, de développer toutes les valeurs qu'il possède. Comme les facultés ou puissances de l'homme lui viennent de ses quatre vies: physique, intellectuelle, morale et surnaturelle, la fin immédiate de l'éducation sera de développer ces quatre vies au maximum.

1. L'éducation physique développera la vie physique de

l'enfant afin de rendre son corps aussi sain et vigoureux que possible.

2. L'éducation intellectuelle développera la vie intellectuelle de l'enfant afin de le rendre capable d'acquérir le plus de connaissances possible et de résoudre les problèmes de tous genres que pose la vie.

3. L'éducation morale développera chez l'enfant la vie morale, i.e. la vie des vertus afin de l'amener à toujours discerner le vrai bien et à le poursuivre indéfectiblement.

4. L'éducation religieuse développera la vie surnaturelle de l'enfant afin de l'amener à vivre conformément à ses croyances (82-84).

Les "agents d'éducation" sont une dimension nouvelle, dans la série des manuels analysés, de la représentation de la situation. On y voit les signes d'une société qui devient pluraliste. L' "agent premier" est Dieu; l' "agent principal" est l'enfant; les "agents de droit" sont la famille, l'Eglise et l'Etat, qui ensemble délèguent la mission éducative à l'école et au maître. Ce dernier doit assurer la concertation et le contrôle des influences concurrentes qui s'exercent sur l'enfant:

> Toutes et chacune de ces forces peuvent avoir, selon les circonstances, une influence décisive sur l'enfant. Tantôt ce sera l'école, tantôt la famille ou un compagnon, tantôt une oeuvre quelconque. Cette influence peut être décisive pour le bien comme pour le mal. Il faut donc de toute nécessité coordonner ces forces éducatrices, afin qu'elles agissent toutes dans le même sens. On n'a pas le droit de laisser la radio, le cinéma, ou d'autres influences détruire celle de l'école, de la famille, de l'Eglise ou de l'Etat (115).

Le modèle d'action décrit systématiquement tous les éléments visés dans le schéma des finalités. Nous retiendrons simplement ici, à titre illustratif, l'idéologie nationaliste et la formation du citoyen; dans les deux cas, on trouve des modifications importantes par rapport aux formulations antérieures de l'idéologie scolaire.

a) *L'éducation civique* "Avec l'influence grandissante des organisations ouvrières et professionnelles sur les gouvernements et la puissance croissante de l'opinion publique, chacun de nous participe de plus en plus à la vie civique. L'abstention est elle-même une participation puisqu'elle permet ou empêche toutes sortes de réalisations. L'éducation

civique est donc un élément de la formation générale de base
que l'école primaire doit donner'' (67).

b) *L'éducation nationale* designe, parmi les objets sociaux de
l'action scolaire, celui qui occupe le statut prédominant. Ce
texte, assez long, pourrait constituer à lui seul, une formulation autonome de l'idéologie nationaliste canadienne-
française de l'après-guerre:

Les valeurs spirituelles qui constituent la nationalité et que nous
avons reçues en héritage sont des biens auxquels nos descendants
ont droit et que, par conséquent, nous avons le devoir de conserver
et de leur transmettre. Or, pour conserver ces valeurs, il faut les
connaître, les aimer, et avoir assez de force de caractère pour les
défendre au besoin et s'imposer les sacrifices qu'exige parfois leur
conservation. Nous savons que beaucoup de nos gens sont ignor-
ants de ces valeurs ou indifférents envers elles et qu'ils les aban-
donnent facilement.

Ces valeurs spirituelles ont besoin d'assises matérielles.
Aussi, le niveau économique d'une nationalité influence-t-il
grandement le développement de ses valeurs culturelles ou autres.
. . . Les relations du national et du politique ne sont pas moins
étroites. . . . Même si notre économie et notre politique étaient des
plus favorables au développement de notre nationalité, la situation
particulière dans laquelle nous sommes rendrait encore nécessaire
une forte éducation nationale. Nous sommes en effet quelques
millions de catholiques de langue française vivant dans un monde
anglo-saxon et protestant plus nombreux et plus puissant politi-
quement et économiquement. Cet environnement est une menace
à notre survivance et à notre épanouissement du seul fait de sa
présence. Une pensée, une culture, et des coutumes différentes
des nôtres nous envahissent continuellement de partout: presse,
revues, radio, cinéma, tourisme, etc. . . . En de telles circonstances, il faut avoir une grande foi dans nos valeurs nationales et
une force morale peu commune pour ne pas suivre la loi du
moindre effort et tout abandonner. Cette foi et cette force morale
nous seront données par l'éducation nationale (68-69).

Les Transformations structurelles de l'idéologie scolaire

Comme nous l'avons signalé au début, nous reprenons ici le modèle qui
a servi pour l'analyse individuelle des manuels. Il faudra donc décrire
les transformations de structure qu'on peut déceler au niveau des

définiteurs, des destinataires, du modèle d'action, des prémisses et des éléments de la situation représentés dans l'idéologie lorsqu'on compare successivement les manuels selon l'ordre chronologique. Le continuum sera défini selon ses deux termes extrêmes.

Les définiteurs

Idéalement, l'idéologue de l'éducation doit donner à ses destinataires une définition quelconque de la société où ils se trouvent. Il doit appuyer cette définition sur une théorie préalable, qu'il élabore par ailleurs. Pour justifier un programme d'action déterminé dans cette situation sociale définie, il faut nécessairement que le définiteur considère cette théorie comme apte à produire automatiquement l'assentiment unanime des destinataires; il faut qu'elle soit placée au-dessus de toute contestation.

Chez Valade, la question de l'éducation est située, si l'on peut dire, au niveau 'politique': il s'agit de convaincre le lecteur de la nécessité sociale d'un bon système d'écoles primaires, pour l'agriculture à la campagne aussi bien que pour l'industrie et le commerce dans les villes. Dans cette idéologie fort sommaire, il n'est pas encore question du maître comme tel. Le définiteur est ici le Bureau de l'éducation, dont le surintendant écrit à titre personnel.

Chez l'abbé Langevin, qui se place également sur le terrain de la contestation, les définitions de la situation ont des implications beaucoup plus complexes par rapport aux définiteurs, qui se trouvent dans une position décrite comme précaire. C'est pourquoi l'idéologue cherche sa garantie dans la divinité, le clergé, et les autorités civiles et scolaires comme pour se pourvoir de l'autorité morale maximum.

Avec le manuel de Rouleau, Magnan et Ahern et celui de Mgr Ross, la situation stratégique des définiteurs passe au second plan, et ce sont l'Eglise et la divinité providentielle qui deviennent les autorités morales auxquelles l'idéologue a recours d'une façon dominante. On peut dire que Mgr Ross, identifiant pratiquement l'Eglise avec sa mission divine, fait de l'Eglise, comme définitrice, une norme historique concrète identifiée avec les intentions de la Providence.

Au point 'final' de l'évolution, on trouve dans le manuel de Vinette une véritable métaphysique des finalités humaines et des valeurs premières: une ontologie des fins de l'éducation. Le définiteur prend ainsi finalement la figure d'une autorité morale radicale, universelle et impersonnelle, parlant le langage d'une vérité incontestable en principe. Au-dessus de tout, il place Dieu et l'Eglise, dont le caractère religieux se transpose également au comité catholique du D.I.P., l'autorité scolaire immédiate du système d'enseignement. C'est donc la confessionnalité du groupe définiteur qui constitue sa solidarité de principe avec cet ordre divin transcendant.

Les destinataires

Dans le manuel de Valade, les destinataires sont désignés d'une façon très englobante: parents, maîtres, et "tous ceux que préoccupent l'enseignement et l'éducation". Ils apparaissent ainsi comme tous ceux qui doivent être intéressés par ce problème général actuel. Ils ne sont pas définis davantage.

Chez l'abbé Langevin, par contre, le maître visé par l'idéologie devient l'élément majeur et le pôle central des valeurs et de l'action. Le définiteur présente ici le portrait minutieusement détaillé d'un statut social concret dont les rôles font l'objet de multiples prescriptions. C'est un maître qui incarne les valeurs communes à un point tel qu'il peut affronter toute contestation et toute exigence morale de la part des groupes d'opposition (les "éteignoirs"). Son statut est cependant subordonné à celui du clergé et des autorités scolaires.

Le manuel de Rouleau, Magnan, Ahern et celui de Mgr Ross présentent une image beaucoup moins précise du statut du maître et des prescriptions de rôles moins cohérentes. En effet, il s'agit moins du maître lui-même, comme personne typique, que des devoirs et fonctions qu'il doit assumer et qui sont définis d'une façon un peu abstraite et "juridique". Dans ces deux manuels, le maître est essentiellement un "chargé d'éducation", un agent délégué dont le statut est nettement subordonné à celui du clergé et des autorités scolaires et nominalement subordonné (mais avec moins de garanties explicites) à celui des parents de ses élèves. En particulier chez Mgr Ross, le destinataire fait figure d'un collaborateur spécial d'un plan providentiel et chargé d'une mission divine dont il est responsable.

Au terme de la transformation, chez Vinette, l'instituteur comme personne s'efface presque totalement devant un système anonyme auquel il est non seulement socialement, mais "ontologiquement" subordonné. Sa fonction relève d'un ordre à la fois naturel et sacral où il ne faut introduire aucune perturbation incompatible avec les intentions du système. Ce qui prend vraiment l'importance majeure ici, c'est bien moins l'instituteur que la hiérarchie et la justification de ses tâches.

Le modèle d'action

Dès les premières formulations de cette idéologie, les tâches et fonctions de l'instituteur s'étagent sur deux plans: la formation des facultés de l'enfant et, à travers lui, l'édification ou la conservation d'une société conforme à un idéal explicite. Chez Valade (ou plutôt, Jean-Baptiste Meilleur), le maître doit former l'élève à des vertus et connaissances qui l'habiliteront à vivre d'une façon socialement utile sa future condition laborieuse. Cette tâche, pour brièvement décrite qu'elle soit, demeure d'un caractère concret et immédiat.

Chez Langevin en particulier, le modèle d'action est présenté comme l'exemple concret du comportement d'un maître idéal. C'est une action concrète dont le but est aisément perceptible dans le prolongement direct des relations sociales du maître, dans son école et dans son milieu paroissial: son statut social est coextensif au reste de la société où il pratique son métier, et qu'il a pour mission d'aider à construire et à conserver.

Dans les manuels de Rouleau, Magnan et Ahern et de Mgr Ross, et davantage dans ce dernier, le modèle d'action est déjà largement dégagé du réseau social immédiat du maître: sa tâche est ''plus grande que lui'', et commence à se définir en dehors de sa personne. Il est l'initiateur de la jeune génération dans une société de règne providentiel. Il fait déjà partie d'un ''système'' articulé sur des normes religieuses centrales.

A l'autre bout du processus, la tâche enseignante apparaît comme la transmission formelle d'un système où la personne sociale du maître disparaît tout à fait devant cette fonction qu'il reçoit pour mission d'exécuter. Son modèle d'action n'est pas un ensemble de comportements concrets mais d'abord un ordre de finalités à la fois ''absolues'' et ''circonstancielles'', appliqué à des éléments choisis de la situation sociale. A la limite, il est fort difficile d'y distinguer ce qui est norme et ce qui est action à exécuter.

Les prémisses normatives

C'est fondamentalement au niveau des prémisses d'une idéologie que se pose le problème de l'unanimité. L'idéologue, en supposant l'unanimité des principes, garantit sa capacité de justifier l'action qu'il veut prescrire dans une situation historique donnée. La façon dont une idéologie structure ses normes définit, comme telle, le type d'unanimité qu'elle suppose implicitement.

On pourrait dire que la systématisation des prémisses varie en sens inverse de l'unité de la représentation de la situation. Si, en effet, l'idéologue sent que l'unanimité sur la définition de sa société devient un consensus de plus en plus précaire, il aura tendance à compenser cette disparité par une nouvelle unité obtenue par la systématisation des principes. Quand une situation historique perd sa signification normative concrète, ce sont des normes abstraites qui serviront à définir la situation pour l'action des hommes. Cette rigidité devient éventuellement une limite aux possibilitiés de développement de l'idéologie et peut annoncer des mutations majeures.

Il nous semble que cette définition de l'unanimité se vérifie dans le cas que nous avons étudié. Au départ, la représentation unitaire de la situation dispense d'une démonstration de principe, et les prémisses semblent disparates. Mais une systématisation croissante des prémissès commence graduellement à déplacer la représentation de la situation, qui devient, à l'inverse de ce qu'elle était au début, de plus en plus disparate et fragmentaire.

Au début, chez Langevin comme chez Valade, les principes invoqués pour la justification et la contestation constituent une sorte d'assemblage empiriste de normes concrètes que nous pouvons bien appeler la 'sagesse commune'. A cette phase de l'évolution de notre idéologie, les prémisses ne sont pas construites en un ensemble organisé: c'est bien un 'assemblage' souple dont la structure interne demeure totalement implicite, et où les auteurs vont chercher des principes lorsque les circonstances définies de l'action semblent l'exiger. On n'y 'raisonne' point: on cite le principe ou le dicton approprié, et tout porte à croire que l'auteur considère ce procédé suffisant pour évoquer l'unanimité des destinataires.

Chez Rouleau, Magnan et Ahern et chez Mgr Ross, on trouve parfois ce type de prémisses justificatrices. Cependant, les techniques de justification se font beaucoup plus systématiques que dans la première phase. Les normes prennent une forme plus abstraite et unitaire, et tous les détails du programme d'action sont explicitement définis comme compatibles avec ce petit nombre de "principes directeurs". L'argument d'autorité y est souvent invoqué, pour bien garantir la conformité systématique du modèle d'action avec la "mentalité chrétienne", la "volonté divine", et l'autorité du clergé.

Avec Vinette, ce n'est vraiment plus un assemblage empiriste de dictons traditionnels; on y est loin de la 'sagesse commune' à structure implicite. Ici, on trouve la construction explicite d'un système abstrait où les prémisses sont organisées pour elles-mêmes pour être ensuite appliquées à des situations selon un ordre hiérarchique de finalités. Ce langage des finalités 'transcende' à la fois les normes invoquées et les objets (ou objectifs) concrets de l'action prescrite.

L'auteur ici semble ressentir le besoin de partir de très loin pour formuler ce qu'il considère comme les termes unanimes de la justification. L'unanimité n'est plus simplement évoquée par allusion ou rappelée brièvement: au contraire, elle doit être créée, construite selon des procédés d'argumentation fort élaborés.

La représentation de la situation

L'action éducatrice justifiée par les prémisses idéologiques est définie par jonction avec des objets précis faisant partie de la situation socio-historique commune aux définiteurs et aux destinataires.

Dans les premières formulations de l'idéologie, les représentations de la situation sont des définitions et des descriptions concrètes, coextensives à la définition du statut social du maître lui-même. Chez Valade, à cause peut-être de la brièveté du texte, cette représentation est très 'globale': la préface évoque les besoins de la société globale en matière d'éducation, notamment pour la préparation aux nouvelles formes de travail dans les milieux urbains (les professions 'mécaniques'). Chez Langevin, l'empirisme minutieux des descriptions est très frappant. La société, malgré ses différenciations en milieux ruraux et urbains et en classes sociales, apparaît—au moins idéalement —comme un tout 'organique', où prédominent ses caractères de société rurale, agricole et traditionnelle. L'unité interne de ces représentations semble impliquer la référence à une situation qui—malgré les conflits et les incompatibilités que l'auteur y discerne et critique au passage —demeure relativement homogène aux yeux du définiteur.

La définition des éléments de la situation se transforme dans la phase suivante, chez Rouleau, Magnan et Ahern et chez Mgr Ross. Les objets sociaux y sont toujours évoqués comme chez les premiers auteurs, à l'occasion de la présentation et de la justification des matières scolaires à enseigner: histoire, religion, géographie, agriculture, etc. Cependant, certains objets sociaux y sont le sujet de très longs textes et développements, doués d'une cohérence propre et traités clairement pour eux-mêmes (le monde rural traditionnel, le nationalisme centré sur la tradition). L'unité de ces descriptions de la situation socio-historique semble provenir moins de leur homogénéité 'horizontale', si l'on peut dire, que de l'affirmation, constamment reprise à l'occasion de chaque élément, de sa compatibilité normative avec un petit nombre de principes religieux: volonté divine, mission providentielle, etc. On y trouve donc déjà une fragmentation partielle (une sorte de 'disjonction latérale') des représentations de la situation.

Avec le manuel de Vinette, ce 'processus' de fragmentation s'accentue encore davantage, au point que la représentation de la situation y a perdu pratiquement toute unité, à ce niveau même de la description. Ce qu'on y trouve, ce sont des idéologies partielles systématiques, organisées en pièces 'détachées', abstraites et cloisonnées entre elles, chacune étant traitée explicitement pour elle-même. Le thème ruraliste et agriculturiste est abandonné tout à fait, de même que la fonction sociale sécurisante de la femme et que le modèle traditionnel de l'orientation professionnelle par la continuité familiale. A ce niveau, l'unité syncrétique de la pensée idéologique apparaît d'une façon flagrante: en effet, l'unité perdue sur le plan 'horizontal' des représentations concrètes de la situation se compense par un effort systématique d'unification sur le plan 'vertical' des prémisses abstraites. Et si l'idéologie donne l'impression d'une représentation unitaire de la situation sociale, c'est par les procédés d'un langage normatif unique (celui des finalités) qui est appliqué à la fois aux prémisses justificatrices et aux objets socio-historiques du modèle d'action prescrit.

Quelques Tendances plus récentes dans l'évolution des idéologies scolaires au Québec

Les formulations successives de l'idéologie scolaire que l'on trouve dans les manuels de pédagogie québecois, jusqu'en 1948, donnent l'image d'une société qui s'urbanise, s'industrialise et se diversifie de multiples façons: une société qui se modernise et qui devient pluraliste, presque 'contre son gré', dirait-on. Du point de vue des pouvoirs scolaires, ces tendances posaient un problème de 'consensus' culturel et idéologique de plus en plus critique: on peut même considérer le manuel de R. Vinette (1948) comme l'ultime effort d'une idéologie de moins en moins 'dominante' dans les faits pour assimiler et 'contenir' la différenciation croissante de la société québecoise et la ramener à l'unité d'une seule vision normative bien caractérisée.

Or, depuis 1948, aucun nouveau manuel équivalent n'a été produit au Québec pour remplacer l'ancien manuel officiel. Un des effets de la réforme de l'éducation dans les années 1960 a donc été une diversification considérable dans les ressources employées pour la formation des enseignants. Entre 1965 et 1972 le nombre des écoles normales est passé d'une centaine à trois seulement, et la formation des enseignants est assurée depuis 1969 par les universités. Même durant cette période chaque école normale pouvait employer, parmi les ouvrages spécialisés cités dans les listes autorisées des programmes officiels, les volumes qui lui paraissaient les plus utiles dans chaque matière. Comme la majorité des manuels en usage sont d'origine européene et américaine et que ces listes autorisées sont assez diversifiées, on ne peut donc plus considérer les anciens manuels *québecois* de pédagogie comme des sources idéologiques encore importantes ou centrales parmi l'ensemble des sources de la pensée pédagogique contemporaine, qui constitue désormais la culture professionnelle de référence des enseignants en formation. Les normes de socialisation professionnelle de ces derniers ont été ainsi fractionnées et 'pluralisées' dans les instruments de formation eux-mêmes et, de plus, les sources d'influences idéologiques se trouvent localisées dans plusieurs 'littéra-

tures parallèles' distinctes: revues de pédagogie et de psychologie
appliquée; documents officiels du Ministère de l'Education; rapports
du Conseil supérieur de l'Education; dossiers, revues, et journaux
pédagogiques publiés par les syndicats des enseignants eux-mêmes et
notamment par la Corporation des Enseignants du Québec (C.E.Q.),
etc.

Comme la tâche d'analyser l'ensemble de cette littérature, avec la
diversité des tendances idéologiques qu'elle recouvre, serait très considérable, nous ne citerons ici que quelques sources *officielles* (puisque
notre étude originale ne portait que sur l'idéologie scolaire officielle du
secteur francophone au Québec) particulièrement importantes, qui ont
précédé immédiatement ou suivi les premières années de la réforme
scolaire des années 1960. De plus, nous ne retiendrons que des textes
qui ont servi à poser un *diagnostic général* sur l'état de la situation de
l'école dans la société québecoise et de son rôle dans ce contexte
nouveau. Ce faisant, nous poserons une hypothèse, également
générale, sur l'évolution récente de l'idéologie scolaire officielle dans
notre société—hypothèse que d'autres chercheurs pourront préciser et
que les développements futurs permettront de montrer fausse ou non.

Le rapport de la Commission royale d'enquête sur l'enseignement dans la province de Québec (1964)

Le rapport Parent a sans doute été le document public le plus influent
dans le monde de l'éducation au Québec durant les années de la
"révolution tranquille". Nous citerons ici deux passages seulement où
le problème de la culture et celui du rôle de l'école ont été posés dans
toute leur ampleur par rapport au contexte d'une société moderne.

> Au lieu du sens restreint donné généralement au mot "culture"
> lorsqu'on parle par exemple d'une "personne cultivée", nous
> avons ici défini la culture comme un univers polyvalent de con-
> naissances (culture humaniste, scientifique, technique, culture de
> masse); chacun de ces univers correspond à un mode de percep-
> tion du réel et à des attitudes mentales, morales et spirituelles qui
> lui sont propres; chacun développe certaines qualités de l'être,
> exerce certaines facultés, active des aptitudes ou des tendances
> particulières. Il devient alors légitime de parler de culture techni-
> que et même de culture de masse aussi bien que de culture
> humaniste et scientifique. Chacun moule la personne humaine
> selon un idéal, des normes et des valeurs caractéristiques. Cette
> diversité humaine témoigne du pluralisme culturel autant que
> sociologique de notre société moderne (vol. 2, 8).

C'est dans ce contexte d'une société définie positivement comme ''pluraliste'', à la fois dans sa réalité et dans ses normes et valeurs culturelles, que les membres de la Commission ont posé le problème général de l'école, dans son double rôle d'*accommodation* aux exigences changeantes de la situation et d'*assimilation* de la diversité plus ou moins anarchique de la culture à une nouvelle unité, par l'harmonisation de ses traits ''polyvalents'':

> Il ne s'agit pas de faire le procès de l'enseignement ni de chercher des coupables, mais de bien voir que toute une civilisation est ici en cause. Les cloisons trop étanches entre les programmes, les distinctions entre catégories d'étudiants et de maîtres, les incohérences du système ne font que refléter l'évolution parfois chaotique du savoir et les exigences de la société moderne. L'histoire de l'enseignement est intimement liée . . . à celle de la science et des conditions de vie; l'école a dû s'adapter à la prolifération des connaissances et chercher à répondre aux besoins de la société industrielle et technologique. Mais le mouvement n'est pas à sens unique: l'enseignement exerce en retour une profonde influence sur l'état des connaissances et les conditions sociales; il est un élément dynamique de la civilisation. C'est ici qu'apparaît sa responsabilité. Se pose alors la question fondamentale qui confronte les éducateurs et tous ceux qui s'intéressent à l'enseignement: dans la crise culturelle et l'évolution sociale de notre civilisation, quelle doit être l'orientation de l'enseignement, dans quelle direction doit se faire la réforme pédagogique? Cette formation générale, en quel sens faut-il l'entendre, quel doit en être le contenu? Comment et par quelles voies doit se faire le passage de la formation générale à la spécialisation? Au-delà de ces questions, c'est la conception d'un type humain dans le contexte de la société moderne qui est un jeu. La réponse à ces interrogations détermine le rôle de l'enseignement dans l'avenir, sa mission culturelle et sociale'' (vol. 2, 10).

Ce qui frappe dans tout cela, c'est que les 'interrogations officielles' du système scolaire québecois sont désormais semblables à celles que toutes les autres sociétés contemporaines industrialisées se posent. La ''polyvalence'' de l'école nouvelle est en quelque sorte la reproduction du ''pluralisme'' qui apparaît conme la caractéristique socioculturelle majeure du Québec durant cette période. Mais on distingue mal, dans ces représentations de la situation et de la culture, les principes ou les 'noyaux' d'une nouvelle unité plus organique dans sa complexité.

La création du Ministère de l'Education

Les débats idéologiques très vifs qui ont précédé et entouré la création du Ministère de l'Education, instrument administratif central de la réforme scolaire, ont été analysés ailleurs (L. Dion, 1967) d'une manière plus complète. Citons seulement un texte de l'éventuel ministre de l'Education, P. Gérin-Lajoie (1963), tiré d'un de ses nombreux discours prononcés durant la célèbre "Campagne du Bill 60":

> Notre salut, notre progrès, notre épanouissement seront oeuvre collective ou ne seront pas. Pas d'émancipation économique fructueuse, pas d'avancement politique, pas de progrès culturel sans un système d'enseignement puissant, organique, dynamique, intégré à la société canadienne-française, lui donnant un stimulant nouveau et en recevant un appui ferme. A ceux qui disent que nous allons trop vite et que nous voulons tout faire à la fois, je réponds que nous avons un retard d'un demi-siècle à rattraper et qu'il est, dans l'histoire des peuples, des moments où il faut tout *faire à la fois*, parce que tout se tient.
>
> Dans cet Occident en progrès foudroyant, dans cette Amérique du Nord anglo-saxonne toute puissante de son nombre et de sa richesse, il y a une place et un rôle pour une nation française, fidèle à son témoignage centenaire, adaptée au continent et au temps. Cette place, nous l'occuperons, ce rôle nous le jouerons, ce témoignage nous le rendrons par un effort de rigueur et de qualité auquel participera la nation entière.
>
> "Bâtir aujourd'hui le Québec de demain": comment cette entreprise n'attirerait-elle pas l'adhésion fervente, la participation enthousiaste d'un peuple réveillé au sens de la dignité et de la liberté?" (140).

Ce passage, dont le style d'argumentation enthousiaste illustre fort bien ce qu'on pourrait appeler l'*esprit* de la "révolution tranquille" à l'époque, est aussi un exemple de recours au sentiment national qu'on ne retrouve plus que très rarement depuis cette période de mobilisation des 'grands espoirs'. On notera que dans ce texte on insiste au moins autant sur la reprise en charge de l'héritage historique de la société québecoise que sur la nécessité pour celle-ci de s'adapter au continent nord-américain et au temps présent. Par la suite, c'est plutôt cet impératif d'*accommodation* à l'environnement dynamique de la société elle-même qui redevient le thème prédominant dans l'idéologie scolaire officielle. Par exemple, voici comment est définie la "vocation nouvelle du Québec'' dans le *Premier rapport du ministre de l'Education* (1965):

> Dès la proclamation du ministère et dans les jours qui ont suivi son assermentation, le ministre de l'Education a déclaré à plusieures reprises que son ministère serait un instrument de base pour réaliser la vocation nouvelle du Québec. Cette nouvelle vocation se confirme et se précise chaque jour davantage: c'est dans la voie de l'industrialisation, du progrès technique et scientifique, de la création originale que le Québec doit résolument s'engager s'il veut continuer à jouer un rôle valable en Amérique (9).

Industrialisation, progrès technique, création originale: ce sont là plutôt des ''impératifs de survivance'' et des directions de rattrapage que des valeurs ou des finalités sociétales proprement dites. Dans cette *idéologie d'accommodation* à la modernité de la civilisation nord-américaine, le *contexte* auquel le Québec doit s'adapter devient le thème central, alors que l'*héritage* socioculturel du Québec lui-même (sans doute parce que cela fait davantage problème) demeure à l'état d'une interrogation ou d'une inquiétude implicite et ne reçoit que peu d'élaboration.

Le Conseil supérieur de l'Education

Le Conseil supérieur de l'Education, créé en 1964 en même temps que le Ministère, tout en s'inspirant fortement du *Rapport Parent* (1965), a contribué à préciser sur certains points l'interprétation de l'idéologie scolaire dominante (rapport 1965/66 et 1966/67):

> On ne peut ignorer . . . que les exigences de la société industrielle—et l'on est presque déjà à l'aube de l'ère post-industrielle!—que l'avènement d'une société dominée par les moyens de communication de masse, que l'avancement dans le domaine des sciences, en particulier dans certaines branches des sciences physiques et de la cybernétique, que l'évolution politique, que les transformations sociales dont l'un des principaux traits est un pluralisme de plus en plus marqué et une tendance à l'égalitarisme social, que la multiplication des contacts avec d'autres sociétés, souvent fort différentes de la nôtre par leur culture, leur mode de vie, leurs religions et leur philosophie sociale et politique, ont profondément altéré le caractère de l'école. Celle-ci s'est démocratisée: elle offre maintenant tous ses services à l'ensemble de la population plutôt que de les réserver à

un petit groupe de privilégiés; c'est que la notion d'élite s'est élargie et qu'elle ne se fonde plus sur des critères limités comme ceux de la richesse, du rang social, de la domination d'un sexe sur l'autre ou de la religion. L'instruction est devenue un droit pour tous et, de ce fait, l'école a acquis une autonomie qu'elle ne possédait pas auparavant (7).

Plus loin, le rapport affirme qu'on doit percevoir l'école comme ''un agent extrêmement dynamique du progrès social et économique'':

Son action ne se limite plus à un groupe limité de jeunes personnes: en effet, les services qu'elle rend à l'ensemble de la population doivent, par l'éducation permanente, se prolonger bien au-delà de l'école secondaire, du collège et même de l'université. L'école, en outre, ne peut plus se confiner au simple rôle de véhicule des valeurs culturelles, le plus souvent entendues au sens de valeurs traditionnelles d'un milieu: en effet, aux paliers les plus élevés du système scolaire, les institutions d'enseignement ont aussi comme tâche de remettre en question, dans un effort systématique et objectif d'évaluation, les divers éléments qui composent le patrimoine culturel d'une société. L'école doit également, par ses nouvelles méthodes d'enseignement, par ses programmes et par le climat intellectuel qui doit y régner, jouer un rôle indispensable, grâce à la formation qu'elle donnera à ses étudiants, dans l'amélioration et même la transformation des conditions sociales, économiques et politiques du milieu. Cette fonction de l'école contemporaine crée pour l'enseignant des difficultés considérables d'adaptation qu'il n'avait sûrement pas à affronter il y a même une génération (8).

D'autres auteurs reprennent des interprétations semblables de cette situation de l'école face au ''pluralisme'' et à l' ''inquiétude''. Par exemple, L.-P. Audet et A. Gauthier (1967), devant cette prolifération d'idéologies et de mouvements nouveaux, affirment qu'il est possible d'y reconnaître certains courants qui caractérisent l'évolution présente: '. . . mentionnons un certain réveil à l'esprit démocratique, l'évolution marquée de l'Eglise catholique sur d'importantes questions d'ordre social, l'ouverture au mouvement d'internationalisme contemporain, le changement d'attitude à l'égard du rôle de la femme dans la société, l'émergence de nouvelles élites et la montée du socialisme'' (216).

Ce sont déjà là des traits un peu plus concrets qui définissent dans quelles directions tendent à évoluer les idéologies contemporaines au Québec et dont le système scolaire devra tenir compte, de plus en plus, au plan des transformations dans les *contenus* normatifs et 'informatifs' des activités et des programmes éducatifs.

Elites nouvelles, idéologies critiques et révisions:
la recherche difficile des justifications unanimes

On mesure bien l'écart qui nous sépare du temps où l'idéologie scolaire servait à préserver les valeurs et le patrimoine d'un réseau de petites communautés rurales contre l'expansion urbaine et industrielle, par où se diffusaient des valeurs et des idéaux 'étrangers', une langue et des religions différentes. On savait bien concrètement et on pouvait définir explicitement au nom de quelles valeurs et de quelles réalités familières on traçait les limites qui départageaient l'univers à préserver et à promouvoir par l'idéologie et les valeurs et réalités 'étrangères' que l'on préférait éliminer ou 'contenir' à distance. Mais cet 'environnement étranger' est devenu envahissant et ses influences multiples, irrésistibles. Nous avons dit plus haut que le manuel de R. Vinette (1948) nous paraissait être l'ultime effort d'assimilation de cette diversité envahissante à l'unité de l'héritage culturel officiellement reçu du passé. Or cette idéologie a éclaté totalement.

Aujourd'hui, on dirait (au moins approximativement) qu'on est passé d'un système idéologique trop 'fermé' et trop rigide, à un système idéologique qui est trop 'ouvert', qui a perdu temporairement ses 'normes centrales' de guidage. On a l'impression de voir assez clairement les exigences d'adaptation scolaire de la société québecoise aux exigences de son environnement: industrialisation, progrès technique et scientifique, démocratisation des institutions, 'création originale', échanges avec d'autres sociétés et emprunts à d'autres cultures. Mais, outre la formulation d'idéaux fort *abstraits*, on distingue mal encore ce que les pouvoirs conçoivent comme devant être les composantes unanimement acceptables de l'héritage sociétal propre au Québec et quelles seraient les contributions originales et les 'spécialités culturelles valables' que le Québec lui-même pourrait développer délibérément et qu'il aurait à offrir dans ces échanges avec les 'autres'. Paradoxalement, l'influence des sociologues québecois et de leur vocabulaire conceptuel (notamment celui du continuum ''société traditionnelle —société modernisée'') a peut-être contribué pour une part à la formulation d'un tel style idéologique abstrait. En d'autres termes, au niveau général où nous avons exprimé la manière dont l'idéologie scolaire officielle définissait le rôle spécifique de l'école relativement à son contexte sociétal et extra-sociétal, l'idéologie qui prévaut actuellement est davantage celle d'une *société moderne* qu'une idéologie du système scolaire proprement *québecois*. D'autres sociétés pourraient adopter, sans difficulté de *consensus*, la plupart des idéaux d'accommodation à la modernité que nous avons cités plus haut. On dirait que l' 'expérience idéologique' du Québec dans les années 1960 a été la *découverte de sa situation moderne*; mais que ce fut, en même temps, l'expérience d'un certain *oubli* de la nécessité d'entreprendre une nouvelle étape dans la *continuité de son patrimoine* socio-culturel particulier.

Les impératifs de la modernisation et les conditions institutionnelles de sa réalisation démocratique ont formé l'essentiel des formulations de l'idéologie scolaire jusqu'à maintenant. Il reste désormais à redéfinir l' 'héritage québécois', à reprendre les orientations jugées encore importantes et essentielles, à les choisir et les trier, à les recréer autrement dans le champ même où se déroulent les débats idéologiques engagés autour d'enjeux plus particuliers et plus concrets et où se résolvent provisoirement les grandes indécisions culturelles d'un peuple. Si le noyau des valeurs centrales à négocier dans le "Contrat social" n'est plus aussi visible ni aussi assuré qu'autrefois, c'est dans ces débats où, entre les idéologies critiques des élites nouvelles et les révisions successives des doctrines officielles en place, émergeront peut-être des termes essentiels et des enjeux définis sur un terrain commun à toute la famille de nos discours normatifs sur l'éducation. Cette situation, cette tâche-problème, est commune aujourd'hui à un grand nombre de sociétés, moyennes et petites surtout. C'est une situation où il n'existe pas de garanties externes, où les enjeux sont lourds et les risques, réels. C'est en partie dans les formulations idéologiques de demain que nous pourrons constater si les décideurs et les créateurs culturels ont trouvé un 'centre de gravité' proprement québécois. Pour l'instant, les débats font toujours rage; et le temps court.

Notes

[1]Ce texte est une version modifiée et mise à jour d'un article antérieur (V. Ross, 1969). L'article précité a été tiré d'une monographie plus complète, dont il représente une version résumée (V. Ross, 1965). Voir aussi: L. Duval (1963); N. Gagnon (1963), dont les études ont fait partie du même programme de recherches sur les idéologies scolaires au Québec.

[2]Cf. F. Dumont (1963a, 158). On trouve un exemple de cette perspective d'analyse dans le même numéro (G. Fortin, 1963): "L'idéologie, forme de rationalisation collective servant à la fois à justifier et à diriger l'action d'un groupe, est sans cesse remise en question par les changements globaux qui se produisent dans le milieu où évolue le groupe" (p. 224).

[3]Notons que les résultats d'une telle analyse peuvent servir ensuite à des analyses plus larges du premier type.

[4]Valade était originaire de la France et s'était établi tardivement au Canada.

[5]Rappelons qu'à l'époque (1865), "Canadiens" désignait spécifiquement les Canadiens *français*.

[6]Les débats idéologiques au cours des années 1960 ont vu entrer dans l'arène des interlocuteurs nouveaux, notamment les étudiants et leurs élites contestataires (E. Bielinski, 1972), et surtout les organisations syndicales des enseignants (voir, par exemple: Corporation des enseignants du Québec, 1972; Association québécoise des professeurs de français, 1970). Sur l'idéologie économique des Québécois, voir l'hypothèse de P. Harvey (1971). Enfin, on trouvera plusieurs études éclairantes dans le recueil de textes sur la sociologie de l'éducation publiée par P.W. Bélanger et G. Rocher (1970).

Bibliography

Association québécoise des Professeurs de français. *Le livre noir. De l'impossibilité (presque totale) d'enseigner le français au Québec* (Montréal: Editions du Jour, 1970).

Audet, L.-P. et Gauthier, A. *Le système scolaire du Québec. Organisation et fonctionnement* (Montréal: Librairie Beauchemin Limitée, 1967).

Bélanger, P.W., et Rocher, Guy, eds. *Ecole et société au Québec. Eléments d'une sociologie de l'éducation* (Montréal: Editions HMH Ltée, 1970).

Bielinski, E. "L'idéologie des contestataires," dans (en collaboration), *L'étudiant québécois: défi et dilemmes. Rapports de recherches* (Québec: Ministère de l'Education et Editeur Officiel du Québec, 1972), p. 313-364.

Conseil supérieur de l'Education. *L'enseignement face à l'évolution sociale et scolaire, Rapport 1965/66 1966/67* (Québec: Roch Lefebvre, Imprimeur de la reine, 1968).

Corporation des Enseignants du Québec. "L'école au service de la classe dominante." Manifeste présenté au XXIIe Congrès de la C.E.Q (Québec: C.E.Q., 1972).

Dion, L. *Le bill 60 et la société québécoise* (Montréal: Editions HMH Ltée, 1967).

Dumont, F. "Notes sur l'analyse des idéologies," *Recherches sociographiques*, vol. 4 (1963), p. 155-165.

Dumont, F. "Idéologie et savoir historique," *Cahiers internationaux de sociologie*, vol. 34 (1963), p. 43-60.

Duval, L. "Quelques thèmes idéologiques dans la revue *L'enseignement primaire*," *Recherches sociographiques*, vol. 4 (1963), p. 201-218.

Fortin, G. "Changements sociaux et transformations idéologiques: deux exemples," *Recherches sociographiques*, vol. 4 (1963), p. 224-227.

Gagnon, N. "L'idéologie humaniste dans la revue *L'enseignement secondaire*," *Recherches sociographiques* vol. 4 (1963), p. 167-200.

Gérin-Lajoie, P. *Pourquoi le Bill 60* (Montréal: Les Editions du Jour, 1963).

Harvey, P. "La perception du capitalisme chez les Canadiens français: une hypothèse pour la recherche," in J.-L. Migué, ed., *Le Québec aujourd'hui: regards d'universitaires* (Montréal: Editions Hurtubise HMH, Ltée, 1971), p. 129-137.

Langevin, J. (prêtre) *Cours de pédagogie, ou principes d'éducation* (Québec: C. Darveau, imprimeur, 1865).

Ministère de l'Education du Québec, *Premier rapport du ministre de l'Education* (Québec: Gouvernement du Québec; Roch Lefebvre, Imprimeur de la reine, 1965).

Québec. *Rapport de la Commission royale d'enquête sur l'enseignement dans la province de Québec. Tome II* (Québec: gouvernement de la province de Québec, 1965).

Rouleau, (L'abbé) Th.-G., Magnan, J.-C., et Ahern, J. *Pédagogie pratique et théorique à l'usage des candidats au brevet d'enseignement et des élèves des Ecoles normales* (Québec: Dussault & Proulx, imprimeurs, 1901).

Ross, (Mgr) F.-X. *Pédagogie théorique et pratique* 3e édition, "Adaptée au nouveau programme" (Québec: Imp. Charrier et Dugal, Limitée, 1924).

Ross, V. "La structure idéologique des manuels de pédagogie québécois," *Recherches sociographiques*, vol. 10 (1969), p. 171-196.

Ross, V. "Analyse de la structure idéologique des manuels de pédagogie." (Thèse de maitrise en sociologie, non publiée. Québec: Université Laval, Département de Sociologie et d'Anthropologie, 1965).

Valade, F.-X. *Guide de l'instituteur* (4e édition, Montréal: Fabre et Gravel, 1856, c. 1853).

Vinette, R. *Pédagogie générale* (Montréal: Editions du Centre de psychologie et de pédagogie, 1948).

III.

Alienation and Radicalization

WHAT distinguishes the collection of papers in this subsection is the regional diversity of the populations chosen and the analytical frameworks used. In examining the development of ideology among students and dirigeants (the intellectual cum-administrative elite of Laval University), Simoneau utilizes an historical-institutional approach. In contrast, Cohen's paper is an interactionist analysis of the reaction of a small group of Newfoundland youth to the attempts by their elders to legitimate their position in the community. Finally, Skogstad's study of an Alberta youth sample deals with a popular theme in sociology, alienation of young people.

Simoneau's paper demonstrates the presence of a noticeable parallelism between the social development of Quebec society, on the one hand, and the ideology of its educational system on the other. Simoneau's methodology is a combination of content analysis of documents and personal interviewing of a total of thirty groups representing the various segments of the University structure. Working within three chronological periods, up to the Second World War, from the Second World War through the 1950's and during the last decade, Simoneau locates somewhat differing strands of ideologies among students and dirigeants. While the students' ideologies are characterized by traditional, syndicalist and libertarian doctrines, those of the dirigeants reflect humanistic, liberal and developmentalist or reformist orientations. Initially, the students shared with the rest of Quebec society adherence to cultural nationalism which manifested itself in the rejection of "foreign" ideas. The second stage of ideological development showed the students to be departing from chauvinistic nationalism and instead opting out for democratic ideals based on secularism. The final period, during the 1960's, is characterized by receptivity to the ideologies of international student movements. Yet, Simoneau goes on to show that this radicalization has been contaminated by the ideology of the dirigeants and the University as a whole which rendered the radical transformation of Quebec society from within the University an impossible task.

Skogstad's paper is an interesting treatment of socialization of Alberta youth into regionalism. She discovers that positive identifica-

tion with the provincial level of government is stronger than that shown toward the federal system, specially among adolescents who come from Conservative homes and those who reside in rural, rather than urban areas. Overall, Skogstad finds, contrary to most current research on American children, that it is possible for young people to develop a negative image of the world of politics at an early age.

The picture portrayed to us by Cohen of a small group of high school seniors residing in a Newfoundland outport community underscores the failure of the leadership in this Newfoundland community to legitimate its authority in the eyes of the young. It is important to note, however, that this rejection of the local leadership, which is characterised by apathy and indifference, is mediated through nostalgic affinity to traditional values, values which symbolize the politics of non-activism.

6.

The Political Context of Childhood[1]

Leaders and Anti-leaders in a Changing Newfoundland Community

Anthony P. Cohen

THIS article examines the failure of antagonistic political elites in a Newfoundland community to mobilize support among a group of children to which each looks for succession. It thus concerns the leaders' inability to transmit their political values to those whom they regard as the key political figures of the young generation.

There are innumerable reasons why, in a society experiencing rapid modernization and undergoing sudden and pervasive socio-economic change, children should come to acquire political values which differ from those of their parents and the adult population. Education and the mass media become more widely available, complicating the diffusion and control of cultural values; materialistic achievement replaces subsistence as the rationale of social life. A less well understood phenomenon, and one infrequently examined, is the modernizing situation in which the political values of children revert to those of an earlier generation, not because of their inherent attractiveness or because of the children's traditionalism, but because the new values are denied credibility by the ways in which they are articulated. It is, perhaps, best thought of as a phenomenon of negative socialisation, in which children reluctantly revert to traditional values as a reaction to the politics which attends the expression of new ones.

It is just such a phenomenon which I attempt to document here. Again, my concern is not to explain why values do not change, nor to identify the most important reasons for their resilience. It is simply to suggest one possible source of their failure to change in a specific cultural-political context. Two opposing groups of leaders in a community seek to legitimate new political forms, and their roles in the generation of these forms, by manipulating popular values; the very nature of their efforts denies them success amongst the children whom they regard both as sources of legitimacy and as potential political successors.

The sample of children whose values and reactions I report here is not representative of children in the community. It is comprised of the educational elite of the town, that small group of sixteen and seventeen year olds which has managed to remain at school until Grade XI, the senior high school grade in Newfoundland. They are, also, close to the community's leaders either through kinship or other forms of parental association. Given these ascriptive and meritocratic attributes, they might well be thought of as heirs-apparent to both sets of leaders in the community and in this respect, their reactions to the contemporary politics of leadership in the community are important. Further, their "elitism" and personification of the much-valued new "educational opportunity" combine to make them, in the leaders' eyes, important sources of approval not least, of course, because of the rhetorical value to politicians of contented and well-served children. The children's proximity to the leaders makes them particularly vulnerable to the politics of leadership, and their receptivity to the antagonistic values of that politics is therefore a matter of some interest from the point of view of socialisation process. Their reaction, let it be said now, is one of apathetic rejection. But if rejection of parental political values by a young elite is not an uncommon phenomenon, it is the indifference and disinterestedness of the reaction which seems to me significant here: there is no organisation for collective dissent, nor articulation of contrary values. It is this implicit expression of the futility of politics, and the consequent reversion to customary non-activist attitudes, which indicates the extent to which the legitimating exercises of the leaders *qua* socialisation process have produced their own failure among the members of this particular "elite" group. Put quite simply, the nature of the contemporary leadership of the community fails both to implant imitative (and, therefore, legitimating) values or to provoke antagonistic forms, among its potential successors.

My purposes, then, are narrow, but in order to pursue them it is necessary to introduce considerations of a wider nature. In the first place, the validity of my argument suggests that the assumptions we commonly make about processes of political socialisation require some qualification. Secondly, I have to describe in some detail the political context of childhood which is the ostensible subject of this article.

The situation I describe, then, is one in which political activists (who, by very reason of their activism, can be culturally distinguished in the general population) fail to implant their own political values in their children. This calls attention to assumptions which have been frequently made about political socialisation processes and invested with universalistic validity. The assumptions I have in mind derive from the "structural determinism" which is postulated by the logic of the functionalist paradigm. The first is that political values transmitted from parents to children may be judged simply to have changed or to have remained the same (see, *inter alia*, Easton & Dennis, 1969; McQuail, *et. al.*, 1968; Jennings & Neimi, 1968; Bruner, 1956) and, secondly, that these values "functionally" reflect the nature of political relations in the immediate community environment (see LeVine, 1960a; 1960b; 1963). The argument of the present paper is that the intergenerational continuity of values may be more apparent than real: the child's reversion to customary values may be a function of his rejection both of his parents' espousal of new ones, and of the prevailing structure of local leadership. But, furthermore, it suggests that to infer continuity or change from the child's ostensible values does not always do justice to the complexities of socialisation process in certain societal situations. An initial source of the misleading universalism which has attended such assumptions may be the stipulative manner in which both politics and socialisation have been defined.

Prior to the recent and increasing refinement of interactionist and processual models in political anthropology, few academic students of politics adequately recognised its diffuseness as process in social life. Thus, definitions of politics have invariably been "fiat"-like—tied to notions of government as either consensual or conflictual domination, or to issues of "public" concern—and wielded to bludgeon social phenomena into arbitrary and empirically insensitive categories of social life.

Such unhappy uses of the word typically inform functionalist and structural studies of political socialisation, which tend to focus on the inculcation of values relating to government, authority and law. It is my contention that the social scientist has to mean rather more than this by "politics." If for no better reason than that the logic of culture suggests that patterns of behaviour are replicated—or, at the very least, are consistent—in diverse areas of social life, should we start with the assumption that the "political" is unlikely to be distinctively located in discrete institutional and processual aspects of a society. Further, whilst acknowledging the possible multiplicity of such aspects, we cannot blithely assume their presence in all societies: politics is manifest in such diverse phenomenal varieties that it defies definition and delineation in universalistic institutional terms. It is in precisely this respect that "politics" as process is misunderstood when tied to notions of government, policy, authority and so on.

The argument about the nature of politics, and about the virtues and shortcomings of its various definitions, is obviously too complex to be dealt with here. Suffice it for now to say that I take the diffuseness of politics in social life for granted; and that in common with the prescriptions of the various "grounded theory" perspectives, I maintain that it is the empirical situations with which one is confronted—and the data one draws from them—which should, so far as is possible, determine the appropriateness of definitions, not the other way around. Thus I would argue that an optimally inclusive framework for the identification of political phenomena in empirical situations can be provided which (a) accommodates the many previous definitions; (b) does not stipulate specific structural referents and loci; which nevertheless (c) imposes paradigmatic boundaries sufficient to give integrity to a concept of "politics," and which (d) is optimally inclusive of social phenomena and of theories and their complementary methodologies. To meet these criteria, I propose to regard activity as political which relates to attempts to create, maintain, or change systems of unequally distributed valued social resources. Political action is not, then, tied to specified resources, but to behaviour associated with their distribution. This framework allows us to conceptualise any such distributive systems as having political significance if the empirical situation so warrants. For example, the two ambitious executives, vying with each other for promotion, may be seen to stand in a political relationship to each other with regard to the scarce resource of promotion. Or, to take a case which falls well outside the conventionally defined area of politics, we may similarly see political content in a relationship between a Newfoundland craftsman and his client, when the craftsman fulfills his client's contract but refuses to accept payment, and thereby becomes politically predominant with respect to the situationally valued resource of obligation (see Chiaramonte, 1970).

Given this framework, then, the political context of childhood embraces a very much wider galaxy of social phenomena than is conventionally considered to fall within the scope of the sub-field of political socialisation. Moreover, there is obvious empirical justification for such eclecticism when that context is a face-to-face community in which the child's elders confront him in a wide variety of roles—a variety which itself underlines the artificiality of the structural taxonomies (e.g. "political" as opposed to "economic" process) with which social science is bedevilled.

The unequally distributed resource with which I am most concerned here is that of legitimacy, and I discuss it in relation to the politics of leadership in a Newfoundland community, and the success with which leaders, extending their struggle for legitimacy from the adult to the adolescent population, manage to mobilise support amongst a particular group of children. The data which support my discussion are drawn from observation of, and frequent and extensive conversations with a group of Grade XI students in one of the community's high schools, whose credentials as a problematic populatin for study I have already suggested.

Regardless of the meaning of politics, the notion of socialisation as the process through which children are introduced into bodies of values which inform and, perhaps, define their societies is sociologically primitive. It implicitly suggests that such bodies of values stand objective and immutable, changing all those with whom they come into contact, without undergoing much change themselves. Against this must be set the principle that the structural contexts of interaction are mediated as a conditioning or socialising force by the interaction itself. It is not simply the structural contexts of interaction which determine the values and expectations which inform the actors' behaviour, for these are also mediated and, indeed, generated by the very process of interaction.[2]

Thus in regard to our present concerns, socialisation is done an injustice if regarded simply as a process in which children come under the influence of pre-existing structural contexts and cultural practices: children have a dynamic and reciprocal relationship with those socialising forces, making and unmaking them, as well as being made by them.

In a situation of intensive change and its attendant cultural instability, we may expect this dynamic element to be increasingly critical. The same will be true of the context's ideological heterogeneity. It goes without saying that in a period of change, the old, or "traditional," is increasingly subject to the challenge of the contextually new. But what is, perhaps, more significant, is that the new is rarely homogeneously defined: it exists in varieties, or versions, until one achieves the cultural sanction of legitimacy and prevails over the others.

This, indeed, is the political context of childhood with which I will deal: one in which traditional and alien values confront each other and finally produce a hybrid behaviour which surprises both of its parents.

The processes by which the leaders attempt to mobilise these children's support are similar to the strategies of legitimisation they employ with respect to the adult population. They may be thought of as "myth management"—or the attempts to manipulate popular values by either sanctifying, or rejecting, prevailing structural arrangements and cultural practises.

My research with the children was part of a larger project concerned with the study of leadership strategies with respect to the legitimisation of political change. In its course, I carried out some fairly extensive work with high school students in Focaltown and in a larger town of the region. In Focaltown, the work consisted of frequent unstructured interviews, games based on simulated political situations, and a questionnaire survey. In this paper, I report the attitudes of my informants in the eleventh grade of Focaltown's Amalgamated High School, based principally on the interviews and informal interaction I had with them during my stay in Focaltown. I have already indicated why I feel this group to be important. I emphasise again that my present concern is neither with the nature of their values *per se*, nor with their similarity to and deviation from those of their peers and the adult population. It is, rather, with the efficacy of attempts by the activist elites to inculcate supportive and imitative values amongst this group of children, in a process which may have implications of some significance for socialisation theory.

At the time this study was made, Focaltown was experiencing rapid growth and had a population of some 3,500 inhabitants.[3] This put it among the larger of Newfoundland's outport communities. It is the "service centre" for the numerous outports and settlements of Herring Bay, on the northeast coast of the island, a status reflected in its modern and comprehensive stores, its high schools, government offices, hospital, and the proliferation of voluntary and denominational associations which thrive there.

Like several other largish communities in central Newfoundland, the rationale for Focaltwn's early growth was not the ubiquitous codfish, but timber—first for sawmills; during the thirties, for pitprops to be used in Welsh coalmines; but primarily, for the paper mills at Grand Falls and Cornerbrook.

But the phenomenal growth of the town's more recent history (75% between 1961 and 1969J) is due to copper. During the period of my fieldwork, there were three coppermines operating in the immediate vicinity, employing upwards of six hundred men, many of them Focaltowners. To be properly appreciated, this wealth of jobs must be set against the chronic unemployment and underemployment which typically informs rural Newfoundland (see Hurwitz, 1968; Wadel, 1973), although pessimistic estimates of the ore's longevity were a constant cause for concern. For Focaltown's merchants, the mines meant a large and relatively affluent clientele with ready cash. And for the more enterprising of these merchants, they created the opportunity to diversify—to break into building contracting, transportation, industrial supply, and, latterly, even manufacturing. For the community as a whole, they provided a strategic resource with which to negotiate for services from the Government, and they meant an influx of middle-class expertise and experience from the mining company executives which complemented the political skills and ambitions of the town's entrepreneurs by contributing to the sophistication of their clubs and associations.

But whilst copper meant growth, it does not explain the present political configuration of the community's leadership, nor the careers of the activists with whom we are concerned. The politics of Focaltown's leadership were well in the making when local copper was thought to have been exhausted by the early mining operations of the last century. It consisted, and still consists, in the confrontation between the old mercantile and ascriptive elite and their followers, and, on the other hand, the new entrepreneurial "middle-class" elite.[4] Traditionally, the leadership of Focaltown lay in the hands of the dominant merchant who, operating his business on the typical credit system, acquired a captive constituency which looked to him for guidance in all secular matters. A predominantly Protestant community, Focaltown lacked the political hegemony of the clergy that is associated with Catholic areas of Newfoundland (see Nemec, 1972; Szwed, 1966). Gradually this merchant came to exercise a monopoly of all leadership roles in Focaltown which he either occupied personally, or through his family and senior employees. His authority and influence derived from his ascriptive status, and his membership of community organisations was virtually *ex oficio*. He rarely used the organisations as vehicles for his political strategies but, rather acted personally and directly. Such was the typical, and culturally legitimate behaviour of the pre-eminent merchant in the outports.

But in 1955 this pre-eminence was challenged when a businessman from a nearby island community moved into Focaltown, against the merchant's wishes, and brought in his wake a number of other entrepreneurs from the locality. As outsiders, these men were free of the obligations that normally accrued to the merchant and his associates, and could therefore afford to be relatively uninhibited in their criticism of him. Furthermore, they were men who sought to build and run their businesses on cash bases, thus helping the new transfer payments which followed Newfoundland's entry into the Canadian Confederation, to undermine the merchant's monopolistic hold on the community's inhabitants. These were men who recognised the financial opportunities offered by Confederation and who grasped the social frills of commerce which they associated with a stereotypical "mainland" culture. They were organisation men, establishing a Lions Club, founding a Chamber of Commerce, rationalising the local school system, collecting for this and pressurising the Government for that. Where the traditional leadership was personalised, theirs was anonymous, shielded by the organisational facades they had created.

The specific issues informing the confrontation are unimportant for our present concerns. It is the contrast in styles to which I wish to draw attention for, indeed, it is around precisely this stylistic contrast that the politics of Focaltown leadership has revolved. I have characterised the styles as falling into broad types which inform the elites' respective strategies. The traditional elite will be referred to as the People's Group, which operates with a style of "cultural extension." The entrepreneurial group will be referred to as the Sophisticates, pursuing a strategy of "cultural substitution."

To some extent, the conflict might be represented as one between tradition and modernity, but one should not make the mistake of associating these respectively with conversatism and radicalism. The People's Group is not *traditionalistic*; it is rather, sustained by the customary values of political legitimacy, and associated with the pre-eminent political force of recent Newfoundland history—Small-woodism—which, in its early days, was radical in every sense of the word. Smallwoodism was born in the movement to take Newfoundland into Confederation and, as such, was composed of sections of rural society working in opposition to the established economic and political groups of the capital, St. John's (see Gwyn, 1968). But from these radical origins the movement, having achieved success, fell into largely pre-established modes of political behaviour. The basic structures were simply altered to accord with the change of incumbency —from paternalistic merchant to paternalistic government—and with the exigencies of political management which it called forth. Just as traditional structures of political behaviour—for example, patronage and local oligarchy—were "extended" to serve modern conditions, so the values which sustained them with legitimacy were similarly extended to legitimise the new order. Smallwoodism, then, and the People's Group as its Focaltown manifestation, were traditional in only this respect: that as a grass-roots, almost populist, political phenomenon, it was able to manage its popular legitimacy through the manipulation of traditional or customary values which were "extended" to new political objects. Their policies were typically represented as having precedents in the past, and were therefore implicitly held to be consistent with those valued elements of the past to which the politicians pragmatically attributed sacrality. There are many and well-known instances throughout the contemporary "developed" and Third Worlds of similar uses of the past to mediate the present and predicted future.

But just as the apparently traditional People's Group is misunderstood if interpreted in terms of conservatism, so are the apparently modernistic Sophisticates if credited with radicalism. The essence of Sophisticate ideology is the right of commercially and professionally successful men to dictate the good of the people. They consider their merit to have been proven by their personal success; they further consider their intrinsic skills to be complemented by the relative scarcity of such talents among the rest of the population. Their right and capacity to decide the common good they therefore judge to be undeniable. But their watchword is rationalisation, and their valued skills are administration and organisation. It is the ethic of Sound Business Sense. And tradition, and the past generally, is clearly not evidence of good business. A societal image of modernity and achievement is called for, and found in the apocryphal entrepreneurial paradise of "the Mainland." The ascriptive past is now judged both irrelevant and prejudicial to the achievement of the new meritocratic order. Here, then, the values of the past are denied, and replaced by those of putative and alien modernity. That is the essence of cultural substitution, and it, too, is a strategy employed in a variety of ideological and cultural contexts.

At this point, let me recall the notion of politics that I set out earlier as behaviour associated with attempts to create, maintain and change systems of unequally distributed valued social resources. The valued resource which is sought in the politics of Focaltown leadership is that of legitimacy, and its by-product with which we are concerned here in the support of the town's young and embryonic elite. The contrasting strategies of cultural extension and cultural substitution may be thought of as alternative approaches to the acquisition of the resource of legitimacy, in the sense that each makes coherent all of its respective elite's behaviour with respect to legitimisation. Thus, their policies and their modes of recruitment, articulation and mobilisation are all consistent with either a culture-extending or culture-substituting strategy, and all can be seen as being directed towards the acquisition of legitimacy.

If we abstract the culture-extending and culture-substituting principles and values from the various aspects of these groups' behaviour, we have something which looks very much like the sociological model of myth. In Malinowski's view, myth serves as a "charter" for social action, investing action of the present with the sacrality of historical precedent, thereby legitimating the present in terms of the past, and, like Durkheim's ritual, continually re-affirming the under-lying principles of social organisation (see, *inter alia*, Malinowski, 1928; 1936; 1963). According to Levi-Strauss, at least one of the prime functions of myth is to reconcile apparent oppositions in social life (e.g. *inter alia*, Levi-Strauss, 1965). Maranda, in a recent discussion, suggests that the analysis of myths is concerned with the ways in which alien structures are reduced to familiarity, and with ". . . the culture-conditioning mechanisms that mould ethnic cognitive systems."[5]

The literature on the sociology of myth is now large and rapidly growing, and the definitions proliferate accordingly. We need not bother here with their particularities, and perhaps their variation is best served by Kirk's comment that ". . . myth as a general concept is completely vague, (implying) no more in itself than a traditional story.

. . .''[6] But, these postulated functions have in common an obvious similarity to the processes I associate here with political legitimisation—the manipulation of values to reduce the unpopular to the popular or, at least, to the tolerable. Disregarding the adequacy of these models as total explanations of myth, it is clear that their common function—most explicitly expressed, perhaps in Malinowski's notion of a charter[7]—is precisely the same as that served by both culture-extending and culture-substituting groups in Focaltown. Both imply systems of order—or resource distribution—from which the principles which constitute their legitimating myths are derived. In cultural extension, the order is that of the indigenous and customary norm; in cultural substitution, it is that of an alien ''modernity.''

The ''myths'' that I derive from the groups' respective strategies are rarely narrated as coherent tales. Rather, they are generally implicit in their behaviour and I infer them accordingly. The roles that children play as audiences, therefore, consist largely in observation of the leaders' behaviour, and in the inferences they themselves make from their direct dealings with leaders.

The assumptions to which I referred at the beginning of this paper suggest that if children display similar values to those of the adult generation this may be taken as evidence of the persuasiveness of the myths in which they are enshrined, and which are transmitted from the adult to the younger generation; the myths should have particular potency when articulated by leaders to their own children or to children closely associated with them. That assumption is not borne out by the children I report here, for their reversion to the customary values of the general adult population in fact constitutes a rejection of the myths articulated by the leaders and accepted by the wider adult population. To put the matter simply, one cannot infer from the *apparent* similarity of values in the young and adult populations that the values, and the potency of leaders' myths, have not changed from one generation to the next. Not only do these children reject the substantive values of these myths; but the indifference and apathy with which they react to them suggests that they also reject the underlying values involved in the assumption of leadership roles and, in so doing, reject the leaders' call to elite status.

In managing myths, leaders obviously seek to propagate values to which they believe their audiences' cognitive and affective proclivities will be most susceptible. But the dynamic nature of the socialisation process, to which I drew attention earlier, suggests that children may develop new modes of cognitive evaluation which makes the efficacy of the leaders' myths problematic. It is clear that the myth managers in Focaltown take no account of such intergenerational differences, and the irony of their consequent failure with the present sample of children is that it is their myths which have themselves changed the ways in which the children perceive the socio-political world. In this respect, the management of myths contributes to its own inefficacy.

This section illustrates some of the instances in which this intergenerational change stultifies the prevailing strategies of myth management, and begins by sketching the situational background to the most basic of cognitive categories—those in terms of which the children identify themselves socially.[8]

Class distinctions in Focaltown are only now being transformed from the elementary divisions of ascriptive elite and mass into the more complex categories of middle and working class. Formerly, the locally-defined correlates of status were far more important elements of popular consciousness than the more common stratificatory components of identity in Western, and particularly European society. The components of status were many and varied, but principle among them were religious denomination and having work, and these tended to coalesce: many of Focaltown's unemployed belonged to the Pentecostal Assembly which, in 1961, accounted for approximately 33.6% of the town's population. Of the remaining Focaltowners, a further 33.6% belonged to the United Church, and 29% to the Salvation Army.[9] A survey I made in 1969 suggests that the Pentecostal Assembly then accounted for some 42% of Focaltown's inhabitants, an estimate confirmed by both of the local school boards.[10] Generally, one associates Pentecostalism in Focaltown with the lower end of the socio-economic scale. Salvationists tend to occupy a slightly higher category, and Anglicanism and Methodism are most concentrated in the upper reaches of the scale. Family size varies similarly: 50% of my survey sample in Focaltown had between four and twelve children, and almost half of these were Pentecostal families. In the Focaltown context, the Pentecostalism suggested rather more than mere sectarian difference: it suggests extreme hardship caused by a tendency to large families and to either very badly paid employment or to no employment at all. Such characteristics acquire a fresh cogency in a society which is suddenly invaded by the values of an exaggerated materialism after a history of deprivation and, often, near-destitution. To the rest of the population, therefore, but particularly to the children, Pentecostalism implies definitely inferior status, an attitude expressed in such extreme opinions as that Pentecostalists are promiscuous, incestuous, and often illegitimate.

The social correlates of denomination therefore underline the antagonisms which were traditionally associated with doctrinal difference. So far as the children are concerned, they have been further exacerbated in Focaltown by the amalgamation of all the denominational school boards except the Pentecostal into one system. The product of this amalgamation was the construction of a superbly equipped high school, whose facilities were almost unique in rural Newfoundland. Children habituated to this luxury had only to look down Main Street to infer its superiority over the obviously inferior Pentecostal school.

It was clear from my conversations with the children that a primary means of ordering their social worlds was into the Pentecostal and non-Pentecostal. The only other pair of oppositions which approached it in importance was whether or not one was a Newfoundlander.

So far as these children were concerned, to be Pentecostal was to have a "spoiled identity" (Goffman, 1968). But they did not reject the stigma itself so much as the underlying social malaise which became manifest in Focaltown in the form of denominational identity. Pentecostalism bespoke not only sectional poverty and unemployment: it somehow stood also for the familiar destitution which afflicted the outports of earlier years and other districts, and whose relief—or its promise—made them ripe for political management of the most exploitative kind. The maintenance of Pentecostalism in Focaltown was important for both groups of leaders. For the culture-extending People's Group, it provided a captive constituency whose diligent electoral support they frequently mobilised. For the Sophisticates, it symbolised the tradition they sought to reject and de-value. It was an identity rejected by the children as part of their general rejection of traditional poverty. But, at the same time, they seemed to feel the injustice of the stigma carried by the identity in the "new" mythical order of the Sophisticates. The children clearly felt unease about the oppositional nature of the identity and blamed both groups of leaders for its implications; that is, for failing to remove the political and material conditions which led them to define themselves in opposition to Pentecostalism.

Insensitive to the children's unease, the Focaltown politicians still emphasise the distinctiveness of the Pentecostal congregation, each in pursuit of his own expediency. That they do so is, perhaps, some indication of the change which has taken place in the values of the younger generation, a change which, because the children's modal identity has not *ostensibly* altered, is more real than apparent. Here, then, we begin to qualify the easy assumptions of socialisation theory: the maintenance of forms or structures does not necessarily imply the maintenance of those values which originally generated and sustained them. In other words, apparent continuity may obscure real change.

This change is manifest in other ways too. Political leadership in Newfoundland has long been sustained by an almost exaggerated

deference. This trait, coupled with the political reticence of Newfoundlanders, goes some way towards explaining the longevity and hereditary nature of leadership. Leaders exploited this deference in extending
their spheres of influence by appropriating diffuse leadership roles to
themselves and their chosen successors. This was the manner in which
the typical oligarchies were maintained and, indeed, is the context for
the present examination of the relations between the leaders and my
sample of children. It is still the case that the son of a respected man
tends automatically to be accorded respect in his own right.[11]

Both groups of leaders in Focaltown pursue the resource of deference, albeit in different ways and with varying degrees of success. But
it is clearly the case that not only does my sample of children fail to
accord them deference; they also reject deference and its structural
bases as valued elements of their social identities. They play down their
superior status largely by indulging intensively in the general activities
through which children compete to become unequal: four devote themselves to their hockey, soccer and basketball teams, and two others
excel in their studies. It is in such manner that they seek respect rather
than through the assumptions others might make of their inequality. In
this regard, they seem to have been successful, for they appear to be
invested by their peers with neither the envious admiration nor resentment one might expect to be reserved, in a deferential society, for those
well born and close to power. In all their activities, they avoid formal
leadership roles: none is an official of his sports teams, nor a member of
the Student's Council. Only one, as Editor of the school newspaper,
has any official position at all. Their rejection of the roles and respect to
which they are ascriptively entitled is never articulated as an explicit
value, but only—as we see later—implicitly, as a symptom of the more
general cynicism with which they regard leadership activity.

Indeed, whilst the adult population tends to defer to leaders *qua*
leaders, the children make a rather more critical evaluation of their
performance as leaders, and attribute respect accordingly. I discuss
their criteria of performance shortly.

A third indication of a change of values is the absence among the
children of commitment to either group of leaders. Whilst it is true that
adult Focaltowners outside the periphery of activism have only a
limited awareness of the intricacies of political alignments in the town's
leadership, they clearly have their preferences which, should the subject be raised, are advocated with all the vehemence of ideological
partisanship. Such commitment is, again, absent among the children:
leaders, to them, are a generic group, distinguished only by the extent
to which the individual species impinge on their lives.

With the general lack of partisanship, there goes the absence of the

kind of confrontations with respect to political change which characterise the politics of the leadership itself in Focaltown.[12] I found this
particularly surprising in view of the fact that my work with the children
coincided with the acceleration of organised opposition to Premier
Smallwood and his local representatives by Sophisticate and other
"modernistic" leaders—amongst whom, in Focaltown, were both the
young Principal, and the most popular teacher of the Amalgamated
High School. The issues of the day—and, for that matter, of history
—appeared to have little currency among the children, their "Current
Affairs" classes evoked no interest. It is clear from responses to my
questionnaires that these children, despite their very much longer
schooling, are much less well informed about the contemporary and
historical politics of Newfoundland on even a basic level than are their
parents.

But perhaps all of these cases are explicated by that one respect in
which the children and their parents differ only in degree in their
observation of the political world: it is in their pursuit of self-interest
and in their reluctance to do anything to ensure its long-term satisfaction. In this regard, adult Focaltowners, like other outporters, are
clientlike: they were the products of a tradition of patronage which held
them passively captive and taught them the political costs of clienthood
which, knowing no alternative, they paid at successive elections. But
their children are more the products of, what Perlin (1971a) has called,
"promissory politics." With a realism lacking among the adult population, the members of my young samples seem to have recognised that
the town's leaders have no effective sanctions with which to coerce
them into support, and therefore expect promises from them for which
they offer no values in exchange. They clearly seek to extract commit-
ments at no cost to themselves and, in this respect, share in an attitude
which appears to inform the young population of Focaltown generally.
For example, the Grade XI students, amongst whom were my informants, felt strongly the lack of a youth centre in town. They had
initiated a request to the Town Council for such facilities with the
response that if they could collect a minimal amount of money, Council
and various individuals would contribute a substantial amount to cover
building and equipment costs. But they made no attempt to collect the
money. Why?

> "We got a right to a club. Why should we go round knocking
> doors for something we got a right to?"

The "right" was a meritocratic one, and the leaders' non-compliance
had to be seen as a denial of their superior achievements as Grade XI
students about to enter university:

Leaders? They hinder teenagers. . . . They promise this and promise that, but you never get it.

Clearly, they were cynical about the politics of leadership at all levels. Talking about Federal politics, of which he admitted ignorance, the most academically gifted of my informants clearly demonstrated the extent to which experience of local leadership culminated in an attitude of cynicism which treats politicians as a generic type. For example,

Everybody voted for Trudeau. They thought he was a superman, but we haven't seen any changes yet. . . . I've always thought that one politician was just the same as another.

And they impute to the *genus* the same kind of self-interest which they display themselves, as well as the resource which makes them regard their own participation and commitment as futile. What are the prerequisites for gaining local office?

Sir, you need rich friends. Then, if you're not fit for anything, you'll get in.

Whatever they referred to as "power," my informants, without exception, regarded money as its essential prerequisite.

I have already made clear my view that my informants are not representative of their age or educational peer groups, and I therefore emphasise that I am making no claims about the cynicism of the young population as a whole. Indeed, there is evidence from data collected among other children to suggest that such political cynicism accelerates with progression up the school. Indeed, their very lack of representativeness makes all the more striking the unanimity with which the members of my sample express this attitude. It was a cynicism which, like politics itself, touched all situations of inequality in their lives, from their influence in family decision-making to the ways in which each sex evaluated the other.

One paradox of this conclusion is that it contradicts the conventional wisdom that children are more idealistic than adults. That is manifestly not the case with this sample. Indeed, quite the reverse. Newfoundland is a society which demands little attempt to conceal the kind of corruption among its managers which is usually euphemistically known as "conflict of interest." Yet it is the parents who appear to retain their idealism and the image of leadership process as being democratic and accessible.

Since these particular children are so close to the leaders, it is perhaps not surprising that they should display such sensitivity to the latters' self-interest. But their negative reaction to leaders' self-seeking and, more generally, to leadership itself, requires some explanation since it appeared with apparent suddenness, without any recognisable external stimulus and, certainly, independently of the "counter-cultural" movements which characterised "youth culture" in other Western societies. In this latter regard, the children shared their parents' emphatic intolerance of what was seen as teenage protest and dissent and, even, of the explicit rejection of parental values and authority. Without exception, they cite their parents as the most important source of influence and most valued source of approval.

It is not enough to remark that the leaders' myths lack efficacy among the children. Rather, I shall argue that they have contributed to their own inefficacy. To illustrate this process, I return to the cases I have raised above.

Culture-extending myths use the past to legitimate the present. They may do this by depicting the past as being black and appalling so that the contemporary situation, however bad it is objectively, appears to be relatively paradaisical.[13] More commonly, however, they are used to extend traditional values to new structures by suggesting that such structures are not really new at all, but are derived from either precedent events, or from the logic of the past. These myths are managed in Focaltown by men who constantly play on their indigeneous origins, on their association with the old mercantile leadership, on the culturally-repugnant assertiveness of the new businessmen's associations and clubs and, generally, on their fidelity to customary political practise. They mediate the new by infusing it with old values. Their most committed support in Focaltown has come from the Pentecostal congregation, not because of the leaders' denominational credentials—they are all members of the United Church—but, rather, because of their association with Smallwood Liberalism (and, secondarily perhaps, because of their *apparent* dissociation from the materialistic endeavour in which the congregants themselves have so obviously failed). Whilst encouraging the rationalisation of the traditionally autonomous denominational school system in Newfoundland, the Smallwood Government, against the largely apocryphal opposition of the other political parties, protected the right of any local denominational school board to declare its autonomy. In Focaltown, the Pentecostal school board had decided not to join the other denominations in amalgamation, but lived in constant fear that, should Smallwood fall from office, they would eventually be compelled to do so. Their local support for Smallwood in the 1969 Liberal leadership campaign was monolithic. The People's Group, as culture-extenders, had inherited—and, in one case, contrived—the mantle of local Smallwood brokers. As such, they enjoyed virtually unflagging electoral support from a core of Pentecostalists at municipal elections, Liberal Association meetings, and so forth.

Essentially, they had to placate the Pentecostalists by pretending that all that had changed in the situation was the ubiquitous proliferation of—usually one-room—schools in the denominationally heterogeneous community. If schools wanted to combine they could do so. But if they chose to remain independent, their right to do so would be respected and defended. The educational system would still be administered by the denominations, only in voluntary association. Nothing, really had changed. And the myth managers themselves went to extraordinary lengths, from financial contributions to the Pentecostal School Board, to allegations of corruption against the—largely Sophisticate—members of the Amalgamated School Board, to propagate the stability and integrity of the Pentecostal schools. But, of course, the situation *had* changed. The product of amalgamation was not the integration of three or four obsolete school rooms: it was the construction of a sixteen classroom high school, complete with library, language laboratory, cafeteria, sports facilities, and full complement of well-qualified teaching staff. The response of the Pentecostalists was to raise by voluntary contribution about one-seventh of the money this school had cost, to build their own manifestly inferior high school. Its staff was inadequate in number and qualifications, the membership of the senior grades was failing to increase satisfactorily, the number of university entrants was negligible. But still the People's Group myth managers taught that nothing had changed.

The Grade XI students of the Amalgamated High School were not only aware of the People's Group's motives in their support of Pentecostalists, but also displayed some intuitive realisation of its implications. This educational dualism was establishing in the cash-based society a more clearly defined caste system than that which had existed among the mass in the traditional merchant-dominated credit society. Their reactions were to despise the People's Group as politicians, and to regard them as totally unable to recognise the needs of their own age-group:

> There's only a Pentecost school here because "X" was mayor and "Y" wanted to be the MHA (both are members of the People's Group). They don't see for their votes they're leaving those kids with a rotten school, and making all of us feel prejudiced to each other. We don't walk home on the same side of the street.

And,

> The Pentecostal school is so they'll all use Z's (People's Group

leader) store. He doesn't give a damn about their education—only about their groceries.[14]

Here, then, the myth managers are failing. Unlike the Sophisticates, they seek legitimacy through public electoral support, so their appeals must be broadly based. Thus, they typically depict the outport population as a homogeneous mass with undifferentiated interests. In fact, these are clearly perceived by the children to be the generalisation of only *sectional* interest. The problems of which the People's Group speak are supposedly those of the community as a whole. The evident consequence of the policy with respect to education, which is one of the most deeply felt issues in Focaltown, is to exacerbate the emergent antagonisms among the young population. The effect of this on my Grade XI informants, who obviously are potential activists in the causes of either group of leaders, is to see the People's Group as advocating a divisive and wasteful anachronism for dubious ends.

On the other side of the coin, however, the culture-substituting Sophisticates fare little better. If anything, their behaviour is subject to even more critical an appraisal by the children, since each of the four Sophisticates has close associations with their school. Apart from their official positions as Principal, and past or present members of the School Board, three of them have identifiable financial interests in the school's progress, two of them as contractors. They are, further, leading members of the Lions Club, which has sought to dominate the political and organisational life of Focaltown, and have adorned the school site with many products of Lion's endeavour: an ice-rink, a swimming pool, and so on. These men base their leadership firmly on their control of organisational activity, rather than on appeals for public support. This strategy is both an expression of ideology, and also a tactic to which they are forced as culturally illegitimate leaders, challenging the *status quo*.

All of my informants were associated with the Sophisticates in other ways too, as relatives, or as the children of associates or employees. And yet this close association has not mellowed their evaluation of the leaders. Their activity in Focaltown is written down to self-interest masquerading as "community service" and "public spiritedness" which are the explicit ethics of Sophisticate ideology. Indeed, this is a common-place reaction to Sophisticate activity, but is particularly surprising amongst these children, firstly because of their proximity to the Sophisticates, and secondly, because one might have assumed their receptivity to the "modernistic" values of Sophisticate mythology.

But whilst Newfoundlanders generally appear to be reconciled to the self-interest of their politicians—indeed, their initial assumption about a would-be leader is invariably that he is self-seeking—the children seem to react with particular bitterness to the cant-like elements of Sophisticate mythology. Self-seeking among the more traditional—culture-extending—politicians is found to be unremarkable, perhaps because it has always been overt and explicit. But it seems to be regarded as intolerable that the supposed reformers and harbingers of modernistic plenty should be similarly, and somehow more spectacularly motivated. *Their* rhetoric about serving the interest of the community is dismissed as malicious humbug. To some extent, of course, this application of differential criteria is explained by the relative legitimacy of the two groups. But it may also derive from the rather more ambitious activity of the Sophisticates, which necessarily concludes in more obvious failure. The cost of a modernistic and reforming stance is that things must appear to change. If they do not, then the myths associated with such a stance lose their credibility.

This tends to characterise the career of the Sophisticates as a relatively coherent group of political activists. In their roles as organisation men, they proclaimed the imminence of great change in respect of employment and communal facilities and, with some notable exceptions, they failed to procure such change. But what was left after these failures was the suspicion, or certain knowledge, that the leaders had themselves benefited.

The confrontation between the People's and Sophisticate's Groups was superficially about socio-political change and development. In fact, it was a dispute about the legitimacy and efficacy of new organisational activity as opposed to the more traditional styles of political management. The Grade XI children, without fully recognising the nature of the conflict, appeared to grasp its marginality, and that of Sophisticate bluster, to the achievement of change in the political life of Focaltown. The Sophisticates carved out spectacular careers for themselves, but for all their alien modernity, entrepreneurial endeavour, and organisational posturing, they came no nearer to achieving the valued goals of the children than did the People's Group. Their fine school was an anomaly when set against the widely expressed desire to stay in or near Focaltown to pursue a traditional subsistence occupation—fishing or logging—if only Provincial economic policy would make it feasible. But given the prevailing policy of large-scale and centralised industrialisation coupled with a disastrous unemployment rate, they were being forced into higher education as an adaptive resource, whose "successful" conclusion would mean their emigration to the mainland where a market for their educational qualifications might be found. The educational opportunity, which parents prized so highly for their children, was almost a millstone around the children's necks, an unhappy compromise between their ideal of a more equitable revival of the past, and the reality of a present and future for which they had no liking and in which they felt displaced. Ironically, it was their less well-educated Pentecostalist peers who would have the "opportunity" of staying home, even if it meant the recourse to welfare to which such a large proportion of the Pentecostal community was subject.

The culture-extenders' failure to reproduce the past whose values they emphasised in their myths denied them legitimacy amongst the children. The culture-substituters' depiction of a highly competitive materialistic, and apparently unattainable future, led to the children's evaluation of them as being both despicable and derisory. It is, then, little wonder that the ideological confrontations between the People's and Sophisticate's Groups, and the values that sustained them, should not be replicated amongst the educated sixteen year-olds of Focaltown.

So far as these children are concerned in their collective roles of audience and prospective leaders, the myths contribute to their own inefficacy. But the extent to which they may be said to actually *produce* contextually new values must be left problematic. I suggested early in this paper that politics should be thought of as diffuse process, reflecting the strategies and values which inform interaction over the whole range of social process. Later, I noted that the cynical "realism" with which these children approach the politics of leadership in Focaltown also appears to characterise their evaluation of all systems of unequally distributed valued social resources. The specific processual and institutional sources of such values must remain pure conjecture. Indeed, the possible multiplicity of such sources itself calls into question the comfortable ways in which sociologists conventionally circumscribe empirical phenomena when examining processes of socialisation.

The sample whose attitudes I report here is not representative of the young population of Focaltown as a whole for reasons which, as I said earlier, make it particularly interesting. Indeed, my conversations with their peers in the Pentecostal High School, and with younger children of all denominations, indicate a somewhat greater tendency to discern "democratic" features in Newfoundland political process, and yet they display a similar resignation to the futility of participation and the possibility of change and reform. The implicit world view of all these children is of a social structure laid down by autonomous power invulnerable to dissenting wills and behaviour. Their reaction, then, is to accept the *status quo* as being largely immutable and to attempt, as *individuals* rather than collectivity, to minimise its derogatory effects. Thus, the ostensible continuity of behavioural forms obscures a real inter-generational change of values.

Perhaps, then, all that distinguishes the sample I report here from the other children of Focaltown, is their decreasing susceptibility to myth management. One might assume their disavowal of parental and religious myths to be a function of their greater maturity, and, indeed as they grow older, they are decreasingly subjected to these myths. But at the same time, and for the reasons I indicate above, they are *increasingly* subjected to the myth management of the community leaders. Yet, their reaction is not one of positive collective dissent, protest or rebellion, but reverts, like the adults', to one of individualistic self-interest.

There is a further paradox here, For the adult population's reaction can be explained by the historical strategies of Smallwoodism and pre-confederation politics of maintaining a dependence on central and pivotal sources of power, such as the merchant at community level or the Government at provincial level, by discouraging the emergence of communal and collective organisation. But these children are the targets of new organisational ideologies manifest in the establishment of local party associations, community-based economic development associations, co-operatives, increasingly assertive trades unions, and the businessmen's clubs, ideologies which were constantly articulated by several of the children's teachers as well as by the Sophisticate myth managers. Yet, as we have seen, their resistance to these messages is not satisfactorily explained by their belief in the myths of the culture-extending People's Group.

My purposes in this article are limited. They have not been to offer an explanation of these paradoxes but, rather, to cast doubt on the facility which we assume to attend the process though which political values are inculcated in the young. Clearly, these children have rejected the values with which the principal opposing groups of leaders in Focaltown—and, by implication, their counterparts at Provincial level—attempt to legitimate themselves, and whose continuity they seek in the children's assumption of elite roles. They had not found an ideological style of leadership which attracted them more. Perhaps the most that can be said is that instead of a group of people, liberated from the traditional bonds of outport life, marching contentedly and unswervingly towards the values of a new materialistic social order, we see a group of nostalgically traditionalistic children reluctantly struggling, with anomic confusion, into a future in which they feel insecure and dominated by leaders and mythologies in which they have no faith.

This phenomenon ought to cast doubt on the universalism of the assumptions about socialisation which I stated at the beginning of this paper. Furthermore, it raises the need for some attention to be paid by sociologists to socialisation process among the young generally, and among its elites, in unstable and rapidly changing societal situations —attention which produces rather more fundamental and empirically sensitive models of the socialisation process than those of unidimensional interaction between the child and the political context of his childhood.

Notes

[1] The study on which this article is based was made during my tenure of a Research Fellowship of the Institute of Social and Economic Research, Memorial University of Newfoundland (1968-70), and supported by grants from the Newfoundland Department of Community and Social Development. The present analysis owes much to the criticisms and advice of Bronwen Cohen and Roy Fitzhenry, who understood its implications rather better than I did.

[2] This principle expresses, somewhat clumsily, the basic postulate of the interactionist tradition in sociology. It is a tradition which has barely touched conventional political sociology, although it has been evident, through the paradigms of exchange and transaction, and the various "processual" analyses of political life, in social anthropological approaches to the study of political phenomena.

Interactionist sociology is generally exempt from the criticisms I made here of socialisation theory. Interactionists have, of course, expressed the fallacy of the "structural determinism" type of socialisation theory by emphasising the phenomenological aspects of those processes through which behaviour is acquired.

[3] Focaltown is a fictitious name. The fieldwork was carried out between September 1968 and August 1969, and during several visits during 1969-70. When I use the present tense, I am, therefore, referring to the situation as it appeared during those periods.

[4] This, and similar confrontations, are documented in Cohen, 1975a. Also see Perlin, 1971b. For descriptions of traditional mercantile ascendancy in Newfoundland outports, see inter alia, Report of the Newfoundland Royal Commission, (1933); Wadel, 1969; Iverson and Matthews, 1968; and, Horwood, 1967.

[5] P. Maranda, ed., Mythology (Harmondsworth: Penguin, 1972), p. 8.

[6] G.S. Kirk, Myth: Its Meaning and Functions in Ancient and Other Cultures (Cambridge: The University Press, 1970), p. 28.

[7] A function, incidentally, accepted by Levi-Strauss, Cf. Leach, 1968: xvii.

[8] I examine more fully the ideologies and strategies which inform identity-management in Focaltown, in Cohen, 1975b.

[9] 1961 census.

[10] Much of this increase will have been accounted for by immigration, but some of it has come from the Salvation Army.

[11] A practice Perlin has aptly called the "Mr. John phenomenon."

[12] It is generally the case that boys tend to be more traditional and parochial in their attitudes than their female classmates. They are less inclined to move

from Focaltown or from Newfoundland, more inclined to identify themselves as Newfoundlanders rather than as Canadians, are more satisfied with the prospect of a traditional subsistence life than the girls. (This might possibly be explained by the traditionally greater mobility of girls as economically superfluous members of the outport household unit). But *within* sex groups there appears to be no division comparable to that of the leadership and its periphery.

[13]Cato Wadel (1970) has noted this as a frequent defensive strategy of Premier Smallwood.

[14]In fact, whilst I was in Focaltown, there was little to indicate that choice of retailer had much to do with sectarian issues. But, shortly after I left, two shops run and patronised almost exclusively by Pentecostalists opened, in competition with stores owned by Sophisticates. There is no doubt that they were largely financed by members of the People's Group.

Bibliography

Bruner, E.N. "Cultural Transmission and Cultural Change," *Southwestern Journal of Anthropology*, Vol. 12, No. 2 (1956), p. 191-199.

Chiaramonte, L. *Craftsman-Client Contracts: Interpersonal Relations in a Newfoundland Fishing Community*, Newfoundland Social and Economic Studies, 10 (St. John's Institute of Social & Economic Research, Memorial University of Newfoundland, 1970).

Cohen, A.P. *The Management of Myths* (Manchester: Manchester University Press, 1975a).

Cohen, A.P. "The Definition of Public Identity: managing marginality in outport Newfoundland following Confederation," in P.F. Neary and G. Story, eds., Vol. on Newfoundland in Confederation (Toronto: University of Toronto Press, 1975b).

Easton, D. and Dennis, J. *Children in the Political System: Origins of Political Legitimacy* (New York: McGraw-Hill, Inc., 1969).

Goffman, E. *Stigma: Notes on the Management of Spoiled Identity* (Harmondsworth: Penguin, 1968).

Gwyn, R. *Smallwood: The Unlikely Revolutionary* (Toronto: McClelland & Stewart, 1968).

Horwood, H. *Tomorrow Will be Sunday* (Toronto: McClelland and Stewart, 1967).

Hurwitz, N. *Seasonal Unemployment in the Province of Newfoundland* (St. John's: ISER, 1968).

Iverson, N. and Matthews, D.R. *Communities in Decline: An Examination of Household Resettlement in Newfoundland*, Newfoundland Social and Economic Studies, 6 (St. John's: ISER, 1968).

Jennings, M.K. and Neimi, R.G. "The Transmission of Political Values from Parent to Child," *American Political Science Review*, Vol. LXII, No. 1 (1968), p. 169-184.

Kirk, G.S. *Myth: Its Meaning and Functions in Ancient and Other Cultures* (Cambridge: The University Press, 1970).

Leach, E.R. "Introduction," in E.R. Leach, ed., *The Structural Study of Myth and Totemism*, A.S.A. Monographs 5 (London: Tavistock Publications, 1968).

Levine, R.A. "The Role of the Family in Authority Systems: A Cross-Cultural Application of Stimulus Generalisation Theory," *Behavioural Science*, Vol. 5, No. 4 (1960a), p. 291-296.

Levine, R.A. "The Internalisation of Political Values in Stateless Societies," *Human Organisation*, Vol. 19, No. 2 (1960b), p. 51-58.

Levine, R.A. "Political Socialisation and Culture Change," in C. Geertz, ed., *Old Societies and New States: The Quest for Modernity in Asia and Africa* (New York: Free Press, 1963), p. 280-303.

Levi-Strauss, C. "The Structural Study of Myth," in T. Sebeok, ed., *Myth: A Symposium* (London: Indiana University Press, 1965).

Malinowski, B. "The Life of Myth," *The Saturday Review of Literature*, Vol. IV, No. 37 (1928).

Malinowski, B. *The Foundation of Faith and Morals* (Oxford: University Press, 1936).

Malinowski, B. "Myth as a Dramatic Development of Dogma," in B. Malinowski, *Sex, Culture and Myth* (London: Rupert Hart-Davis, 1963), p. 245-255.

Maranda, P. "Introduction," in P. Maranda, ed., *Mythology* (Harmondsworth: Penguin, 1972).

McQuail, D., *et al.* "Elite Education & Political Values," *Political Studies*, Vol. XVI, No. 2 (1968), p. 257-266.

Nemec, T. "Political Patronage and Brokerage Among the Newfoundland Irish," (Paper presented to the *Workshop on Local-level Politics in Newfoundland*, St. John's Institute of Social & Economic Research, Memorial University of Newfoundland, 1972).

Newfoundland Royal Commission. *Report* H.M.S.O., Cmd. 4480, 1933).

Perlin, G.C. "Political Support in the Transitional Society: Newfoundland in the Smallwood Era," (Paper presented to the *Colloquium on Community Aspects of Political Development*, St. John's: Institute of Social and Economic Research, Memorial University of Newfoundland, 1971a).

Perlin, G.C. "Patronage and Paternalism: Politics in Newfoundland," in D.I. Davies and K. Herman, eds., *Social Space: Canadian Perspectives* (Toronto: New Press, 1971b).

Szwed, J. *Private Cultures and Public Imagery: Interpersonal Relations in a Newfoundland Peasant Society*, Newfoundland Social & economic Studies, 2 (St. John's Institute of Social & Economic Research, Memorial University of Newfoundland, 1966).

Wadel, C. *Marginal Adaptations and Modernisation in Newfoundland*, etc., Newfoundland Social & Economic Studies, 7 (St. John's Institute of Social & Economic Research, Memorial University of Newfoundland, 1969).

Wadel, C. "Social & Economic Development in Newfoundland: An Outsider's Point of View," (St. Johns: *mimeo*, 1970).

Wadel, C. *Now, Whose Fault is That? The Struggle for Self-Esteem in the Face of Chronic Unemployment*, Newfoundland Social and Economic Studies, 11 (St. John's: Institute of Social & Economic Research, Memorial University of Newfoundland, 1973).

7.
Adolescent Political Alienation

Grace D. Skogstad

Introduction

AS a field of study, political socialization has been marked by a delineation of explanatory usefulness between two models of learning: the psychocultural model, and role theory. Psychocultural theory has been generally accepted as most appropriate to explain political socialization during childhood; role theory, to explain political learning during adolescence. As a direct consequence of this delineation of responsibility, political socialization has been conceptualized as a cumulative process marked by a persistence of early learning. This process is most markedly evident in studies of images of political authority. At a very young age, children acquire highly idealized and positive images of the central authority figures. These positive images, having been acquired uncritically and unconsciously, persist into and throughout adolescence, becoming increasingly less void of political content, and possibly somewhat more critical, though remaining positive enough to continue to be described as *supportive* (Easton and Dennis, 1969; Hess and Torney, 1967; Dawson and Prewitt, 1969).

The premise of the persistence of early learning has been questioned and found wanting. Observed disparities between adolescent and parental attitudes suggest that later experiences do upset early learning (Niemi and Jennings, 1968). However, the assumption of the longevity of benevolent images of and faith in political authority figures remains, as yet, untested. Indeed, researchers of political socialization have been so bent on examining *supportive* attitudes that the very notion of youth being alienated from the political system is akin to suggesting an entirely new perspective on political socialization. It is this perspective that is adopted in the research reported here. This is a study of adolescent political alienation. While both the elementary school child and the college student have been the foci of political socialization research, the pre-college adolescent has been ignored. This research is an attempt to rectify that negligence.

We begin by rejecting the generality of a description of the political socialization process as a cumulative one characterized by the persistence of early learning. Propositions about these two characteristics are more properly regarded as hypothetical rather than axiomatic for the following reasons: first, the foregoing description arises out of research which has ascertained only images toward specified institutional figures. By not giving children the opportunity to comment upon the informal trappings of the political system, such as interest groups, researchers may have deprived children of the opportunity to reveal disenchantment with political authorities. Second, while it is conceivable that the early acquired loyalty to a regime may endure for life (diffuse support), less tangible attitudes, for example, feelings of affect and faith in political authorities, may not be sustained as the child's political self develops. This second claim is grounded in (a) evidence that with increasing age and experience the child's enthusiasm for political authorities wanes (Greenstein, 1965). Early support for the regime is adopted in the presence of a restricted perception of the political system (Adelson and O'Neil, 1966). As the child grows older, he develops loyalties to political subgroupings. The result may be that he perceives his loyalties to political groups to be in conflict with his loyalty to the political system. And, (b) the older, more politically informed individual may perceive incongruence between political norms and political realities and become disenchanted.

Third, the picture of political socialization as a cumulative and homogenous process is drawn from studies of white, urban, middle-class children in the United States. The process of political socialization in a Western Canadian province may well differ with respect to both the content and agents of socialization for two reasons: (a) the role of the school in inculcating supportive attitudes appears to be less explicit and well defined in Canada than in the United States; (b) the political systems of Canada and the United States differ in two important respects. While both Canada and the United States are federal systems of government, separatist sentiments and third party electoral support play a larger part in the Canadian political system than in the American, thereby suggesting a greater orientation in Canada to the provincial sphere. Also, the President of the United States has a clearly visible position in the American government; there is greater room for confusion and ambiguity about the role of the Canadian Prime Minister, who owes his position to his party's relationship with the House of Commons. The visibility of authority figures may be important in establishing contact with the political system (Easton and Dennis, 1969).

Fourth, evidence of political sub-cultures within a country suggests that the political socialization process may vary across social class and residence. Children in the Appalachian region of eastern Kentucky did not regard the American President with the same benevolence as children in large urban centres (Jaros *et al.*, 1968). The description of political socialization as a homogenous and cnsensual process among the adolescents of a particular country is thus cast in doubt.

The Sample

It was out of a desire to test the applicability of the American model in light of the foregoing criticisms, that in June, 1970, students between the ages of twelve and eighteen were asked to complete questionnaires designed to examine their feelings of political alienation. The population of 1354 students was drawn from one rural and two large urban schools located in communities in Alberta with working- and middle-class backgrounds. The town is located in a farming district. As Tables 1 and 2 show, the distribution of the rural and urban populations with respect to age and sex is similar, with the exception of their being almost twice as many grade ten urban students as grade ten rural students.

Religious, income, and political differences exist. As ascertained from the students' responses, the mean family income of the study group as a whole is $6,762; for the rural group, the figure drops to $5,728; for the urban group, it rises to $7,868. Forty-five per cent of the rural population, as compared to fourteen per cent of the urban population of students reported their family income as less than $6,000 annually. The two urban schools are both Roman Catholic, whereas the rural school is more Protestant than Catholic. Using occupation as a second measure of social class (in addition to income), it can again be seen that the urban students tend to have middle-class backgrounds, and the rural students working-class backgrounds. Table 3 gives the distributions of fathers' occupations.

The rural community has a background of voting Progressive Conservative. Indeed, over three-fourths of the students in the rural area described their fathers' party identification as Progressive Conservative. Over four-fifths of the urban students saw their father as identifying with the Liberal Party. These differences across the two study groups provide the opportunity, if in fact political socialization is a different process across different social climates, for different political attitudes to be acquired by children in the two different schools.

The decision not to sample pre-junior high-school students was a deliberate one. Adelson and O'Neil have documented the inability of the pre-thirteen-year-old to appraise political events for their social as well as personal consequences (1966). It is difficult for the researcher to identify the student whose support for the political system is

TABLE 1

Grade Distribution in the Rural and Urban Populations (percentages)

	Rural (N=749)	Urban (N=584)
Grade		
7	15	16
8	18	14
9	19	12
10	17	32
11	17	17
12	14	9
Total	100%	100%

TABLE 2

The Sex Distribution in the Rural and Urban Populations (Percentages)

	Rural (N=749)	Urban (N=584)
Sex		
Female	51	54
Male	49	46
Total	100%	100%

TABLE 3

**Distribution of Father's Occupation in the
Rural and Urban Populations (Percentages)**

Occupation	Rural (N=731)	Urban (N=549)
Professional	5	6
Business/Managerial	12	22
Clerical	2	8
Skilled or Semi-Skilled	10	33
Unskilled	13	26
Farmer	48	0
Farmer and other employment	3	0
Other (Unemployed, Retired Deceased)	7	5
Total	100%	100%

t=3.9 significant for 899 degrees of freedom beyond the .0001 level.

specific—contingent upon favourable policy outputs—rather than diffuse because of the very real possibility of the student's disapproval of a political policy being based upon personal considerations and not upon considerations of the beneficial or detrimental nature of that policy for the majority of the citizens. In addition, if one can assume the comparability of the cognitive development of Canadian and American school children, it is not until the seventh or eighth grade that ". . . the child has acquired a considerable ability to identify and describe the varying kinds of political roles and to distinguish them from the parental role."[1] Only then does the adolescent begin to orient himself toward impersonal political objects (such as institutions) and away from personal authority figures.

Political Alienation: A Theoretical and Empirical Construct

The Theoretical Construct

The exploration of feelings of political alienation focuses upon personal and structural dimensions of legitimacy beliefs and the relationship between the two dimensions (Easton, 1965). The belief that ". . . the occupants of the political authority roles have a right to command and the other members of the system a duty to obey" is based mainly, suggests David Easton, upon assessments of the personal qualities of the political leaders and perception of the extent to which political structures (or, more precisely, the political authorities occupying those structures) are fulfilling appropriate and worthy purposes. (p. 208) As the theoretical juxtaposition of the politically supportive individual, the politically alienated individual is one whose images of the personal and structural aspects of political authority are unfavourable or negative.

Scepticism or disbelief in the legitimacy of political authorities has been generally held to stem from feelings of political powerlessness (Seeman, 1959; Finifter, 1970). If feelings of powerlessness are one characteristic of the alienated, it is resentment against these feelings that is major in distinguishing the politically alienated individual from the apathetic (Schick, 1964). The politically apathetic individual is ambivalent or neutral with respect to the political system, if he is conscious of it at all. The alienated individual, however, holds negative attitudes about objects of the political system. The resentment of the alienated person has an external focus—the political system, or more specifically, the political authorities who either do not allow the individual to assume the role that would enable him to be effective in politics, or are not behaving so as to execute the individual's will without his having to perform an active political role. This perception of a discrepancy between what is the case and what ought to be the case has been conceptualized as political normlessness. The politically alienated individual then is the man who feels powerless and resents it.

Is the individual who is estranged from the political system but who does not believe in the effectiveness of political action properly described as politically alienated? Given that adolescents sampled here have not yet had the opportunity to test the effectiveness of political action in the attainment of highly valued goals, it seems sufficient to accept negative feelings towards political authorities and dissatisfaction with their behaviour as indicating adolescent political alienation. A belief in the relevance of political action is useful in hypothesizing whether hostile feelings will be externalized or internalized.

The Empirical Construct

Political alienation, as the dependent variable in this study, is measured in terms of the following variables: political ineffectiveness, dissatisfaction with national governmental outputs, dissatisfaction with provincial governmental outputs, and disaffection with institutionalized governmental power. Attitudes about the provincial and national governments are assessed separately in order to compare political disenchantment with the two different governments. The five-item measure of political ineffectiveness is the largest factor which emerged from a factor analysis of a four-item political effectiveness index and a four-item political cynicism index adapted from *The American Voter* Study.[2] Dissatisfaction with national (provincial) governmental outputs is measured by the question: "On the whole, do you think the activities of the National (Provincial) Government tend to improve the living conditions of Canadians and make their lives more pleasant, or does the National (Provincial) Government tend to make things worse?" A response of "tend to make things worse" indicated a high dissatisfaction with national (provincial) governmental outputs.

The measure of disaffection with institutionalized governmental power was devised to indicate both feelings of ineffectiveness and dissatisfaction with the distribution of political influence in the political system. The student was allowed to establish what constitutes an unfair amount of influence in political affairs and to judge political groups and actors against the standard he himself had set. The respondent assessed the relative influence of a number of specified political actors by positing their location within a set of concentric circles, the centre of which represented the location of the important decision-makers in Canadian politics and the outer boundary of which symbolized the location of the non-influential. The student then judged whether a given actor possessed, relative to the other political actors, "too much influence," "too little influence," or "the right amount of influence."[3]

In addition to these measures of political alienation, three political variables are included as intervening variables: sense of relevance of the national government, sense of relevance of the provincial government, and sense of citizen duty. Measures of a sense of relevance of the government were included because of the supposition that a given individual's belief in the salience of political action is a function of the propensity of the society as a whole to address itself to the political system in the resolution of non-political conflicts and the achievement of social goals. A further premise is that whether feelings of disenchantment will result in passivity and withdrawal or in extra-systemic behaviour (violence, for example) is a function of the individual's belief in the salience of political action (Czudnowski, 1968). The individual who does not find the political system relevant to the achievement of his goals ought not to become non-supportive of political authorities or the political system when confronted with unfavourable governmental policies. Non-supportive behaviour (either of the system or the authorities) ought to result only where governmental policies (or authorities) are perceived to be obstructing the individual's goals, that is, where governmental action is disadvantageously relevant to the individual. The measures of a sense of relevance of the government, then, are predictors of the internalization or externalization of political alienation feelings.

We were reluctant to regard a low sense of citizen duty as a measure of political alienation for two reasons: 1) the belief that the attitude may well be a political norm so much a part of our political culture as to be analogous to the feelings of loyalty toward one's country that are engrained in children from a very young age; and 2) if the lack of a sense of obligation to vote measures anything at all, it probably measures alienation from the "politics" process rather than from the political system. Voting may be regarded rationally as less effective than other channels of influence. However, since voting and following politics in the media are two of the cheapest political acts, and a failure to perceive an obligation to be interested in politics and to vote could indicate not only a low potentiality to participate but also a feeling that politics is not worth one's while, the variable is included in this study.

The measures of sense of relevance are adapted from *The Civic Culture* study,[4] and the two items measuring citizen duty ascertain attitudes about citizen obligations to "vote in every election" and "follow politics and community affairs."

The Distribution of Political Alienation Feelings

Feelings of political alienation are not frequent enough to allow us to describe the study group as a whole as "politically alienated." Nevertheless, two factors lead to the conclusion that political alienation is not a meaningless concept among these Alberta adolescents. Firstly, a comparison of the frequency of reported antagonistic feelings in the Alberta study group and negative sentiments reported for roughly comparable groups of American children suggests a higher frequency of alienation feelings among the Alberta study group. Almost one-third of the Alberta sample feel politically ineffective. Of two separate samples of American adolescents, no more than one-fifth could be described as moderately or highly politically effective (Jennings and

Neimi, 1968). The Alberta students overwhelmingly temper their praise of the Governments' activities, with three-quarters of the group opting for the "sometimes improves, sometimes not" response when queried as to whether the national and provincial governments generally tend to improve conditions. The notion of citizenship of the Alberta group seems not to entail an obligation to participate by voting should that act inconvenience one.

Assuming that the realities of the Canadian and American political structures are such that there exist only minimal differences in the actual (as opposed to the theoretical) ability of the Canadian and American citizen to be effective in political affairs, the findings here suggest that political myths about democratic government may be neither so fully inculcated nor so immune to reality testing among Canadian adolescents as among American adolescents. If the assumption of the comparability of American political structures is erroneous so that different levels of political effectiveness feelings reflect rational appraisals of differing abilities to influence the course of political events in the two countries, is their higher frequency in the Alberta study group not necessarily to be construed as indicating political alienation? Whether feelings of political ineffectiveness are to be interpreted as negative attitudes is contingent upon the co-occurrence of political ineffectiveness alongside malevolent political attitudes whose formation is seemingly more independent of the nature of the political structures than political inefficacy.

Secondly, there is sufficient attitudinal consistency among individuals who hold negative attitudes toward the government to conclude that their antagonistic attitudes are not simply random responses, the consequence of an unclear and amorphous picture of governmental authorities. The individual who feels politically ineffective and disaffected with governmental authorities tends to be less satisfied with the activities of the provincial and national governments than the politically effective student who is not disaffected with governmental authorities.[5]

What is the focus of resentment of the politically alienated adolescent? The negative sentiments are directed more toward the federal government than the Provincial government. Adolescents sampled here feel that the provincial government is both more relevant and more satisfactory at improving conditions than is the national government. Only 6 per cent of the students feel the provincial government "worsens conditions," but 14 per cent feel the national government does. 70 per cent afforded the provincial government with "a great deal" or "fair amount" of relevance, whereas only 59 per cent saw the actions of the national government as that important. This orientation to the provincial, rather than the national sphere of politics, is in contrast to the finding of Easton and Dennis that the American child first becomes immersed at the national level of politics.

Political Alienation as a Dependent Variable

Previous Research

If adolescent political alienation is to be understood within the context of political socialization theory, it seems important to determine its antecedent and causal factors. Among the determinants of supportive attitudes isolated by students of American political socialization are other political attitudes, personality traits, and sociological and familial factors.

Political awareness, political activity, and political information have been found to be related to satisfaction with governmental authorities. Students who are knowledgeable about their political representation have been observed to have higher feelings of political effectiveness than students not so informed (Harvey, 1967). Adult samples have shown both political interest and political knowledge to be negatively related to feelings of political alienation (Seeman, 1959; Clarke, 1959).

Age, sex, social trust, and social isolation are non-political variables whose bearing upon political alienation feelings has been documented. Misanthropy, or a lack of social trust, has been used as both a measure and a predictor of political alienation (Aberbach, 1969; Finifter, 1970). When social isolation was posited as a component of alienation from society, a low but statistically significant relationship was found between alienation and rural background (Dean, 1960; 1961). Students integrated into high-school extra-curricular activities have been found to feel politically effective, have an expectation of future political participation, and believe in the legitimacy of political institutions and political parties (Sonnenburg Lewis, 1962).

Differing political attitudes in adults due to sex differences have been documented on samples of American children and teenagers and they affirm that boys are better informed, more politically active, and stronger believers in a citizen duty to participate than girls are (Greenstein, 1965; Hess and Torney, 1967). No sex differences in "basic attachment, loyalty, and support of the country" have been noted (Hess and Torney, 1967) even though there is evidence that the political alienation of men and women may be dimensionally different (Finifter, 1970). With respect to differences in supportive beliefs due to age, there is evidence both that supportive beliefs wane and strengthen with increasing age. Hess and Torney (1968) document the stronger feelings of political effectiveness and higher performance ratings of leadership figures among the older students. On the other hand, Greenberg found a decreasing tendency among white and black children as they grow older to see government as "protective and nurturant." The deterioration of favourable images of paternalism-benevolence is especially marked for black students between grades three and seven, but then the trend is reversed with black students in grades seven to nine recovering confidence in the government, especially the national government. These racial developmental differences have led Greenberg to suggest that the support of the black child is specific and that of the white child diffuse (Greenberg, 1970).

Political dispositions included here as explanatory variables are politicization, political information, and political party identification. Politicization is a measure of the student's political interest, frequency of political discussion and leadership of opinion during discussions of political matters.

Age, social trust, social isolation, and sex are the four nonpolitical variables whose effect upon alienation feelings is examined. An adaptation of Rosenberg's "faith in people" scale constitutes the measure of social trust.[6] Two items dealing with feelings of being out of the centre of things at school and with physical isolation from friends and family comprise the measure of social isolation.[7]

Political Attitudes and Political Alienation

Political awareness and knowledge mitigate political alienation feelings. As Table 4 indicates, the highly politicized student, like the well-informed student, believes that the national and provincial governments' actions improve conditions affirms the relevance of both the federal and provincial governments, and asserts a citizen obligation to vote and participate politically. It is the individuals who are low in political information and uninterested in politics who report the "worsening effects" of governmental action, feel the impact of the federal and provincial governments upon their lives to be little or non-existent, do not feel it the duty of the citizen to participate in politics, and are dissatisfied with the amount of control government institutions have in deciding how affairs in Canada should be run.

The politically informed and politicized student, as Table 4 indicates, is neither more nor less politically efficacious than the uninformed and unpoliticized one. Hence, neither politicization nor amount of political information permit us to predict whether the individual will

TABLE 4

Summary of Strength of Relationship (Gamma) between Political Alienation Measures and Politicization, Political Information, Grade, Social Isolation, Parents' Political Interest, and Parents' Political Activity (N=1354)*.

	Politicization	Political Information	Grade	Social Trust	Social Isolation	Parents' Interest	Parents' Activity
Political Ineffectiveness				.21			
Satisfaction with National Government	.26	.21	.18	.22	.42	.17	
Satisfaction with Provincial Government	.33	.32	.21	.20		.27	
Relevance of National Government	.37	.22	.21			.41	.19
Relevance of Provincial Government	.36	.26	.24			.38	.16
Disaffection with Governmental Authorities		.21	.14				
Duty to be Politically Interested	.42	.27	.18			.38	.24
Duty to Vote	.17	.15	.21			.38	

* Blank cells represent non-significant relationships (at the .005 level).

experience feelings of ineffectiveness in politics. In addition, participative orientations have no bearing upon whether the individual is disaffected with governmental authorities.

Reported political party identification does distinguish the alienated from the supportive adolescent. At least two important findings emerge: 1) Children who claim to have no party preference or to prefer a political party other than the four traditional ones, are more likely to believe that the national government ''makes things worse;'' 2) children identifying themselves as Liberal are both much more satisfied with the policy outputs of the national government and less disaffected with the power of the national government.[9]

It is significant that the focus of negative sentiments is the national government and not the provincial government. Differences in satisfaction with provincial governmental outputs occur, but they are between party identifiers and non-party identifiers and not between identifiers of different political parties.

To what extent do these adolescent attitudes reflect the governmental position of the Liberal Party in Ottawa? Would Liberal supporters reverse their positions regarding the beneficial impact of actions of the national government if there were an NDP Government in Ottawa? The possibility is not remote, insofar as self-identified Liberals are slightly less likely to perceive both the relevance of the national government upon daily affairs and a citizen duty to participate.

Non-Political Attitudes and Political Alienation

When political alienation is examined across grades, the trend which emerges is that older adolescents are more supportive of the government than younger students. Beliefs in the benevolence and relevance of both national and provincial governments, a duty to be interested in politics and community affairs and to vote, and approval of the decision-making power of sanctioned authorities are stronger among older adolescents than younger. Table 4 reports the relationships between political alienation and grade. (Grades seven, eight, and nine are combined to form a junior high-school group and grades ten, eleven, and twelve to form a senior high-school group.)

The important exception to the trend of older students being more supportive is that senior high-school students have neither higher nor lower feelings of political effectiveness than junior high-school students. This raises the possibility either that feelings of political ineffectiveness in political affairs have their sources in factors unrelated to maturational trends, or, as discussed earlier, that political myths are not so important a part of the political culture examined here as they seem to be in the American political culture.

Do feelings of social trust and social integration dispose the student toward satisfaction with governmental authorities? Yes, but the effects of the variables are independent and not so uniform as appears to be the case among American groups. The socially integrated and socially trusting individual (as opposed to the socially isolated and misanthropic student) is more likely to be satisfied with governmental outputs. Table 4 shows that misanthropy, but not social isolation, is related positively to feelings of political ineffectiveness and of scepticism regarding the legitimacy of governmental power.

There are no startling differences in the political alienation feelings of male and female students. Again, this is in contrast to groups of American children and adults.

Family Background and Political Alienation

One would expect parents for whom politics is more salient to emit more cues both direct and indirect. Cue giving would structure the political orientations of the child, and, in the absence of rebellion, bolster parent-student correspondence.[10]

Similarly sociological factors such as residence, educational level, and occupational status of his parents should affect the political socialization of the child, for he inherits a social climate that has already helped to shape his parents' political attitudes.

While the familial political climate encompasses such attributes as the amount of political interest and discussion, the homogeneity of the parents' political attitudes, the parents' sense of political effectiveness, and the consciousness of the family efforts at political socialization, parents' political interest and parents' political activity are the only two aspects examined here.

Social Climate   Rural-urban residence is a more important factor than father's occupational status or parents' educational levels in determining political alienation. Students residing on farms possess less positive attitudes toward government and politics than students who live in the large city. Table 5 shows some of these differences between the extreme groups. Compared to city and town students, farm students feel somewhat less politically effective, are more inclined to believe that the national government tends to make things worse rather than better, and are also disaffected with the amount of power of national governmental institutions and authorities. However, sense of relevance of both levels of government, satisfaction with policy outputs of the provincial government, and belief in duty to vote do not differ significantly across residence.

TABLE 5

Political Alienation Differences Across Residence (Percentages)

	Farm	Town	City
National Government Improves	6	11	10
National Government Worsens	16	11	11
Low Political Ineffectiveness	29	40	31
High Political Ineffectiveness	36	40	31
Low Disaffection with Governmental Authority	16	28	28
High Disaffection with Governmental Authority	33	25	26

Parents' Political Interest and Activity: The parental political climate does not *directly* affect the political alienation of the child. The connection, as will be shown later, is indirect. The child who describes his parents' political interest and activity as high does not feel more politically effective, is not more satisfied with the amount of power governmental authorities have in running Canadian affairs, and does not have a greater belief in a citizen obligation to vote than the child whose parents are reported to be uninterested and inactive in political affairs. There is, however, a positive relationship between the intensity of parents' political interest and adolescent perception of the national and provincial governments as having "a great deal" or "fair amount" of relevance upon daily affairs. And, interestingly, parents' political interest is strongly positively related to the belief that the activities of the provincial government tend to improve things, but only slightly with the adolescent's satisfaction with the activities of the national government. Parents' political activity is related to neither.

A Multi-Variate Analysis of Political Alienation

This paper has thus far completed two tasks. The first was to draw out the empirical interrelationships among the dependent (political alienation) variables. The second was to investigate the effects of predictor variables (personality and background characteristics) upon the dependent variables. When a third task, the computation of the intercorrelations among the predictor variables showed a network of very strong interrelationships, the possibility of many of the previously reported relationships being spurious or intervening, rather than direct, seemed great. Thus, a second study of the predictor variables upon the political alienation measures was undertaken for two reasons: firstly, to ascertain very generally the *relative* importance of these independent variables in accounting for the variance in each of those dependent variables posited here to be measures of political alienation; and secondly, in achieving the former goal, to shed light upon the nature of all associations—their direct, intervening, or confounding nature.

Diagrams I-IV present schematically the major linkages of the independent variables to satisfaction with national government's activities (I), satisfaction with provincial government's activities (II), political ineffectiveness (III), and disaffection with governmental authorities (IV). The linkages represent prediction equations in the sense that only those independent variables that *directly* account for the largest proportion of variance in the dependent variable are linked to the dependent variable in the diagram. These linkages have been arrived at after all variables found earlier to be associated with a given dependent variable, have been regressed upon that dependent variable.

Several findings of interest emerge from these regression analyses. Firstly, other political alienation measures are generally more useful than personality and background variables in directly accounting for dissatisfaction with the activities of the national government, political ineffectiveness, and disaffection with governmental authorities. Secondly, the effect of personal and background variables upon political alienation attitudes is not direct, for the most part, but mediated through a sense of the relevance of the provincial government. There are exceptions here, of which one is political party identification, which have a direct bearing upon the belief that the national government worsens things. Thirdly, whereas satisfaction with the provincial government is a direct function of political information, political awareness, and perception of the relevance of the provincial government, dissatisfaction with the national government's activities is not. The implication here is that negative sentiments toward the national government will not be altered by the growth of political knowledge and awareness. Fourthly, residence has no *direct* effect upon political alienation feelings. Instead, this variable is mediated through political party identification. This suggests that if the political socialization process which gives rise to negative sentiments is a consequence of different social climates, it is not because residence directly affects political attitudes but rather because different individuals residing in different environments assume different levels of political awareness

DIAGRAM I

Linkages of Predictor Variables to Satisfaction With National Government's Activities

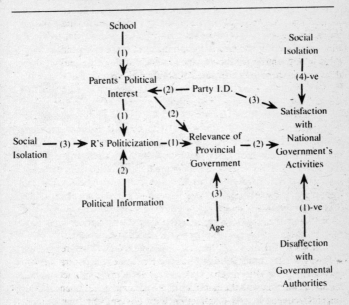

—(1)—▶ strongest predictor (accounts for the largest proportion of variance).

—(2)—▶ second strongest predictor (accounts for second largest proportion of variance).

—(3)—▶ third strongest predictor (accounts for third largest proportion of variance).

—(4)—▶ fourth strongest predictor (accounts for fourth largest proportion of variance).

-ve   refers to a negative relationship between the predictor and dependent variables.

DIAGRAM II

**Linkages of Predictor Variables to Satisfaction
with Provincial Government's Activities**

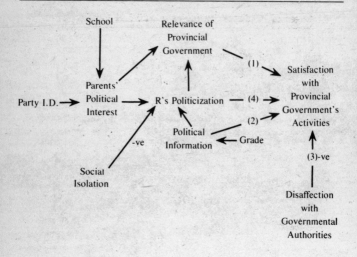

Only the relative strength of direct predictive linkages to Satisfaction with the Provincial Government's Activities is given. The other linkages are as presented in Diagram I.

DIAGRAM III

Linkages of Predictor Variables to Political Ineffectiveness

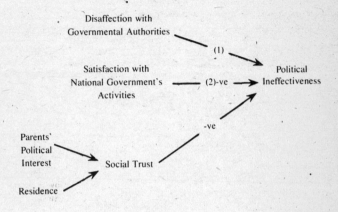

Only the relative strength of variables directly predicting Political Ineffectiveness is given.

DIAGRAM IV

Linkages of Predictor Variables to Disaffection with Governmental Authorities

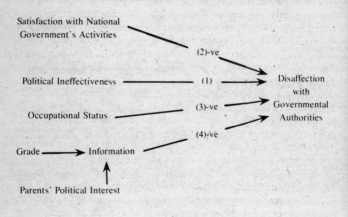

Only the relative strength of variables which directly predict Disaffection with Governmental Authorities is outlined.

and different political party identifications, which, in turn result in different political attitudes.

Conclusions and Implications

Theorizing about the utility of the concept of political alienation, and, concomitantly, the nature of the political socialization process in a Western Canadian province has beenmade possible by this research. Political alienation has proved to be a valid concept among the population of students investigated here. While estrangement from the political system is not widespread, such estrangement as exists seems to be the result of feelings of powerlessness and perception of governmental non-responsiveness. This is consonant with our theoretical conceptualization of political alienation. Two political alienation variables, dissatisfaction with national governmental outcomes and disaffection with the power of governmental authorities, account for the largest proportion of the variance of political ineffectiveness. The two best "predictors" of disaffection with the power of governmental authorities are political ineffectiveness and dissatisfaction with the actions of the national government.

However, it appears unlikely that whatever alienation from the federal government that exists will manifest itself as an active force. Given that dissatisfaction tends to be linked with little political interest, little political information, weak participative inclination, and non-recognition of the salience of political action, it seems that alienated adolescents withdraw from the political arena leaving it to the more politically satisfied adolescents.

This research has raised the very real possibility that the nature of the political socialization process in Canada is different from that in the United States. Dissimilar political attitudes and participative dispositions prevail. These seem to be, in part at least, a consequence of the influential impact upon the development of the political self of factors hitherto given short shift. Beginning with a less benevolent image of governmental authorities, the Alberta school children continue to hold less positive attitudes toward their political authorities and institutions than their American counterparts. The rare frequencies of supportive attitudes and participative orientations within the group lead us to speculate that even the well-informed and politically interested Alberta student seems not to feel so politically effective, so admiring of his government's activities, and so conscious of a citizen duty as we have been led to believe his American counterpart is. Political partisanship and residence emerge as factors not to be ignored in any analysis of political socialization, and with their emergence, the researcher is cautioned that environmental factors, such as residence, may be compounded with political predispositions, such as political partisanship, to affect directly political consciousness and thereby determine political attitudes. If this research has clarified anything about the nature of the process of political socialization in Canada, it is that it is intricate.

Notes

[1] D. Easton and J. Dennis, *Children in the Political System* (New York: McGraw Hill, 1969), p. 271.

[2] The items comprising the political ineffectiveness index and their factor loadings on the single factor are these:

1. Politicians spend most of their time getting re-elected or re-appointed.   .558
2. Voting is the only way that people like me and my family can have any say about how the government runs things.   .430
3. Canadian politics is really controlled by a small group of powerful politicians who pretty much do what they want.   .667
4. People like me and my parents don't have any say about what the government does.   ,631
5. I don't think public officials care much about what people like me and my family think.   .636

[3] The ratings of the twelve political actors by the students were factor-analysed. The Varimax rotation yielded three factors which were labelled Political Actors, Big Companies, and Self. In subsequent analyses, indices constructed from the latter two factors were unrelated to political alienation measures. Hence, only the index constructed from the assessment of the political influence of the Prime Minister, the House of Commons, the Cabinet, the New Democratic Party, the Governor-General, and the Liberal Party was retained.

[4] "How much would you say the actions of the Provincial Government affect the daily lives of you and your family? a great deal? a fair amount? only a little? not at all?" The question was repeated for the National Government.

[5] The reported gamma's are: Political Ineffectiveness by Satisfaction with Provincial Government -.21; Political Ineffectiveness by Satisfaction with National Government -.37; Political Ineffectiveness by Disaffection with Governmental Authorities .34; Disaffection with Governmental Authorities by Satisfaction with Provincial Government -.37; Disaffection with Governmental Authorities by Satisfaction with National Government -.26.

[6] A Likert scale of Social Trust was constructed from these three questions:

(1) Generally speaking, would you say that most people can be trusted, or that you can't be too careful in dealing with people?

(2) Would you say that most of the time people try to be helpful, or that they are mostly just looking out for themselves?

(3) Do you think most people would try to take advantage of you if they got a chance or would try to be fair?

[7] Two items were used to measure Social Isolation:

(1) How close do you usually feel to the centre of things at school?

(2) How do you spend most of your spare time alone and on the weekend?

[8]21 per cent who give no party identification and 27 per cent who identify with a party other than the four traditional ones, as compared to 15 per cent National Democrats, 13 per cent Progressive Conservatives, 11 per cent Social Credit identifiers, and 7 per cent Liberals responded "makes things worse."

[9]16 per cent of the Liberal Party identifiers said that the national government improves conditions, compared to 8 per cent Progressive Conservatives, 8 per cent who chose a fifth party, 6 per cent National Democrats, 5 per cent Social Crediters, and 5 per cent who did not know their party identification. 33 per cent of the Liberal Party identifiers were lowly disaffected with governmental authorities. The comparable figures for students identifying with other political parties are: 23 per cent of those who don't know their party identification, 20 per cent with no party preference, 20 per cent with a fifth party preference, 20 per cent of the Progressive Conservative Party identifiers, 15 per cent of the Social Credit identifiers, and 10 per cent of the National Democrats.

[10]M.K. Jennings and R.G. Niemi, "The Transmission of Political Values from Parent to Child," *American Political Science Review*, Vol. 62 (Mar. 1968), p. 181.

Bibliography

Aberbach, Joel. "Alienation and Political Behavior," *American Political Science Review*, Vol. 63 (Mar. 1969), p. 86-99.

Adelson, Joseph and O'Neil, Robert. "The Growth of Political Ideas in Adolescence: The Sense of Community," *Journal of Personality and Social Psychology*, Vol. 4 (Sept. 1966), p. 295-306.

Almond, Gabriel and Verba, Sidney. *The Civic Culture* (Princeton: Princeton University Press, 1963).

Campbell, Angus, *et al. The American Voter* (New York: Wiley, 1960).

Clarke, John P. "Measuring Alienation Within a Social System," *American Sociological Review*, Vol. 24 (1959), p. 849-852.

Czudnowski, Moshe. "A Salience Dimension of Politics for the Study of Political Culture," *American Political Science Review*, Vol. 62, No. 3 (Sept. 1968), p. 878-888.

Dawson, Richard and Prewitt, Kenneth. *Political Socialization* (Boston: Little, Brown and Co., 1969).

Dean, Dwight. "Alienation: Its Meaning and Measurement," *American Sociological Review*, Vol. 26, No. 5 (Oct. 1961), p. 753-758.

Dean, Dwight. "Alienation and Political Apathy," *Social Forces*, Vol. 38 (Mar. 1960), p. 185-189.

Easton, David. *A Systems Analysis of Political Life* (New York: Wiley, 1965).

Easton, David, and Dennis, Jack. *Children in the Political System* (New York: McGraw Hill, 1969).

Finifter, Ada. "Dimensions of Political Alienation," *American Political Science Review*, Vol. 64, No. 2 (June 1970), p. 389-410.

Greenberg, Edward S. "Children and Government: A Comparison Across

Racial Lines,'' *Midwest Journal of Political Science*, Vol. 14, No. 2 (May 1970), p. 249-275.

Greenstein, Fred. *Children and Politics* (New Haven: Yale University Press, 1965).

Harvey, Teddy G. ''A Multi-Dimensional Analysis of Patterns of Adolescent Political Socialization.'' (Unpublished M.A. Thesis, University of Hawaii, 1967).

Hess, Robert D. and Torney, Judith. *The Development of Political Attitudes in Children* (Chicago: Aldine, 1967).

Jaros, D. *et al*. ''The Malevolent Leader: Political Socialization in an American Subculture,'' *American Political Science Review*, Vol. 62, No. 2 (1968), p. 564-575.

Jennings, M. Kent and Neimi, Richard G. ''The Transmission of Political Values From Parent to Child,'' *American Political Science Review*, Vol. 62 (Mar. 1968), p. 169-184.

Schick, Allen. ''Alienation and Politics.'' (Paper presented to the 1964 Annual Meeting of the American Political Science Association Meetings, New York, September, 1969).

Seeman, Melvin. ''On the Meaning of Alienation,'' *American Sociological Review*, Vol. 24, No. 6 (Dec. 1959), p. 783-791.

Sonnenburg, Lewis, Helen. ''The Teen-age Joiner and His Orientation Toward Public Affairs: A Test of Two Multiple Group Membership Hypotheses.'' (Unpublished Ph.D. Dissertation, 1962).

8.

Idéologies étudiantes, doctrines universitaires et système universitaire: Contribution à l'étude du mouvement étudiant au Québec

Richard Simoneau

English Abstract

THE influence of continental European sociology on the perspectives of French-Canadian sociologists is apparent in the contribution of Simoneau. A central feature of such a tradition, usually ignored in most North American sociological literature, is the conscious attempt to situate the phenomena under investigation into a proper historical context.

Simoneau examines the shifts in student ideology at Laval University as a function of both the internal structure of the university and the actual changes taking place in Quebec society. The University, through its *dirigeants* (a term used earlier by the Italian sociologist, Antonio Gramsci, to denote a hegemonic cultural elite) becomes a basic agency for interpreting French-Canadian society and legitimating the dominant value system.

Although Simoneau discovers a change in the framework of the student ideology, moving away from agrarian values to secularism and cultural nationalism and finally to an espousal of radical views on the Quebec social order, the end result of the students' effort is an "unconscious effort for integration" into the mainstream of French-Canadian society.

In spite of continual confrontation with the dominant ideology, it appears that the students, like all other social groups, are the carriers of specific interests. Contrary to Mannheim's notion of "free floating intellectuals," Simoneau notes that here too the intellectuals are coopted into working within the system.

Introduction

LES étudiants ont joué un rôle politique et idéologique de premier plan dans la société québecoise au cours de la dernière décennie.

Quelques années avant 1960 les premières luttes pour la démocratisation du système d'éducation et la modernisation des institutions politiques québécoises ont contribué à mobiliser et à unifier divers groupes universitaires demeurés jusqu'alors sans orientations autonomes et dont les intérêts se limitaient souvent au folklore estudiantin.

Les premières années de la période de la "Révolution tranquille" fourniront au mouvement étudiant l'occasion d'effectuer de multiples gains. La généralisation des organisations syndicales en milieu étudiant est facilitée, sinon encouragée, par un régime politique soucieux d'ouverture et de concertation. En retour, la faction avant-gardiste du parti au pouvoir, néo-nationaliste et technocrate, bénéficie de l'appui fervent des étudiants, qui la pressent d'accentuer le rythme et l'étendue des réformes et combattent vigoureusement tous les partisans d'un retour en arrière.

Intelligentsia, groupe de pression, mouvement social, les étudiants font alors figure d'alliés et d'opposants au régime néo-libéral: ils négocient au sommet avec les grands commis de l'Etat; ils organisent, à la base, des grèves et des marches de protestation; ils envoient de l'argent aux ouvriers grévistes; ils font parvenir leurs mémoires et leurs télégrammes aux chefs politiques.

Mais au milieu de la décennie, le glissement progressif du régime au pouvoir vers des positions conservatrices, puis la victoire électorale des forces de droite au scrutin de 1966, incitent les étudiants à reviser leurs orientations. N'ayant plus accès au pouvoir, désenchantés et désorientés, ils se replient dans une opposition de plus en plus virulente qui se nourrit de nouveaux thèmes: le combat de la bureaucratie étatique, les luttes internationales contre l'impérialisme, la crise de l'université, les conflits de générations.

La révolte étudiante internationale qui survient en 1968 a un impact notable en milieu québécois. Les mois d'automne, période d'apprentissage de la contestation autochtone, sont l'occasion d'un bouillonnement idéologique inusité. Les organisations syndicales et les journaux étudiants se sabordent joyeusement pour satisfaire les exigences de la gauche et de la droite. Les groupuscules se démultiplient, la polarisation des tendances s'accentue comme jamais auparavant.

L'éclectisme des mots d'ordre et des stratégies étudiantes favorisent alors toutes les prétentions. Les revendications nationalistes (Québec français, McGill français); les demandes de services (résidences, cafétérias, transports, examens, notes de cours) permettent au mouvement de rester un certain temps sur sa lancée. Mais en l'absence de leaders et d'organisation, les discours, les manifestes, les journées d'études, les occupations symboliques ont tôt fait de le consumer. Récupéré en partie, depuis, par les forces souverainistes, dominé par les multiples courants de la nouvelle culture, le mouvement étudiant québecois est devenu, au cours des dernières années, singulièrement passif. Comment cela s'explique-t-il?

Position du problème:

La notion de mouvement étudiant, on le sait, recoupe un ordre multiple de phénomènes. L'impact international des luttes étudiantes de la dernière décennie, la variabilité de leurs manifestations, la diversité de leurs objectifs rendent malaisée toute généralisation sur la nature du mouvement et obligent à considérer en chaque cas les caractéristiques des divers groupements nationaux et les traits spécifiques des diverses sociétés où ils s'insèrent.

Le dossier des analyses du mouvement étudiant et de l'université se présente conséquemment sous un jour complexe. Devant l'universalité et l'ampleur du phénomène, les commentateurs ont été amenés à épuiser—sinon, parfois, à confondre—tous les registres d'explication. D'innombrables approches existent, dont les degrés de pertinence, d'intérêt, de rigueur, fort variés, ne peuvent être discutés dans le cadre de ce court article.[1] Nous nous bornerons dans ce cas-ci à résumer les quelques hypothèses ayant orienté notre propre analyse.

D'un côté, voulant éviter d'assimiler le mouvement étudiant québecois à un groupe restreint d'agents (son avant-garde), à un type particulier de discours, à une séquence d'événements précis, nous avons cherché, au départ, à identifier la multiplicité de ses formes différentielles, au plan institutionnel et au plan historique.

Nous avons analysé les diverses caractéristiques du mouvement telles qu'elles se manifestent dans un environnement précis, l'université; plutôt que de considérer l'action du groupe étudiant isolement, nous avons étudié les *rapports* qu'elle entretient avec l'action du groupe institutionnel concurrent, celui des dirigeants universitaires; nous avons enfin cherché à voir comment les actions des deux groupes, et leurs interrelations, peuvent être modelées par les éléments du contexte institutionnel et socio-historique où elles s'inscrivent.

Pour les fins de notre étude (Simoneau, 1972), nous avons défini le mouvement étudiant comme étant principalement orienté vers l'action idéologique. Pareille hypothèse, croyons-nous, renvoie à l'analyse des formes les plus manifestes et les plus caractéristiques du mouvement, tel qu'il est apparu au Québec au cours des dernières décennies. Elle n'exclut en rien, ainsi qu'on le verra, l'éventuelle étude des autres dimensions pertinentes du mouvement, tout comme elle n'interdit pas le renvoi, au terme de la démarche d'analyse, à d'autres registres d'explication.

Méthodologie

Du mouvement étudiant québecois nous n'avons étudié que les seules dimensions universitaires et, plus particulièrement encore, les aspects qu'il a pris dans une institution, l'université Laval de Québec. Le lecteur devinera les incidences d'un tel choix sur la portée finale de l'analyse, de même qu'il discernera aisément l'ordre des contraintes et des motifs coutumiers, essentiellement pratiques, nous ayant obligé à effectuer ce choix.

Une partie de notre matériel d'enquête fut recueillie lors d'un programme d'entrevues réalisé au printemps de 1969. Une trentaine de groupes, comprenant chacun de cinq à dix répondants, furent alors interrogés. C'est d'abord le souci d'un inventaire exhaustif des orientations du milieu étudiant contemporain qui nous fournit le critère de sélection; l'on rencontra des groupes de facultés (grandes et petites, professionnelles, culturelles et scientifiques), des groupes à vocation intellectuelle (journalistique, religieuse, théâtrale, etc.), des groupes d'action (exécutifs, animateurs, occupants), d'autres à caractère spécifique (nouveaux arrivants, gradués, résidents, etc). Un schéma d'entrevue semi-directif, touchant les problèmes de la pédagogie, de l'organisation universitaire, et de la société québecoise, fut alors appliqué.

Ainsi qu'il est souligné plus haut, il nous apparaissait nécessaire de relier la recherche sur les idéologies étudiantes contemporaines à une analyse plus exhaustive des idéologies émanant du système universitaire. Une histoire comparée des doctrines universitaires, tant celles des dirigeants que celles des leaders étudiants, devait nous permettre de dégager la nature des rapports idéologiques entre les deux groupes à diverses périodes historiques et de saisir la spécificité de l'état présent.

L'on choisit donc d'analyser les journaux étudiants, vu leur intérêt et leur facilité d'accès. Le journal *Le Carabin* et son continuateur immédiat *Le Quartier Latin* furent retenus. L'on étudia plus de la moitié de tous les numéros publiés depuis le début des années trente, concentrant davantage notre attention sur un certain nombre d'éditions annuelles jugées importantes.

Dans le cas des dirigeants, la quasi-totalité de leurs publications (livres, essais, mémoires, communiqués) disponibles à la bibliothèque générale de l'université Laval furent dépouillés.

En raison des contraintes posées par la qualité des matériaux et des informations que nous y cherchions, l'on eut recours à des méthodes différentes pour l'analyse des doctrines et des entrevues. L'étude des doctrines devait permettre d'identifier les principales séquences de développement des idéologies des deux groupes; vu l'abondance et l'hétérogénéité du matériel, l'on opta pour une approche monographique. Dans le cas des entrevues, étant donné le très haut degré de redondance du message parlé et la parenté manifeste des "discours" avec les doctrines déjà analysées, l'on choisit une méthode de type sémantique.

Les Périodes de l'histoire universitaire

L'histoire des doctrines universitaires ne constitue qu'une partie de l'histoire de l'université; elle s'y articule et s'en dissocie, la précède et la prolonge. Loin d'être un simple reflet des autres pratiques, l'idéologie a sa cohérence propre et elle est soumise à des règles de fonctionnement qui lui sont spécifiques. L'on a donc cherché au départ à identifier les périodes de l'histoire idéologique de l'institution. L'on a distingué trois grandes périodes idéologiques, chacune étant caractérisée par la dominance d'une doctrine particulière chez les dirigeants et chez les étudiants. Il n'y a pas de *coupure* chronologique précise entre les périodes que l'on a identifiées; il existe plutôt des *intersections* plus ou moins larges entre des ensembles qui s'inscrivent toujours en parallèle, les uns avant de se retrouver en position dominante, les autres avant de décliner.

Pour l'ensemble des périodes l'on a relevé six types de doctrines, que l'on a identifiées de la manière suivante: dans le cas des étudiants: 1) la doctrine traditionnelle, 2) la doctrine syndicale, 3) la doctrine libertaire; dans le cas des dirigeants: 1) la doctrine humaniste, 2) la doctrine libérale, 3) la doctrine du développement.

Nous avons analysé de la même façon en un second temps, l'histoire de l'institution. Ayant recours aux données sur les procédés de gestion et les types de production caractéristiques de l'université à divers moments de son histoire, nous avons retrouvé, ici encore, trois périodes qui ne sont point sans correspondance avec les séquences idéologiques préalablement identifiées. Pour ces périodes les repères chronologiques sont approximativement les suivants: de la fondation de l'université Laval au XIXe siècle jusqu'aux années de la seconde guerre mondiale pour la première période, l'après-guerre et les années cinquante pour la seconde, la dernière décennie pour la période la plus récente.

Avant de procéder à l'analyse des doctrines des dirigeants et des étudiants, nous présenterons d'une manière succincte les principales données sur l'histoire de l'université Laval.

L'histoire de l'institution

i) Première Période

L'université de la première période revoit toutes les caractéristiques du système d'enseignement traditionnel. Elle accorde le primat à l'humanisme, avec lequel elle conjugue toutefois une orientation nettement 'professionnaliste': le secteur des humanités et des professions libérales anciennes regroupe en 1940 soixante-cinq pour cent de la clientèle étudiante; Laval produit trois fois plus de théologiens, deux fois plus de médecins et d'avocats que l'université canadienne moyenne de la même époque. L'institution a un mode de recrutement élitique (sélection par le B.A.) et un très faible volume de production (elle ne compte que 785 étudiants en 1940). L'enseignement, axé sur la tradition et la technique, fait abstraction de toute recherche: en Droit, l'on consacre plus d'heures à la religion et à la comptabilité qu'au droit comparé; en Lettres, un professeur enseigne à lui seul toutes les langues modernes. La pédagogie magistrale et charismatique à laquelle sont soumis les étudiants s'assortit d'une foule de réglementations et de contraintes autoritaires dont la mise en oeuvre est facilitée par la taille alors minime de l'organisation (voir Simoneau, 1972 pp. 183-210).

La fonction qu'assume l'université dans la société de l'époque est en partie conforme à celle sur laquelle insiste sa doctrine. L'institution a une fonction idéologique qui s'apparente à l'exégèse et dont le but est d'assurer la reproduction d'une culture et d'un système d'institutions scolaires, religieuses, culturelles, alors totalement contrôlées par l'Eglise catholique québecoise. Mais l'institution a aussi une fonction de reproduction proprement sociale: elle favorise le maintien d'une hiérarchie sociale et d'un ordre social séculaires, en assurant le renouvellement de cette élite petite bourgeoise ancienne, essentiellement formée de médecins et d'avocats, qui monopolise le pouvoir au sein des institutions politiques et des diverses communautés locales. Sa production de clercs et de petits notables s'assortit de la formation d'une maigre main d'oeuvre technicienne, spécialisée dans les opérations économiques alors dominantes (bois, électricité, mines), qui sert d'intermédiaire au plan économique (comme la petite bourgeoisie professionnelle, au niveau politique) entre l'industrialisateur étranger et la main-d'oeuvre autochtone. Au moulin à papier numéro 1 de Cantonville[2] que décrit Everett Hughes vers 1940, vingt-quatre des vingt-cinq administrateurs sont anglophones; le vingt-cinquième, francophone, est le plus important médecin de la ville.

ii)Deuxième Période

L'institution universitaire connait de multiples changements à la deuxième période: diversification d'une production qui est désormais autant axée sur les professions de type scientifique, administratif ou technique (cinquante-cinq pour cent de la clientèle) que sur les professions libérales; développement de la recherche et des études graduées; élargissement considérable du recrutement (étendu au secteur des écoles secondaires publiques). Tous facteurs qui se traduisent par une croissance notable des investissements universitaires (ils décuplent en quinze ans), par une augmentation rapide des effectifs (ils quadruplent), et qui supposent maint changement dans les procédés de direction et de gestion des ressources de l'institution.

Les transformations qui affectent l'université vers les années cinquante doivent être mises en corrélation avec celles que connaît le Québec depuis l'après-guerre: urbanisation rapide, croissance économique favorisée par la concentration industrielle et l'innovation technologique, gonflement du secteur tertiaire, extension du régime salarial, américanisation de l'idéologie et de la culture québecoise par le biais des modes de consommation et des médias de communication.

L'influence de ces multiples changements ne s'exerce pas d'une façon mécanique sur l'université. Celle-ci répond aux nouvelles demandes du marché, des corps professionnels et des groupes intellectuels suivant sa logique propre: elle met sur pied de nouvelles disciplines (séculières, expérimentales, techniques), recrute différemment ses professeurs et ses clientèles étudiantes, diversifie ses méthodes et ses activités, en rehausse le statut, les exigences. S'efforçant d'acquérir le visage de l'université moderne, Laval s'intègre au circuit universitaire international, et sa doctrine, désormais, met l'emphase sur le libéralisme, le positivisme, le cosmopolitisme.

Comme on le verra, la doctrine universitaire à la deuxième période nous renseigne plus ou moins fidèlement sur la hiérarchie réelle des fonctions qu'accomplit l'institution. Elle donne, en premier lieu, un sens aux pratiques contradictoires d'une université libérale partagée, à l'instar de toutes les autres, entre les exigences intellectuelles et les impératifs d'ordre pratique et soucieuse de concilier les deux dans sa gestion de façon à préserver sa légitimité et sa rentabilité sociale.

Mais la doctrine masque aussi certaines contradictions particulières, caractéristiques d'une institution insérée dans une société alors en transition et où existent de multiples décalages entre l'économique et le politico-idéologique. Les procédés de recrutement de l'université, élitiques ou démocratiques selon les secteurs, les orientations de son enseignement, humaniste clérical, ou séculier—positif selon les facultés, desservent à la fois les intérêts de la nouvelle petite bourgeoisie urbaine et de l'intelligentsia libérale montante et ceux d'une petite bourgeoisie de souche rurale encore dominante dans la plupart des institutions politiques et culturelles québecoises. La doctrine universitaire de la deuxième période confère à l'institution une vocation d'*universalité* et de *neutralité*, image métaphorique qui est bien la plus pertinente pour masquer l'éclectisme de son fonctionnement.

iii) Troisième Période

L'idylle séculaire qui eut cours dans la plupart des sociétés entre l'intelligentsia libérale, l'Etat parlementaire bourgeois et le capitalisme de marché, chacun évoluant de façon autonome à son propre niveau, n'a jamais eu lieu au Québec. Libérée sur le tard d'un régime politico-idéologique isolationiste et obscurantiste, l'université des années soixante tombe graduellement sous la coupe d'un Etat néo-libéral interventionniste qui fait fi, à son tour, de ses prétentions à l'autonomie et à l'universalisme. L'idéologie d'une université constituant une fin en soi aura été aussi bien niée par la petite bourgeoisie ancienne, fervente d'ordre, que par la nouvelle classe dominante, soucieuse de productivité et de développement.

Au début de la décennie soixante l'université Laval connait une période de croissance effervescente, bénéficiant des retombées de la réforme du système scolaire public à laquelle elle parvient un temps à échapper. Elle accumule les effectifs, les crédits, les infra-structures, complète l'organisation de ses facultés et de ses départements, développe considérablement le secteur de la recherche et des études graduées, modernise son administration.

Mais, en contrepartie des ressources sans cesse croissante que lui consent l'Etat, l'université doit rendre des services: il lui est demandé de rationaliser sa gestion, de maximiser son utilité en épousant les objectifs de la réforme scolaire, en planifiant son développement, en réduisant ses coûts.

La doctrine des dirigeants universitaires de la troisième période, verra-t-on, répond positivement aux demandes nouvelles exprimées par l'Etat. La formation de la main-d'oeuvre scientifique et technicienne, la promotion de l'éducation permanente, la participation aux travaux de développement, l'engagement concerté avec l'Etat et l'industrie dans la recherche sont les objectifs que s'assigne une institution désireuse de prouver sa capacité d'intervention et son utilité sociale.

L'université veut accentuer le rythme de ses réformes afin de mieux rationaliser son activité. Il lui faudra trouver le moyen de transformer rapidement des structures d'enseignement et de recherche qui, en dépit des intentions proclamées, restent encore fortement inspirées d'une éthique libérale (recherche pure, mono-disciplinarité, etc.). Elle devra, de même, parvenir à planifier d'une quelconque manière une production surabondante de main-d'oeuvre qui rencontre de moins en moins la demande et qui, sur-qualifiée par rapport aux besoins du marché, se retrouve déçue dans ses espoirs de mobilité. Elle devra mettre un frein à la croissance pléthorique de ses dépenses d'enseignement et de recherche, augmenter le rendement d'investissements qui iront en se raréfiant alors que croîtront de plus en plus les clientèles.

Ces problèmes, comme on le sait, ne sont point spécifiques à l'université québecoise. Mais ils se posent ici avec une plus grande acuité qu'ailleurs. La société québecoise connaît de sérieux problèmes de développement économique (secteurs à faible niveau de croissance, de capitalisation, d'innovation, d'entrainement) qui sont en grande partie dus à sa situation périphérique dans l'ensemble nord-américain. Passée l'ère de la "révolution tranquille" et du "qui s'instruit s'enrichit" credo d'une petite bourgeoisie optimiste et ambitieuse, de plus en plus de québecois s'interrogent sur la pertinence d'une stratégie de développement si peu planifiée et qui accorde une telle importance à l'éducation, qui n'est et ne demeure qu'un prérequis.

Avec l'idéologie de la rationalisation, l'université québecoise inaugure un nouveau cycle de réformes. Mais est-il sûr qu'il ne s'agira, cette fois-ci, que de réformes?

L'histoire des doctrines universitaires

L'histoire des doctrines universitaires recoupe en partie celle de l'université; elle a précisément pour fonction de donner un sens aux pratiques dominantes au sein de l'université aux différentes périodes.

Mais les diverses doctrines élaborées par les dirigeants universitaires et les étudiants ne sont pas de simples reflets ou de purs effets de ces pratiques. Elles ont leur signification propre et leur efficacité propre. La mise en parallèle des doctrines universitaires et des modes de gestion de l'université montre qu'en tous les cas ce que l'idéologie révèle est tout aussi important que ce qu'elle masque.

L'étude comparative des doctrines dominantes au sein du groupe étudiant et du groupe dirigeant aux différentes périodes permet d'identifier les rapports existant entre les deux catégories d'agents; ces rapports de type idéologique sont relativement autonomes des conditions institutionnelles; ils n'en produisent pas moins des effets déterminants sur l'action des agents ainsi qu'on pourra le voir.

i) Première Période

La doctrine étudiante et la doctrine des dirigeants, à la première période, privilégient un ordre identique de principes et paraissent dérivées toutes deux d'une seule et même idéologie pré-industrielle, à forte saveur religieuse et culturelle.

Les deux doctrines insistent, en effet, au plan sociétal sur la sauvegarde des traditions culturelles autochtones et le rejet des idées 'modernes' ou étrangères, la défense de l'économie artisanale et agricole et le refus du capitalisme, la préservation de l'organisation sociale communautaire et l'indifférence envers l'Etat et l'ordre juridico-politique.

Résumons-nous. Sous son triple aspect politique, social, religieux, l'erreur de la civilisation moderne peut se ramener à ceci: matérialisme et divinisation de l'homme dans le domaine religieux, mercantilisme industriel sous sa forme capitaliste ou socialiste, démocratie égalitaire dans le domaine politique (*Le Carabin*, 1941-42: 13-15).

La doctrine étudiante du premier moment n'est, de fait, qu'une copie malhabile de la doctrine des dirigeants, laquelle est toute entière tributaire de l'idéologie du nationalisme religieux dominant dans la société d'alors.

Notre patriotisme consiste à nous imprégner de cette hiérarchie de valeurs selon laquelle nous sommes attachés d'abord et avant tout à notre religion, ensuite à notre culture qui nous inspire d'être loyaux même au-dessus des divisions de classes, de partis, de groupements et d'intérêts (*Le Carabin*, 1952-53: 20-23).

Les deux doctrines définissent bien sûr d'une même façon l'institution universitaire: la vocation de l'université est de conserver et de transmettre le savoir plutôt que de le découvrir; la culture universitaire est constituée de savoirs purs, gratuits, généraux; les enseignements spécialisés, techniques, professionnels n'y occupent qu'une place subsidiaire.

La tâche séculière de l'université traditionnelle étant subordonnée à sa mission religieuse, les sciences et les savoirs universitaires seront entièrement tributaires de la théologie et de la philosophie catholique.

Il est entendu que l'ordre social est impossible sans un ordre intellectuel et l'ordre intellectuel ne se conçoit pas sans un principe: Dieu (Bruchesi, 1953:41).

On ne sait pas assez qu'une déviation dans l'ordre des premiers principes peut compromettre l'ordre économique lui-même (Paquet, 1920:13).

L'université traditionnelle oeuvre à la survivance de la race en préservant la culture autochtone de l'influence des philosophies malsaines et des idéologies étrangères: le matérialisme, le modernisme, le positivisme, le protestantisme. Elle fournit aussi à la société les élites dont celle-ci a besoin. Visant, suivant la conception de Jaspers (1959) à former non pas "la classe dominante" mais "l'aristocratie de l'esprit" nécessaire au gouvernement du peuple, l'université traditionnelle ne peut bien sûr pas être ouverte à tous.

Les dirigeants traditionnels, suivis en cela par les étudiants sont "contre l'accessibilité générale à l'université," (Bruchesi, 1953: 65, 80, 102) idée qu'ils croient résulter "d'une certaine méconnaissance du but de l'université" (Lebel, 1961:2). Ils invoquent l'argument théologique qui explique l'accession à l'université par les desseins mystérieux de la Providence:

> C'est une institution qui doit être regardée comme un patrimoine commun et dont les plus humbles fils de cultivateurs et d'ouvriers peuvent un jour être *appelés* non seulement à recueillir les fruits mais à gravir les sommets (Paquet, 1920:29).

Les états d'inégalité intellectuelle et économique qui séparent les diverses couches de la société sont d'ailleurs entrevus comme naturels, inévitables, par une pensée sociale autochtone qui valorise l'ordre et la paix sociale, la solidarité de toutes les classes dans la promotion d'une même mission religieuse et nationale.

> Peu importe que nous soyons des travailleurs manuels ou des travailleurs de l'esprit, tous nous devons collaborer ensemble. . . . Une université prospère est une garantie pour la vie morale, intellectuelle et matérielle d'un peuple (Comité d'aide à Laval, 1945:14).

Au plan pédagogique la conception des dirigeants traditionnels n'est que la répétition des grands principes synthétisés par Newman au XIXe siècle: le professeur n'instruit pas le futur praticien; il l'éduque, façonne son caractère, sa culture, ses comportements.

> L'université laisse dans la pensée et dans l'âme de ses élèves une empreinte . . . faite non seulement de savoir technique, mais de curiosité intellectuelle, de probité morale, de distinction de manières. Il se crée dans le monde une élite qui marche en tête de tous les groupes (Paquet, 1920:8).

De son côté l'étudiant se soumet volontiers au maître, comme il s'identifie aux aînés, comme il est solidaire de l'élite dirigeante, à laquelle il croit d'ores et déjà appartenir.

Toutes les valeurs, tous les schémas d'action étudiants étant prescrits par l'autorité ne subsistent en marge d'une doctrine d'emprunt que des intérêts folkloriques bien caractéristiques du milieu estudiantin traditionnel: goûts prononcés pour l'esthétisme, l'érudition, les loisirs, l'humour et les 'divertissements' anodins, les relations sociales. Les préoccupations prosaïques des carabins, les dissertations livresques des idéologues révèlent, chacune à leur manière, le conservatisme de pensée du groupe étudiant traditionnel, son absence d'autonomie face aux autorités institutionnelles et à la classe dirigeante dans la société d'alors.

ii) Deuxième Période

Les rapports entre la doctrine étudiante, celle des dirigeants, et l'idéologie dominante dans la société québecoise pouvaient être aisément schématisés à la première période. Les doctrines de la deuxième période, parce qu'elles s'inscrivent dans des lieux différents, entretiennent des rapports beaucoup plus fluides et plus ambigüs. Nous commencerons par résumer les principaux traits de chacune.

Une affirmation de l'autonomie et de la spécificité des intérêts étudiants, une conscience aigüe des multiples retards de la société québecoise, une adhésion quasi inconditionnelle à tous les programmes de réforme et de rattrapage, telles sont les lignes de force de la doctrine syndicale.

Depuis l'après-guerre les journalistes étudiants revendiquent sans cesse, avec de plus en plus de fermeté, le droit à la liberté d'expression et la dissidence, et ils exercent de nombreuses critiques, chaque fois plus franches et plus virulentes, contre le régime en place, dominé par la petite bourgeoisie professionnelle de souche rurale:

> Corruption, nausée, démagogie, abêtissement populaire . . . c'est la politique (*Le Carabin*, 1949-50: 24-1).
> La bouillabaisse nationaliste et cléricale . . . servie à grands chaudrons à toute une génération a stérilisé et conformisé une assez grande partie de l'élite actuelle pour qu'il ne soit pas exagéré de parler de démission. Quand je dis élite, je dis ceux qui ont l'argent, les pouvoirs, les respects et qui laissent mûrir les abcès par complicité ou aveuglement (*Le Carabin,* 1957-58: 17-12).

Ils réclament la démocratisation du pouvoir, la modernisation des institutions, la réduction des écarts entre les groupes sociaux, une utilisation rationnelle des ressources.

Les intellectuels étudiants se révèlent alors partisans du socialisme et de l'ouvrièrisme; ils croient en même temps à la légitimité de l'Etat et de ses institutions supports. La référence aux classes défavorisées leur fournit surtout un indice exemplaire de la non-intégration de la société et un bilan concis des réformes à opérer.

Après 1960, hésitant entre l'opposition et l'intégration, les étudiants s'attacheront à promouvoir les politiques réformistes de la nouvelle élite urbaine dirigeante, y voyant autant d'étapes d'un processus de changement dont il leur sera parfois difficile de voir le terme et la forme accomplie.

Les étudiants, sous le régime duplessiste, combattirent fermement l'idéologie du nationalisme culturel. Qu'après 1960 ils se découvrent soudainement indépendantistes ne doit pas faire illusion. Ils ont toujours rejeté l'idée *traditionnelle* de la nation et tout ce qu'elle connottait: xénophobie, obscurantisme, cléricalisme. Fidèles à leur projet social, rebelles à tout chauvinisme, ils trouvent dans le thème nouveau de l'indépendance l'idée d'un dépassement du réformisme à courte vue et celle de l'édification d'un Etat démocratique à proximité des citoyens québécois.

Tôt regroupés en syndicat,[4] essayant de lier étroitement leur engagement au niveau institutionnel aux luttes sociales et politiques qui se déroulent au dehors, les étudiants font porter l'essentiel de leur action sur les problèmes d'éducation.

> Afin que tous les étudiants soient sur le même pied au point de départ nous réclamons la gratuité universitaire. La valeur individuelle fera les frais de la différenciation ultérieure (*Le Carabin*, 1957-58: 17-2).

> Que les étudiants prennent conscience que leurs problèmes ne sont que des aspects étudiants des problèmes nationaux (*Le Carabin*, 1966-67: 0-2).

Après le renversement du régime duplessiste en 1960 et les débuts de la réforme du système d'éducation public, la lutte pour la modernisation et la démocratisation de l'institution universitaire sera poursuivie de plus belle, de l'intérieur, contre les valeurs surannées de l'idéologie naguère dominante: l'autoritarisme, le cléricalisme, les intrigues et les trafics d'influence, la mauvaise administration. Les étudiants ne veulent pas saborder l'université; ils demandent qu'elle s'adapte au plus tôt à la société nouvelle que l'on est à construire. Ils exigent une université publique, non-confessionnelle, moderne et productive, vouée à la science, assumant ses responsabilités sociales, contribuant au progrès intellectuel et à la croissance. Et ils revendiquent en même temps le droit de participer aux décisions.

> Car l'université, en fin de compte, c'est qui? Nous les étudiants. On peut toujours inventer des machines à administrer . . . mais des machines à recevoir un enseignement universitaire . . . enfin ce n'est pas pour tout de suite (*Le Carabin*, 1966-67: 0-4).

Pareille revendication laisse sceptiques les dirigeants universitaires; car ces derniers croient toujours que l'université constitue ''une communauté naturellement orientée vers le bien commun''. Mais pour le reste les dirigeants de la deuxième période se retrouvent souvent d'accord avec les étudiants. Ils réclament, d'une manière différente il est vrai, la démocratisation de l'accès à l'université, mais ils reconnaissent la nécessité de mesures sélectives, comme les étudiants d'ailleurs.

Les peuples les plus civilisés sont ceux qui ont le plus richement outillé leurs universités et les ont remplies d'un plus grand nombre d'étudiants (Université Laval, 1954:2).

Ils ne nient point la vocation de développement et de croissance de l'université mais la subordonnent à une mission plus fondamentale, à caractère scientifique et spéculatif. Savants et intellectuels libéraux, ils croient que l'université doit être affranchie à la fois des idéologies extérieures et des contraintes d'ordre pratique; ils se considèrent comme des arbitres, dont la tâche est d'analyser objectivement les conflits et les problèmes sociaux plutôt que de s'y mêler.

L'universitaire est le plus autonome des hommes, libre dans ses préférences intellectuelles, c'est-à-dire dans le choix de l'objet de sa recherche, libre dans ses attitudes pédagogiques. (Farlardeau, 1951:3).

Ils invoquent les valeurs du pluralisme intellectuel, de la rationalité, et de l'objectivité scientifique, de l'universalisme de pensée, qui sont les assises de l'université libérale moderne.

La doctrine des dirigeants est apolitique; elle n'est que la théorie des modes de conservation et de diffusion de la science. La doctrine étudiante est sur-politisée. Mais les deux ne sont point pour cela appelées à se heurter de front. La comparaison des textes des deux groupes nous permet de découvrir sous les différences de ton, de style, de vocabulaire, la même adhésion à un ensemble de principes qui se situent à l'antithèse des doctrines de la première période. La doctrine des dirigeants, qui insiste sur les valeurs d'équité, de rationalité, de modernité, fait somme toute référence aux mêmes formes de légitimité que la doctrine étudiante. Toutes deux renvoient, en dernière instance, à une idéologie des libertés fondamentales, de la démocratie parlementaire, de la croissance rationnelle, de la mobilité individuelle contrôlée, qui est caractéristique des sociétés libérales modernes. Cette idéologie, qui a nourri le mouvement d'opposition de la petite bourgeoisie urbaine au régime duplessiste, aura une position dominante dans la société québecoise après 1960.

L'on ne saurait, bien sûr, induire du fait de l'adhésion commune aux mêmes formes de légitimité, l'impossibilité de divergences et d'affrontements entre les étudiants et les dirigeants. Observons qu'il existe une situation de rivalité, de concurrence entre deux groupes qui ont leurs intérêts propres, mais point de véritable lutte idéologique. Les traits les plus virulents de la doctrine syndicale sont décochés contre une doctrine traditionnelle qui a tendance à perdurer. Par contre le débat entre les doctrines contemporaines (syndicale, libérale) tend à porter beaucoup plus sur les modalités que sur les principes, et les deux groupes s'y découvrent à la fois partenaires et rivaux.

iii) Troisième Période

Une situation toute différente prévaut à la troisième période. Les dirigeants se définissent ici comme des hommes d'organisation: l'université est d'abord un système privé de travail, qui définit ses propres orientations, mais qui sert aussi des finalités externes objectives, celles-là dictées par l'intérêt général de la société. La doctrine étudiante considère l'université comme un rouage et récuse d'emblée tout rapport d'appartenance à l'organisation; elle veut s'inscrire directement au niveau culturel et politique. Les dirigeants sont partisans de la rationalité et du pragmatisme; les étudiants se situent sur le terrain de la lutte idéologique absolue. Au système des hiérarchies fonctionnelles privilégié par les uns s'oppose l'individualisme anarchique des autres. Les deux doctrines ne sont point comparables l'une à l'autre: leur rapport n'est pas contradictoire mais contraire.

Considérons brièvement les principaux traits de la doctrine des dirigeants. Celle-ci emprunte une grande partie de ses concepts à la théorie scientifique de l'organisation:

> L'université a-t-elle encore une initiative propre? Ou est-elle devenue simplement le lieu où jouent des influences et des déterminations disparates provenant du milieu ambiant (Université Laval 1968:12)?
> Ce serait avant tout à l'intérieur de structures permanentes et adéquates que pourrait être assumée la tâche complexe de promouvoir un développement dynamique et harmonieux de l'université (Université Laval, 1966:4).

Il importe selon les dirigeants que l'université s'adapte au changement, qu'elle y joue même un 'rôle-moteur'. Tout en assumant ses fonctions traditionnelles (conservation du savoir, enseignement), elle doit se définir de nouveaux objectifs propres: la recherche, l'éducation permanente, la participation à l'aménagement régional, un enseignement de nature prospective.

A l'idée traditionnelle d'autonomie-retrait de l'université les dirigeants opposent les notions d'innovation, de spécialisation et de coordination des activités universitaires à l'échelon global de la société québecoise.

Au plan interne, l'université est définie comme devant être une organisation à la fois efficace et efficiente, centralisée au plan de la gestion, rationnelle dans sa division des tâches, pourvue de canaux de communication adéquats, de mécanismes d'inventaire et de correction qui lui permettent de s'adapter avec souplesse au changement. N'énumérons que certaines assertions exemplaires: la pratique pédagogique, naguère considérée sous l'angle de la tradition et du charisme professoral doit désormais être traitée scientifiquement, évaluée et corrigée en fonction des critères de productivité, d'économie, d'efficience. L'élimination périodique et progressive des étudiants, source de gaspillage, doit être remplacée par la sélection à l'entrée. Au problème de la contestation l'on doit appliquer la solution des ''human relations'': participation, ''counselling,'' aménagement agréable de l'environnement.

L'université s'efforce de résoudre la crise engendrée par le jeu contradictoire des pressions externes et les conflits internes; si elle veut survivre, il lui faut de toute urgence refaire son unité interne et justifier son action face à la société.

La doctrine étudiante libertaire qui prédominera un certain temps dans des journaux sur le point de disparaître prend en tous points le contrepied des thèses précitées. Elle constitue aussi la négation d'une doctrine syndicale encore fortement enracinée dans le milieu étudiant.

Parce qu'elle était le fait d'une intelligentsia mandatée par une organisation, la doctrine syndicale ne pouvait s'épargner ni la référence aux institutions en place, ni le rappel des contraintes inhérentes à la situation du groupe, ni le renvoi aux possibilités légitimes ou légales de lutte. Et il importait peu que l'organisation syndicale soit écartelée entre la base, non-militante, et le sommet, paralysée par le corporatisme du plus grand nombre, récupérée par les administrations, contrainte au pragmatisme et au réformisme, prisonnière de la négociation, du compromis et du court-terme. L'intelligentsia s'efforçait de repenser sans cesse plus adéquatement ses règles de fonctionnement.

Le même constat, suivant la doctrine libertaire, justifie le sabordement de l'organisation syndicale et l'adoption d'un schéma d'action insurrectionnelle et spontanéiste.

> Une minorité agissante, structurée ou non, peut faire bouger tout le campus (*Le Carabin*, 1968-69: 14-7).

Plutôt que de se plier aux contraintes 'objectives' de la situation économique, politique, idéologique, les étudiants doivent faire surgir les conditions propices au combat.

La doctrine libertaire veut définir les vecteurs de la lutte antitechnocratique et anti-universitaire. Formulée d'une façon sommaire et expéditive, elle est d'abord la manifestation d'un style encore à la recherche de sa théorie. Et ce style est doublement caractéristique de la situation d'une avant-garde affranchie des contraintes de l'organisation et continuellement contaminée par les nouveaux modèles élaborés par le mouvement international et les idéologues étrangers.

La doctrine, versatile et syncrétique, conjugue tous les "ismes" dans sa production: Marx et Marcuse, Mao et Reich, Guevara, la nouvelle gauche américaine, et l'underground s'y trouvent réconciliés.

> Ce combat oppose deux camps: ceux qui veulent produire et ceux qui veulent fleurir (*Le Quartier Latin*, 1969-70: 5-46).

De même le raisonnement confond continuellement l'analyse du social et de l'individuel il ramène tout à l'idéal et aux instances fondamentales de la personnalité: le sexe, l'affectivité le jeu, le rêve. Il s'agit d'abord de changer l'homme, de faire violence aux structures les plus communes de la perception. La démonstration s'en remet aussi bien à l'intuition qu'à la logique, au mythique (le recteur autoritaire, le politicien asexué, le policier simiesque) qu'au réel.

> Le Carabin se prononce pour la créativité (*Le Carabin*, 1968-69: 5-5).
>
> L'anarchie, c'est faire ce que tu es, et rien d'autre. C'est l'art. C'est ce qui n'est pas platte (*Le Quartier Latin*, 1969-70: 3-25).
>
> La révolution—ce puissant orgasme social—comme une vague ourlée va accoucher de liberté (*Le Quartier Latin*, 1969-70: 3-35).

La société industrielle et ses institutions sont bien sûr rejetées en bloc; ce n'est que par un reflexe incident que la doctrine vilipendera au passage l'ordre économique capitaliste et la démocratie libérale étatique, la 'rationalité' moderne, la morale chrétienne. Contre l'ascèse, la standardisation, la fonctionnalité, la productivité, la doctrine libertaire prend parti pour l'hédonisme, la spontanéité, l'égalité, la révolution permanente:

> L'objectif poursuivi peut se résumer ainsi: remettre la totalité du pouvoir et des choix à des unités de base qui soient de véritables unités de vie sociale en sorte que les citoyens deviennent eux-

mêmes les seuls responsables de leur vie personnelle et collective (*Le Quartier Latin*, 1969-70: 7-45).

L'abolition des institutions existantes, la quête d'une société 'heureuse' constituent des objectifs de longue durée. La nécessité de l'action à court-terme est par ailleurs un impératif inéluctable, parfois difficile à conceptualiser. La doctrine se situe alors d'une façon malaisée entre l'utopie et la réforme: il faut certes détruire l'université, mais comment le faire sans tomber dans le réformisme? L'on parle alors de possibilités de politisation au niveau de la pédagogie. Mais les revendications à ce niveau affectent-elles tellement le système universitaire? Ont-elles véritablement des incidences plus globales?

Et de même, que faire au niveau sociétal? Les militants doivent-ils se couper de toutes les possibilités immédiates d'action? Ils croient trouver une solution dans l'alliance tactique (et provisoire?) avec les forces de la social-démocratie souverainiste et les technocrates, qu'il faudra bien porter au pouvoir, un jour, avant de songer à les renverser!

Oscillant entre la révolte culturelle, l'engagement de type réformiste, et l'individualisme, la doctrine libertaire triomphe momentanément dans les médias étudiants parce qu'elle englobe tout. Consumée peu à peu par les querelles théoriques et les luttes d'intellectuels enclins au jeu gratuit de la démarcation (v. g. le congrès de dissolution de l'UGEQ en 1969, la disparition du *Carabin* et du *Quartier Latin*), elle conduisit le milieu étudiant à une situation de repliement, de désorganisation, d'impasse politico-idéologique dont il n'est point encore parvenu, deux ans après, à se relever.

Les doctrines et les discours.

Voyons très brièvement quels rapports existent entre les doctrines recensées ci-haut et les différents discours étudiants que l'on retrouve à l'époque récente dans l'institution universitaire.

L'analyse des entrevues nous a permis d'identifier cinq grands types de discours, chacun dominé par une doctrine ou une idéologie caractéristique.

Le premier type de discours, qui est formulé par le plus grand nombre de groupes étudiants interrogés, fait référence à l'idéologie de la modernisation et du réformisme; grandement contaminé par la doctrine étudiante *syndicale*, ce discours récupère au surplus presque tous les thèmes d'une doctrine universitaire *libérale* que les dirigeants ont aujourd'hui dépassée. Les étudiants réformistes se veulent contestataires; ils sont des adeptes de la co-gestion ''responsable'' et de la contestation ''positive''.

Un deuxième type de discours, dominé par une idéologie techno-cratique, n'est que la réplique, plus transparente et plus intransigeante, de la *doctrine du développement* formulée par les dirigeants de la dernière période. Toutefois, à la différence des dirigeants, les étudiants font passer le développement social en premier lieu et l'université en second. Un troisième type de discours, inspiré d'une idéologie profes-sionnelle, donne un exemple typique de l'intégrisme politique et intel-lectuel de certaines strates étudiantes; les agents, qui veulent s'identifier de façon rigide à l'autorité institutionnelle, se situent en fait à l'opposé de celle-ci; ils reprennent toutes les thèses des doctrines de la *première période*.

Restent deux derniers types de discours mettant l'accent sur l'opposition idéologique, qui sont le fait de l'intelligentsia étudiante. L'un, qui fait la critique des modèles sociaux d'intellectualité, n'est que la répétition de cette pratique séculaire d'intellectuels opposés à tout académisme; affranchi des idéologies dominantes mais privé de tout support politique, le discours n'est que l'idéalisation d'une condi-tion étudiante dont il veut ignorer le caractère transitoire et la fonction d'apprentissage, que la valorisation d'une culture qu'il voudrait uni-verselle et objective. L'autre, dominé par l'idéologie de la révolte, reprend les grands thèmes de la *doctrine libertaire*; s'exerçant à évaluer les stratégies employées naguère et les raisons de leur échec, il exprime un fort sentiment de désabusement et d'impuissance; des agents font valoir la nécessité de faire table rase et de tout recommencer à zéro; d'autres hésitent entre l'indifférence et la poursuite de la lutte au dehors de l'université.

L'examen des discours, aussi succinct soit-il, fait ressortir plusieurs phénomènes. Observons d'abord que les diverses formes de l'état présent, qu'une analyse superficielle tend toujours à privilégier, ont, en tant qu'objet, un statut relativement secondaire. En réalité ce sont les doctrines universitaires, tant actuelles que passées, qui parais-sent être les principaux *moyens de production* des discours étudiants.

L'on se rend compte, à l'examen des discours, que les formes idéologiques traditionnelles ont encore largement cours dans le milieu étudiant contemporain, que ce soit sous une forme directe ou trans-posée (v. g. les doctrines traditionnelles, libérales, et syndicales). Se manifeste par cela la durabilité des structures idéologiques, l'efficacité propre d'un travail idéologique qui s'effectue toujours dans le *temps long*.

L'on s'aperçoit que le rapport entre les discours et les doctrines étudiantes, entre celles-ci et les doctrines des dirigeants universitaires, est essentiellement non symétrique; la très grande partie des formes idéologiques étudiantes sont contaminées, sinon dominées par les doctrines des dirigeants universitaires. Se trouve infirmée, de ce fait, cette théorie de la classe étudiante, ou de la conscience de classe étudiante, qui prête aux agents des tendances idéologiques essentiellement axées sur l'innovation et le radicalisme.

Pour sûr, le groupe étudiant conserve une relative autonomie, *en théorie*, à cause de sa distance vis-à-vis le milieu d'origine et l'avenir professionnel. Mais cela, on l'a bien vu vaut point pour tous les étudiants (v. g. l'idéologie de la profession, l'idéologie technocratique).

Et que vaut en réalité cette condition de relative autonomie, qui est permise, garantie, limitée institutionnellement par les structures universitaires? Les mécanismes libéraux de gestion et de socialisation ne sont-ils pas toujours les plus efficaces? Pour la majorité des strates étudiantes le jeu de l'affranchissement et de la distance tourne vite à l'illusion, victime d'un cercle vicieux: car les idéologies étudiantes réformistes n'apparaissent être que des variantes d'une idéologie scolaire réformiste elle-même tributaire de l'idéologie dominante dans la société.

Par ailleurs des idéologies minoritaires, d'une facture plus radicale, subsistent toujours dans le milieu étudiant. La lutte que prétendent assumer ces dernières procède d'un malentendu. Car, ainsi que le souligne Bourdieu (1969) ''la liberté de se libérer des contraintes scolaires n'appartient qu'à ceux qui ont suffisamment assimilé la culture scolaire pour intérioriser l'attitude affranchie à l'égard de celle-ci''. Les stratégies de mobilisation de la masse étudiante contre l'université élaborées par son élite intellectuelle n'auront toujours qu'un rendement aléatoire, leur faible fécondité étant fonction de leur irréalisme.

Il arrive parfois que la méprise de l'avant-garde trouve son pendant dans l'illusion des masses. Notre analyse des discours étudiants (1972) nous avait permis de constater une dominance marquée des revendications ''contestataires'' dans les divers sous-ensembles idéologiques; la révolte étudiante, l'intellectualisme, le réformisme de type libéral ou technocratique, le corporatisme, et le professionnalisme le plus prosaïque s'alimentaient *tous* de contenus idéologiques contestataires, essentiellement polysémiques. Ainsi s'explique, par exemple, que les occupations de cafétéria, les revendications pour la mixité dans les résidences, les grèves pour les bourses et les transports aient pu mobiliser d'une manière sporadique le milieu étudiant dans son ensemble, les théories des leaders et le corporatisme du plus grand nombre se niant l'un et l'autre, sans pour cela se combattre.

Ainsi comprend-on de même que des luttes symboliques aux objectifs et aux mots d'ordre ambigüs menées par l'aristocratie étudiante (Québec français, McGill français, co-gestion, auto-gestion) aient pu soulever l'intérêt d'une petite bourgeoisie étudiante avant tout préoccupée par les débouchés, le calendrier, les cadences et les primes du travail universitaire.

Comme toutes les autres catégories sociales les étudiants sont porteurs d'intérêts spécifiques. Ces intérêts nourrissent des revendications caractéristiques qui sous-tendent à la fois des conflits et une hantise inconsciente de l'intégration. Il n'est pas facile pour les étudiants d'échapper à l'emprise de l'institution universitaire et aux contraintes idéologiques et culturelles que celle-ci ordonne. L'intelligentsia étudiante, qui a cru bon au cours des années récentes d'aller poursuivre le combat au dehors, l'a bien compris.

Notes

[1] Voir l'excellent dossier critique publié dans *Sociologie du travail* (1969), p. 287-335.

[2] En réalité Drummondville, petite ville industrielle de la région des Bois-Francs (voir Hughes, 1945).

[3] J. Bruchesi, *L'université* (Québec: PUL, 1953), p. 41.

[4] Il existe depuis fort longtemps à Laval une association regroupant les étudiants des diverses facultés, l'AGEL. Traditionnellement, l'association s'est surtout occupée de services et de loisirs. Vers la fin des années cinquante, elle commence à se préoccuper des problèmes d'éducation. S'inspirant des thèses qu'a développé l'UNEF (étudiants français) depuis l'après guerre, l'AGEL—et de même, quelques autres associations étudiantes québécoises—se donne une idéologie syndicale, qui définit l'étudiant comme un jeune travailleur intellectuel, ayant des intérêts professionnels à défendre, un rôle social et politique à exercer.

Après 1960 les organisations syndicales se multiplieront en milieu étudiant; les associations universitaires, après s'être retirées de la FNEUC(Fédération nationale des étudiants universitaires canadiens), créeront l'Union générale des Etudiants québécois; l'UGEQ, à son apogée, regroupera 58,000 étudiants des universités et des collèges du Québec.

230   POLITICAL SOCIALIZATION

Bibliography

Bourdieu, Pierre et Darbel, Alain. *L'Amour de l'Art* (Paris: Editions de Minuit, 1969).

Bruchesi, Jean. *L'université* (Québec: PUL, 1953).

Comité d'aide à Laval. *Manuel des Orateurs* (Québec: Université Laval, 1948).

Falardeau, Jean-C. *Grandeur et Misère de la Liberté académique* (2. éd., Québec: 1951).

Hughes, Everett. *Rencontre de Deux Mondes* (Montréal: Parizeau, 1945).

Jaspers, Karl. *The Idea of the University* (Boston: Beacon Press, 1959).

Lebel, Maurice. *Quelques Considérations sur le Rôle de l'Université au XXe siècle* (2e éd., Québec, 1961).

Le Carabin, 1941-42, volume I et II, 20 numéros.

1949-50, volume X, 29 numéros.

1952-53, volume XIII, 26 numéros.

1957-58, volume XVIII, 26 numéros.

1966-67, volume XXVII, 50 numéros.

1968-69, volume XXIX, 43 numéros.

Le Quartier Latin, 1969-70, volume LII, 16 numéros.

Paquet, Mgr L.A. *L'Oeuvre universitaire* (Québec: Imprimerie de l'Action sociale, 1920).

Simoneau, Richard. *Les Idéologies étudiantes, les Doctrines universitaires et l'Idéologie dominante* (Québec: Université Laval—LETMOS, 1972).

Sociologie du travail. "Crise de l'université, mouvement étudiant et conflits sociaux," Numéro 3 (Paris, 1969), p. 287-335.

Université Laval, *Mémoire de l'Université Laval à la Commission Tremblay* (2e éd., Québec, 1954).

Université Laval. *Rapport du Comité de Planification* (2e éd., Québec, 1966).

Université Laval. *Un Projet de Réforme pour l'Université Laval* (Québec: PUL, 1968).

IV

Nationalism and the Canadian Duality

MORE than any other pressing issue in Canadian political life, nationalism seems to occupy a central place. Both papers in this section address themselves to the theme of nationalism in Canada. The first paper by Harvey et al. focuses on national loyalty, idealization of Canada, desire for autonomy, anti-Americanism and aspirations of Canadian youth for national power. The second paper by Lamy probes an equally fundamental aspect of Canadian political life, the French/English duality.

What emerges from the study by Harvey et al. is a strong feeling of nationalism reaching the level of xenophobia among one-half of their Ontario high school sample. This feeling is accompanied by a strong idealization of Canada, with close to three-quarters of the sample echoing the feeling that Canada is "one of the most respected countries in the world." It is not surprising, however, to find a strong desire among the adolescent sample that Canada should charter its own independent course, by freeing herself from the U.S. influence. This attitude of national autonomy is accompanied with an ethnocentric reaction towards the U.S. which manifests itself in anti-Americanism.

An essential pre-requisite to a stable functioning of any political system is the presence of a shared meaning of, or an identification with, political symbols. Lamy finds this to be lacking in the case of English- and French-Canadian adolescents. What typifies the French group is a strong sense of regionalism and a marked sympathy with separatist movements. The latter is specially true among older age groups. The English-Canadian group from Ontario exhibits a strikingly different type of orientation. The main identification is with the federal, and not provincial, level of government. It must be emphasized, however, that this latter finding does not extend to all of English-Canada, as Skogstad's study of Alberta children demonstrated in the previous section. In spite of these differences, both the English- and French-Canadian groups in Lamy's sample ranked the ethnic problem as the major problem facing Canadians.

9.

Nationalist Sentiment Among Canadian Adolescents: The Prevalence and Social Correlates of Nationalistic Feelings.

Ted G. Harvey, Susan K. Hunter-Harvey and W. George Vance

Introduction

NO attentive reader of major Canadian newspapers is likely to have missed the impact of nationalism in moulding Canadian political and economic controversy during the past several years. Foreign (meaning mostly American) ownership has become a controversial issue. Nationalist movements have emerged in the forms of the Committee for an Independent Canada and the Waffle faction of the New Democratic Party.[1] Governments have cautiously adopted a moderate concern with restricting foreign influence in media and economy. Canadian-American diplomatic relations have been strained because of internal swelling of Canadian nationalist sentiment.

Great furor has mounted over the past few years regarding other aspects of Americanization as well: the complex controversy regarding Americans teaching in Canadian universities, American domination of the media and absorption of the Canadian publishing industry, and the hiring of Americans to fill important public posts.[2] Controversy over such issues has generated such responses as government commissions and minor changes in regulatory policy vis a vis media and foreign investment. Yet those most vocally advocating Canadian nationalist positions seem largely unsatisfied by what many regard as "showcase" efforts at pacifying the public. In this connection, it is unclear exactly what potential this current mood of nationalism has for the future. Does its apparent acceleration portend the mobilization and institutionalization of nationalist sentiment? Or is it merely a case of ritualistic "foot-dragging" on the not-so-gradual, and perhaps not-so-unpopular, round to continental union?

If nationalist issues have increasingly become a major preoccupation of the Canadian public mind, young people have become no less a focus of public attention. The key roles played by young people in political protest, drug use and abuse, education, and as newly enfranchised electors are among the major factors responsible for current concern with youth. It is in the merging of these two phenomena —nationalism and youth—that we find our principle research foci. We want to raise some questions which will link these two themes and serve as a framework for increasing our understanding of current Canadian nationalist sentiment. The study of youth is *essential* in this respect since it allows us to get closer to the socialization process within which nationalist sentiments are formed and provides important insight regarding the citizenry of tomorrow.

Some Questions About Adolescent Nationalist Sentiment

What is the nature and prevalence of nationalist sentiment among youth in Canada today? Do adolescents think that maintaining Canada's sovereignty and independence is a central priority for the 1970's? Or are questions of foreign investment, American economic-cultural influence, and Canadian independence in general of little concern? Do they adhere to traditional nationalist-patriotic sentiments? Do they aspire to greater independence for Canada vis a vis the United States? Are their images of Canada glorified or idealized? Are they anti-American in an ethnocentric-xenophobic sense? Are the nationalist sentiments they *do* hold connected to a notion of Canada as a potential world power? Might we say that a significant portion of today's young Canadians are "nationalist?"

Important questions can also be raised regarding the structure and origins of nationalist sentiments. Do nationalist sentiments form an integrated pattern or syndrome so that individuals who adhere to one nationalist perspective are likely to adhere to others as well? To what extent are different nationalist sentiments learned in different social milieux and in different social circumstances? Do such characteristics as sex, ethnic origin, religion, and social class have significant effects on the emergence of nationalist sentiments? This study—a social-psychological study of nationalist views of youth—cannot give us direct or complete answers to such questions.[3] It may, however, by illuminating the attitudinal and behavioural bases of current nationalist sentiments, tell us something of the *potential* of contemporary Canadian nationalism.

Goals in the Study of Nationalism

The authors view the study of nationalism as significant both to the present Canadian political scene and for theory and policy as well. This is primarily because of the relation of nationalism to questions of war and peace. Nationalism has lain at the root of most of the major international conflicts of the past two centuries, and its attendant sentiments would seem to characterize the entire history of human conflict. Christiansen, in an illustrative social-psychological study concludes, "A certain degree of nationalism (patriotism) is generally a necessary precondition for the displacement of aggression towards foreign affairs."[4] Indeed, nationalism and international conflict would seem to be virtually inseparable. Little wonder then that the understanding, erradication, or to a lesser degree, positive channelling of nationalism have been taken by peace researchers as central avenues towards the elimination of war.

Yet, as noted earlier, nationalism has broader implications than those it holds for questions of war and peace alone. Nationalism is associated with outlooks of a beneficent sort as well. For example, the cultural identity and integration necessary for the emergence of nationalism (Doob, 1964; Katz, 1965) is essential as well for the functioning of society per se. Loyalty to the nation, unless replaced by some sub-national or supra-national loyalty, is essential for the maintenance of common "rules of the game" for political processes and for the maintenance of the political system itself.

In nationalism's purely international implications, moreover, and even in instances where nationalist movements have resulted in military conflicts, it is difficult to view all of its by-products as evil. Movements of national liberation in the underdeveloped world, largely sparked by nationalist aspirations, for example, have done much of positive note to place more of humanity on an equal political footing and to maximize the life chances of individuals in those countries to prosper, create, and achieve. The study of nationalism is thus a complex matter: researchers need to determine its origins and causes and simultaneously try to find out how, if at all, its positive/benign effects may be separated from its destructive/malignant effects.

This particular study, with the above cautions in mind, focuses on several aspects of nationalist sentiment among Canadian youth. First, we consider the conceptualization and measurement of nationalism and outline the design of the study. Second, we answer some questions regarding the prevalence of nationalist sentiment among Canadian youth. Third, we turn to a consideration of social factors contributing to the learning of nationalist sentiments.

Conceptualization, Method, and Design of the Study

Conceptualization and Measurement of Nationalism

The fact that diverse notions have been prominent in the development of theories of nationalism has not prevented the emergence of a more or less common understanding of the term. This seems to be the case even though nationalism carries multi-layered meanings at the levels of individual belief system, national ideology or consciousness, and social movement, and even though relatively unique or variable historical-spatial configurations of nationalism have been the rule.

Some definitions are illuminating in this respect:

Nationalism is a state of mind in which the supreme loyalty of the individual is felt to be due to the nation-state.[4a]

Nationalism will always involve more than simply interest in political and national questions. There must be a certain devotion to national symbols and a certain loyalty to national institutions. . . . National loyalty need not be connected with illusions of national grandeur and superiority; nevertheless such illusions have often been regarded as a characteristic feature of modern nationalism.[4b]

The nationalistic syndrome includes . . . strong favorable reactions to numerous subjectively distinctive aspects of an identifiable society as well as other reactions, usually unfavorable in part, to one or more foreign societies. [4c]

Most treatments of nationalism consider one or more of three basic elements. These are national consciousness (especially national pride), national ethnocentrism (including xenophobia), and national aspirations (national self-interest).[4d]

Nationalism is the active solidarity of a larger human collectivity which shares a common culture or a common fund of significant experiences and interests, conceives of itself as a nation, and strives for political unity and self government.[4e]

The themes (see Symmons (1968) for a more elaborate treatment of previous conceptualizations) suggested in these definitions have developed in a number of ways in behavioural studies of nationalism.

Central to most definitions of nationalism is the notion of *affect for the nation*. Affect for the nation and symbols of nation implies solidarity, feelings of identification with fellow nationals, feelings of alienation from (or hostility towards) non-fellow-nationals, and *loyalty* to the nation, including a willingness to endure personal sacrifice for its goals. Often this dimension of loyalty-affect is simply labelled "patriotism" or in its extreme forms "super patriotism." Usually it is viewed as inextricably interwoven with notions of ethnocentrism (Đoob, 1964). Studies of nationalist sentiment focused on the examination of patriotism are typified by Christiansen's (1959) study of nationalism, personality, and international orientations.

A second major theme of nationalism involves *national aspiration*—especially aspiration towards independence, power, or towards the attainment of greater national power where power status is lacking or uncertain. National aspiration implies desire for national political autonomy and distinctiveness as well as the general enhancement of material and other national interests. At the same time it may encompass desire for power as manifest in "national greatness" or the supression of national aspirations of members of other nations. Studies of nationalist sentiment focusing on desire for national independence or power are typified by Terhune's (1964, 1965) studies of nationalist orientation and Forbes' (1972a) analysis of Separatist sentiment among Quebec youth.

Unfortunately, much of this research lacks continuity or is based on unsatisfactory conceptualization and measurement. This is particularly the case where nationalism is a priori equated with conservatism, racism, or authoritarianism. This study began, therefore, with two more basic questions: what are the primary dimensions of contemporary Canadian nationalism? How do *young people themselves* cluster their thoughts about nationalist issues?

The authors approached these questions in the following way. First, a broad universe of over three hundred items relating to nationalist attitudes and beliefs was generated from previous nationalism scales (Christiansen, 1959; Delamater *et al*., 1969; Ferguson, 1942; Terhune, 1964, 1965), from general discussions of contemporary Canadian nationalism (for example, Russell, 1966; Clarkson, 1968; Royal Bank, 1967) and combined with other, original items generated by the researchers. Second, two samples of university students rated the relevant sub-sets of the items by the Thurstone equal appearing intervals method and responded to the items in an agree-disagree format. These responses were then factor analysed (Vance, 1971; Harvey and Vance, 1972). Through this procedure we delineated four of the five measures of nationalist sentiment examined in this paper. (A fifth indicator was fashioned on a priori grounds.) Third, items reflecting these dimensions were selected on the basis of pre-testing conducted with university students and were administered in a questionnaire to 1,955 Ontario high-school students whose responses were subsequently factor analysed.[5] Four dimensions of nationalist orientation were indicated by the factor solution settled on by the researchers as best satisfying the criteria of simple structure and inter-pretability. These modes of nationalist sentiment were named *National Loyalty* (hereafter N-Loyalty), *National Idealization* (hereafter N-Idealization), *Anti-Americanism*, and *Desire for National Independence* (hereafter D-Independence).[6] Before describing these dimensions we should note that the basic scale development procedure (Vance, 1971) led to the conclusion that certain other nation-related sentiments (for example, orientations towards Britain and the Com-monwealth, national unity, Quebec separatism, provincial power and autonomy, military-economic power, and citizenship) were largely tangential to core dimensions of Canadian nationalist sentiment. These results, along with corresponding findings of Forbes (1972b), lead us to the tentative view that our basic scales map out in a reasonably thorough way the major dimensions of Canadian nationalism. These we feel are the central dimensions of nationalist sentiment likely to become manifest in other attitudes or behaviour or likely to be relevant to the emergence of any potent nationalist social movement. The four nationalism scales will be only briefly described here as their content and development is thoroughly explicated elsewhere (Harvey and Vance, 1972).

The *N-Loyalty* scale is a cluster of eight items regarded as reflect-ing traditional patriotism (see Table 1). These items tap such commit-ments to the nation as support for compulsory national service, flag waving, the learning of citizen roles, and "fighting and dying" for one's country. National pride is the major theme of the *N-Idealization* scale, national idealization being the tendency to "ascribe chiefly positive traits to one's own nation" (Christiansen, 1959). The N-Idealization items laud Canada as a "solver of social problems," a "just society," and a "most respected" country with a high degree of social harmony—in effect a country with few equals in the world in these respects. The positive side of ethnocentrism conveyed by N-Idealization is counterbalanced by the negatively ethnocentric at-titudes of the *Anti-Americanism* scale. Its items constitute a highly negative (if incomplete) characterization of Americans and American society per se. In the scale items, Americans are portrayed as "ill-mannered," "self-centred and greedy" and prone to leaving "bad impressions" in their wake, while American society is labelled "cor-rupt." That xenophobic Anti-Americanism is a central aspect of the new Canadian nationalism will be shown later. The *D-Independence*

TABLE 1

Level of agreement and disagreement for items in the Nationalism scales, Supranationalism and Militarism.*

	Agree	Uncertain	Disagree
National Loyalty			
I am a Canadian first, last, and always.	64%	20%	16%
"O Canada" should be sung before every public event.	55	20	25
People who don't like Canada should leave.	53	15	31
Every Canadian should be willing to fight and die for Canada.	51	21	28
For a young person, learning how to be a good citizen is more important than almost anything else he or she learns.	49	22	29
A good Canadian will stand behind Canada whether Canada is right or wrong.	37	17	47
More people should fly the Canadian flag outside their homes and display flag decals in their car windows.	35	32	33
It should be compulsory for all young people to serve Canada either in the military or in some non-military capacity such as the Canadian University Service Overseas (CUSO).	16	15	69
National Idealization			
Canada is rightly one of the most respected countries in the world.	78%	18%	4%
Canadians have developed a way of living together that works as well as any.	67	19	14
Canada comes closer to a 'just society' than just about any other nation.	46	35	20
Canada has done a much better job than most countries in solving or alleviating social problems.	45	32	23
Anti-Americanism			
By and large, Americans are self-centered and greedy.	40%	22%	38%
American society is the most corrupt society in the Western World.	35	27	38
Americans leave a bad impression wherever they go in the world.	31	20	49
In general, Americans are the most ill-mannered of all people.	18	27	56
Desire for Independence			
The closer Canada's relations with the United States, the better off we'll be.	15%	20%	65%
The government should stop at nothing to reverse the American takeover of our economy.	65	15	21
The infusion of American culture is one of the most dangerous threats to Canadian society.	60	21	19
Canadian ownership of all Canadian industries and resources is worth achieving even at the expense of reduced prosperity in our economy.	58	22	20
It is a good idea to limit 'American content' on Canadian television and radio.	54	16	31
Canadians should gladly accept a 25% reduction in income should that be necessary to free Canada from the influence of the United States.	39	31	30
Foreign investment erodes Canada's independence far in excess of the good it does.	32	42	26

* "Strongly agree" and "agree" responses are merged in this table, as are "strongly disagree" and "disagree" responses.

scale expresses a strong desire for Canada's freedom from American economic and cultural influences. Its seven items, five of which refer explicitly to the United States, verbalize such current nationalist views as limiting American television and radio content, regaining control of the economy by whatever means necessary, stopping American takeover "at all costs," and denouncing foreign investment and American cultural imperialism in general. Although our D-Independence scale is rooted conceptually in Terhune's (1964) scale, unlike Terhune's scale it does not include the desire for international power. To evaluate aspiration for national power, we used an a priori indicator of that aspiration (hereafter D-Power).

Desire for National Power. The reader will recall that our scale development procedures suggested that D-Power orientations were tangential to Canadian nationalism. However, observing that national power in some form has traditionally been a mainstay of the independence of nations and a concomitant of nationalist sentiment, and suspecting that D-Power outlooks are distinct from those of D-Independence (Vance, 1971), we developed an a priori indicator of aspiration for national power. This indicator was comprised of a single item in which each subject indicated how much power he or she would like Canada to have in 1990 in relation to a select rank ordering of nations by projected national power. Students could rank Canada in a way reflecting its current international power (low) or, if they so desired, they could rank it high—among the projected super-powers of 1990.[7] Response patterns of the high-school sample suggest that this indicator taps an important dimension of nationalism—one which is not quite so central to Canadian nationalism as the four dimensions discussed above, yet an indicator which illustrates an important dimension of Canadian national feeling.

In addition to the five indicators of nationalist sentiment just discussed, the survey administered to the high-school sample included numerous questions relating to supranationalism, militarism, political outlook and politicization, political knowledge, foreign policy perspectives, family relations, anomie, self-esteem and faith in people, and social-demographic characteristics.[8]

Sample

The survey was administered to 1,955 high-school students in late spring, 1971. The questionnaires, which were anonymous, were administered by teachers to students in grades nine to thirteen. Only six questionnaires were spoiled or very incomplete.[9] Seven schools representing distinct sections of Ontario (southwestern, central, and eastern Ontario) were included in the sample. One school was located in a rural area, one in a small town, and the remaining five in urban areas. Six of the schools were public and one was a separate school. Our sample gives us considerable confidence regarding the generalizability of our results. While it is not random, it is in several ways far more satisfactory than typical samples used in political socialization research. It is, of course, only a sample of English-speaking Canadian young people from one province. Even so, we will find it useful to speculate as to the generalizability of our findings for nationalist sentiments of English-Canadian young people generally, and English-speaking Canadians as a whole. For obvious reasons having to do with the meaning of nationalism in Quebec (see Forbes, 1972a), we wish to make explicit that we do not see our inferences as necessarily relevant to French-Canadian youth.

Mode of Analysis and the Presentation of Statistics

For purposes of analysis our sample was dichotomized into high groups and low groups for each dimension of nationalist sentiment. Thus the sample was divided into a high N-Loyalty group and a low N-Loyalty group and similarly for N-Idealization, Anti-Americanism, D-Independence and D-Power. Relatively *natural* cutting-points for delineating these groups were chosen because of our desire to explore as carefully as possible the direction and prevalence of nationalist sentiment. Therefore these categories should be considered as non-arbitrary partitionings of the sample according to nationalist feeling.[10]

Tables presented in the section of the paper on some correlates of nationalism have the following characteristics. Each sub-table of Tables 4 and 5 is a representation of the cross-tabulation of an independent variable by one of the indicators of nationalist sentiment. Each sub-table is partial in that it shows percentages for the high nationalist group only, for reasons of economy of presentation. The reader can, should he or she wish, compute the percentages for the low nationalist group by taking the difference between each percentage given and one hundred per cent. As would normally be the case, the X^2 presented for each sub-table is always computed from the complete sub-table.[11]

The Prevalence and Organization of Nationalist Sentiments

The Prevalence of Nationalistic Sentiments

In this section we consider the degree of nationalistic sentiment displayed by our sample of young Canadians by looking (1) at patterns of responses to individual items from the nationalism indicators; and (2) at patterns of overall responses to scales.

National Loyalty.   Do adolescents adhere to what we normally think of as traditional nationalistic-patriotic sentiments? The answer to this question is a definite "yes." One-third or more of the sample agree with 7 of 8 N-Loyalty items (Table I), even though the items tend toward traditional symbolic, patriotic, and even "super patriotic" commitment to Canada. This pattern, moreover, cannot be attributed to acquiescent response Set. In the 1970's, an era of supposedly heightened cynicism, 64 per cent of the sample agrees with the traditionalist items, "I am a Canadian first, last, and always." Intense patriotic feeling is also apparent in the agreement by one-half or more of the sample with the statements: " 'O Canada' should be sung before every public event" (55 per cent); "People who don't like Canada should leave" (53 per cent); and "Every Canadian should be willing to fight and die for Canada" (51 per cent). A near majority (47 per cent) reject the unequivocal statement "A good Canadian will stand behind Canada whether Canada is right or wrong," while there is a fairly even split about displaying the Canadian flag. Only the item relating to compulsory national service is rejected by a majority (69 per cent). Overall these responses seemed to reflect a strongly nationalistic outlook —especially when the proportion taking the neutral response for each question is also taken into account. High levels of national patriotism and loyalty to symbols of the nation-state are manifested by a majority of the students surveyed.

National Idealization.   Do the students in the sample hold an idealized or glorified image of Canada? The answer is unequivocally "yes"; our sample *is* characterized by a very strong commitment to N-Idealization. None of the scale's four statements is rejected by a large proportion of the students. The idealized response to "Canada is rightly one of the most respected countries in the world" is taken by 78 per cent of the respondents. Fewer students (46 per cent) see Canada as more of a "just society" than most other nations. Yet even after the October, 1970, Quebec crisis, 67 per cent of the students agree that "Canadians have developed a way of living together that works as well as any," while 45 per cent agree that "Canada has done a much better job than most countries in solving or alleviating social problems." In sum, N-Idealization sentiments are intensely and widely held by the adolescents surveyed.

Desire for National Independence.   Do the students aspire to greater independence vis-a-vis the United States? The answer to this question is again unequivocally "yes"—a surprising result, given the concreteness of the items and given the image reinforced in the mass media during the last few years of "independence advocates" as a minority (and near fringe) group.

    In response to the statement "The closer Canada's relations with the United States, the better off we'll be," 65 per cent of the students disagree, indicating that they reject Canada's traditional interdependence with the United States. The government should "stop at nothing to reverse the American takeover'' of the Canadian economy is the feeling of 64 per cent. These are indications of intense sentiment, reflecting a great deal of antipathy towards American economic control. The "infusion of American culture" is one of the most "dangerous threats" to Canadian society according to 60 per cent, while 58 per cent feel that "Canadian ownership of all Canadian resources and industry is worth achieving even at the expense of reduced prosperity in our economy."

Responses to these items make it apparent that the Canadian adolescents surveyed are overwhelmingly concerned with Canada's relationship with the United States. That 54 per cent feel it is a good idea to "limit American content on Canadian television and radio," and that 39 per cent feel that "Canadians should gladly accept a 25 per cent reduction in income should that be necessary to free Canada from the influence of the United States," attests in the strongest possible way to the prevalence among adolescents of sentiment in favour of a Canada free of American economic and cultural domination.

Anti-Americanism. Are Canadian students anti-American in the ethnocentric-xenophobic sense of the term? The answer to this question is that many are, yet these sentiments are far less prevalent than those relating to the three previously discussed dimensions of nationalism. The fact that 40 per cent of the sample agree with the statement "By and large, Americans are self-centered and greedy," while 35 per cent agree that "American society is the most corrupt society in the Western World," and 31 per cent agree that "Americans leave a bad impression wherever they go in the world" lends credence to the ingroup-outgroup, "us versus them" colorations which many theorists have attributed to nationalism (see Symmons, 1968).

While it is possible to detect anti-American sentiment in the general population, and while anti-American sentiment is often expressed by certain ongoing social movements in Canada, the tenor of this sentiment has not been as xenophobic as the statements agreed to by this sample. The stereotypic responses casting Americans as "greedy," "corrupt," and "ill-mannered," reflect intense disaffection for Americans in general on the part of a much larger proportion of the sample than was anticipated. This, we suspect, suggests that much greater latent hostility towards Americans exists among Canadian populations than has yet been appreciated. While such hostility may provide a supportive undercurrent for the emergence of general nationalist sentiments, its xenophobic and negative orientation reflects a possible moral flaw in the fabric of Canadian adolescent nationalism.

Desire for National Power. Do Canadian adolescents manifest a tendency to desire national power? More importantly, might we say that they would like to see Canada as a "world power?" Common insight into Canadian political life and history suggests they should not. Rather, it is the reputation for "quiet diplomacy" and the image of Canada as a "middle power" that comes to mind. Our pre-testing, moreover, indicated that Terhune's notion of national power was not scaleable for our sample, except when restricted specifically to notions of independence.

Surprisingly, a strong tendency to desire greater national power is characteristic of the sample. More than half of the students (54 per cent) ranked Canada in such a way that we have classified them as desiring "super-power" status for the Canada of the future. Only 9.6 per cent aspired to little or no increase in Canada's power. This is surprising particularly as the aspirations seem unrelated to current international realities. But, on closer examination, the strong orientation towards power manifested by our adolescent sample fits in well with the overall pattern of nationalist outlook exhibited.[12]

Overall Prevalence of Nationalistic Sentiment.   Viewing the question in an overall fashion, might we wish to say that Canadian adolescents are generally "nationalistic"? This question can be illuminated by examining Table 2, where the percentages taking nationalistic and non-nationalistic positions on the various nationalism dimensions are indicated. Attaching numbers to such concrete labels as "nationalist" or "non-nationalist" is, of course, both difficult and somewhat arbitrary. We will engage in such categorizing, however, because of the importance of the prevalence question. Students were categorized as *Strong Nationalists, Moderate Nationalists, Moderate Non-nationalists*, and *Strong Non-nationalists* on each dimension using the natural cutting-points discussed above.

As can be seen in Table 2, our procedure results in a fairly clear answer to the question posed and one which is consistent with our item-by-item discussion of prevalence. N-Loyalty sentiments are accepted by a majority of the students, 12.6 per cent falling into the *Strong Nationalists* group and 45.4 per cent falling into the *Moderate Nationalists* group. Fully 29.7 per cent of the sample agree with all of the N-Idealization items, and altogether 76.3 per cent fall into the strong and moderate nationalist positions regarding N-Idealization. An amazing 26.2 per cent of the sample agree with all of the D-Independence items, with 73.0 per cent altogether assuming a nationalist position regarding D-Independence. Finally, 14.6 per cent of the sample agree with all of the Anti-Americanism items while a larger portion, 24.7 per cent, reject them all. Almost 15 per cent of the adolescent sample can be characterized as extremely xenophobic in outlook, and 35.5 per cent are generally anti-American in outlook.

TABLE 2

Levels of prevalence of nationalist sentiment for each of five Nationalism dimensions.

	Strong Nationalists	Moderate Nationalists	Moderate Non-nationalists	Strong Non-nationalists
National Loyalty	12.6%	45.4%	28.8%	7.2%
National Idealisation	29.7	46.6	11.5	1.7
Desire for Independence	26.2	46.8	16.9	3.7
Anti-Americanism	14.6	21.9	28.4	24.7
Desire for Power	54.1		45.9	

In general, then, Canadian adolescent opinion is shown to be overwhelmingly nationalistic. Canadian adolescents strongly endorse N-Idealization (76.3 per cent), and D-Independence (73.0 per cent), adhere somewhat less strongly to the traditional sentiments of N-Loyalty (58.2 per cent), and display a strong (although minority) undercurrent of anti-Americanism (36.5 per cent). Consistent with these positions regarding the central dimensions of Canadian nationalism is a clear aspiration for the emergence one day of Canada as a world power (54.1 per cent).

In summary, we have shown that young people are not only very *conscious* of nationalist issues, but also that a large portion of the sample are *committed* nationalists. The tendency among youth to idealize Canada is exceptionally strong, as is an intense desire to preserve and promote Canadian independence in the face of a perceived American threat. Youth generally endorse the jingoistic or chauvinistic type of sentiments—"my country right or wrong," "fight and die for Canada"—that typify nationalistic fervor, yet in a way that is much tempered by more concrete and positive sentiments. Lastly, we perceive something of a departure from classic nationalistic feeling: a tendency to constrain somewhat ethnocentric hostility towards the "national enemy" or "outgroup" (the United States). Anti-Americanism is found to be widespread and important, and yet at the same time it can be seen as playing a somewhat secondary role in the pattern of Canadian adolescent nationalism.

The Organization of Nationalist Sentiments

The question of organization of individual nationalist sentiments complements that of prevalence in increasing our understanding of Canadian adolescent nationalist sentiment. That our indicators of nationalist sentiment do not comprise a single dimension of nationalist outlook was suggested earlier in the section dealing with conceptualization and measurement of nationalism. Yet our analysis of prevalence suggests that Canadian adolescents are generally nationalistic: nationalist feelings seem to "go together."

But do nationalistic outlooks form a pattern or syndrome when examined in a more statistically sophisticated manner? This question is important for two reasons. First, we can hardly say that nationalism is prevalent if its attendant sentiments cannot be found simultaneously in many individuals (Forbes, 1972b). Second, if nationalist sentiments do form a syndrome, we may infer from our data that the distribution of these sentiments is likely to be one where a certain portion of young people will hold a consistent nationalist outlook or "belief system" (Rokeach, 1960; Converse, 1962; Sartori, 1969) and a much larger group will manifest selected nationalist outlooks only. This is consistent with Converse (1962) as well as a wealth of theory on attitudes, belief systems, and behaviour (see, for example, Rokeach, 1968). If we find such a pattern of attitudinal consistency, we can posit a greater potential for mobilization of nationalist sentiment than would be the case if nationalist sentiments were randomly interrelated.[13]

Examination of the correlations among dimensions of nationalist sentiment (Table 3) provides an answer to our question regarding consistency of sentiments. All of the nationalism dimensions are positively correlated. Although the correlations are variable (one is not significant at $P = .05$, and they range from a low of Gamma $= .04$ to a high of Gamma $= .59$), all are in the direction indicated by the syndrome hypothesis.

Examination of the intercorrelations among the scales provides further insight into the nature of each dimension and the pattern as a whole. N-Loyalty seems central to the pattern since it correlates most strongly with the other dimensions. N-Loyalty correlates most highly with N-Idealization (.56), followed by D-Independence (.45), Anti-Americanism (.35), and D-Power (.25). Predictably, Anti-Americanism correlates very strongly with D-Independence (.59). Finally, as we might have predicted from our discussion of scaling, D-Power seems least central to the syndrome as a whole.[14]

To determine more carefully whether the pattern detected visually among the correlations indicated existence of a nationalism syndrome, the several nationalism dimensions were factor analysed (along with Supranationalism and Militarism). These factor-analytic results clearly reaffirm our conclusion that our indicators cohere in a general nationalism syndrome. A two factor solution shows all five indicators to load on a single nationalism factor (Table 3). All of the loadings are .65 or higher, with the exception of D-Power (.38). N-Loyalty seems most central to the general nationalism factor with a loading of .74, but equally significant loadings characterize the other components of the dimension, D-Independence (.66), N-Idealization (.65), and Anti-Americanism (.65). A three-factor solution, extracted to examine more closely the two themes of nationalist sentiment suggested by the higher correlations of the correlation matrix, shows the nationalism syndrome to be characterized by two extraordinarily coherent patterns—the first relating to traditional nationalist sentiments of D-Power, N-Loyalty, and N-Idealization, the second interrelating more radical nationalist sentiments of D-Independence and Anti-Americanism.

Our analysis of the patterning of adolescent nationalist sentiment shows that a *nationalism syndrome* underlies their orientations to questions of loyalty, independence, power, anti-Americanism and so on. Not only do young people widely adhere to nationalistic positions

TABLE 3

Nationalist sentiments as a syndrome.

Correlations between Nationalist variables and supranationalism and militarism. Factor analysis of dimensions with two and three factor solutions.

(Varimax rotation)

	NL	NI	DI	AA	DP	Two Factor Solution		Three Factor Solution		
						I	II	I	II	III
N-Loyalty	1.0	.56**	.45**	.35**	.25**	(.74)	.27	.33	(.69)	.22
N-Idealisation		1.0	.27**	.22**	.19**	(.65)	-.09	.28	(.65)	-.01
D-Independence			1.0	.59**	.09**	(.66)	.31	(.82)	.11	-.05
Anti-Americanism				1.0	.04**	(.65)	.40	(.84)	.08	-.04
D-Power					1.0	(.38)	-.28	.15	(.71)	-.06
Supra-Nationalism	.02	.01	.06	.13*	.02	.09	(-.59)	.04	.19	(-.79)
Militarism	.25**	.09	.04	-.09	-.04	.22	(-.72)	-.05	.28	(.74)

** X^2 significant at $P \leq .001$
* X^2 significant at $P \leq .01$

TABLE 4

Sex, grade, religion and ethnicity by nationalist outlook

	High N-Loyalty	High N-Idealization	High D-Independence	High Anti-Americanism	High D-Power
Sex					
Male	58.7%	78.4%	76.1%	55.1%	43.2%
Female	57.5	74.3	70.0	38.5	65.3
Chi square (x^2) =	.2	4.2	8.83	52.8	74.8
Significance (P) =	ns	.05	.01	.001	.001
Grade					
Grade 9	53.4	71.8	71.8	41.7	56.6
Grade 10	63.5	75.0	68.5	40.3	59.8
Grade 11	58.1	78.7	76.8	48.3	56.4
Grade 12	53.5	76.2	73.9	51.9	48.3
Grade 13	55.0	76.1	73.4	56.0	39.6
Chi square (x^2) =	12.8	3.8	10.9	20.6	21.4
Significance (P) =	.02	ns	.05	.001	.001
Religion					
Catholic	65.2	82.2	72.4	43.7	54.6
Protestant	60.3	76.2	73.2	47.1	54.3
No religion	39.5	70.6	75.4	50.0	53.2
Chi square (x^2) =	48.1	14.6	.8	3.0	
Significance (P) =	.001	.001	ns	ns	.1
Ethnicity					
Canada	61.5	83.8	70.9	44.7	65.5
Britain	59.0	76.2	74.5	48.1	53.8
Europe	55.7	72.8	71.9	45.6	48.9
Anglo-European	58.0	76.3	72.8	45.5	55.7
Chi square (x^2) =	1.9	7.8	1.5	1.4	9.6
Significance (P) =	ns	.05	ns	ns	.05

in a symbolic sense, they do so on pressing contemporary economy and independence issues as well. Their views, moreover, reflect a level of patterning indicative of considerable potential for mobilization to action.[15]

Some Social Correlates of Nationalism

With a view toward arriving at a fuller understanding of Canadian nationalism and increasing our understanding of nationalism in general, let us explore some of the linkages between nationalist sentiments and individual life experiences and circumstances.

Only a few references to nationalist sentiments are to be found in the political socialization literature. Dawson and Prewitt (1969) for example, suggest that the development of nationalist orientations is best viewed as part of the normal process of individual political maturation. Piaget and Weil (1951) suggest that it is normal for children to develop an early affection for their country of birth or "homeland," and the universality of these patterns is shown by Lambert and Klineberg's (1967) study of children's views of foreign peoples. Doob (1962, 1964) views the development of patriotism as universal because of the desire of all people to preserve their cultural heritage. Such generalizations cannot, however, be viewed as presenting adequate guidelines for the delineation of specific, well-founded research hypotheses. Political socialization researchers have primarily focused their attention on the learning by children and adolescents of a very limited set of cultural-political norms and values. Attention has been largely limited to the learning of such selected aspects of political culture as: attitudes towards authorities and leaders, partisan stances, feelings of political efficacy, and knowledge of politics. (For general reviews of this literature see Dennis, 1967; Baker, 1971; Harvey, 1972).

Only recently, in the study of student activism, has any suggestion been made as to why some students initiate and participate in social movements (Jackson, 1971; Burgess and Hofstetter, 1971; Halleck, 1967; Lipset and Altbach, 1967), and this literature, although concerned with questions of linkage, has not focused upon nationalism per se. Research on the political socialization of international outlooks, an under-researched area in any case, has tended to focus upon the emergence of attitudes towards "foreign peoples" and international images (Lambert and Klineberg, 1967) and views of war and peace (Cooper, 1965, Alvick, 1968). Unfortunately, in this area too, guidelines for the study of nationalism are lacking.

The purpose of this section is to relate Canadian nationalist sentiment to variables which may tell us something about the origins of nationalism in social circumstance. We will explore a number of interfaces between individual social circumstance and nationalist stance. Space, unfortunately, does not allow detailed consideration of these matters. Extrapolation, moreover, from theoretical literature in this area to our own concerns must of necessity be sketchy. For these reasons we will attempt to deal briefly with the following two questions. (1) How do such diverse indicators of circumstance and origins as sex, grade, religion, and ethnicity relate to the emergence of nationalist sentiments? (2) How does socio-economic status (hereafter SES) relate to nationalist sentiment? Answers to these questions may tell us more about the nature of contemporary Canadian nationalist sentiment and give us deeper insights into the socialization and learning of nationalist perspectives per se.

Sex, Grade, Religion, Ethnicity, and Nationalist Sentiment

Sex is an important indicator of nationalist sentiment for four of our five nationalism dimensions (Table 4). Males tend generally to be more nationalistic than females although they differ little in N-Loyalty. The greatest difference in this direction is found for Anti-Americanism: 55.1 per cent of the males are high in Anti-Americanism, compared to only 38.5 per cent of the females. Males are likely as well to be higher than females in D-Independence and N-Idealization. Contrary to this trend, females are much higher (65.3 per cent) than males (43.2 per cent) in D-Power. These findings correspond to others showing males to be more nationalistic or patriotic (Delameter *et al.*, 1969; Harvey, 1967). Considerable research has suggested that males generally assume a more political role (Greenstein, 1965). We found males to be more politicized in our Ontario sample as well. This may explain greater male concern for nationalist issues and thus their greater tendency to adopt a nationalist stance. This consideration, however, does little to explain the curious centering of this male-female difference on Anti-Americanism and D-Power. This would seem to merit further research.

Grade is also significantly associated with four of our five nationalism variables. D-Power and Anti-Americanism are most closely related to grade. There is a clear increase in Anti-Americanism as grade increases. D-Power, on the other hand, declines with grade, suggestive of complex effects of maturation and increased ability to appraise reality. D-Independence and N-Loyalty show a weak and irregular relationship to grade—D-Independence increasing slightly as grade increases and N-Loyalty declining slightly as grade increases.

These findings suggest that nationalist sentiments in general are fairly well established for our Ontario sample by about grade ten or so.

Religion is significantly related to only two of our nationalism indicators. Catholics are more likely to be high in N-Loyalty (65.2 per cent) than Protestants (60.3 per cent) who in turn are generally higher in N-Loyalty than those with no religion (39.5 per cent). A slightly larger margin separates Catholics (82.6 per cent) from Protestants (76.2 per cent) regarding N-Idealization, while those with no religion are least likely to idealize the nation (70.6 per cent). This pattern might have been predicted on the basis of general associations between social-political conservatism, religion, and religiosity. Since patriots have traditionally coupled "God" and "country" in expressions of loyalty, it is consistent that Catholics or Protestants tend to be more loyal to Canada and tend to idealize Canada more than those reporting no religious affiliation. Given the generally more symbolic and ritualistic nature of the Catholic church, it seems consistent as well that Catholics tend to be more loyal and prouder of their country than Protestants. The fact that this pattern does not obtain for other dimensions of Canadian nationalist sentiment supports, we suspect, the view that Anti-Americanism and D-Independence probably are interwoven with more radical political outlooks than are other nationalist orientations. In fact, *non-significant* but interesting trends regarding Anti-Americanism and D-Independence support this view. In both cases Catholics are the least likely to exhibit nationalist outlooks; those with no religion are most likely to be high in Anti-Americanism or D-Independence.

Ethnicity is significantly related to two of our nationalism dimensions, N-Idealization and D-Power. Our analysis shows that those claiming *Canadian* origins are highest in N-Idealization (83.8 per cent) and D-Power (65.5 per cent), possibly because of identification with the nation, although the effect of generation in Canada on these sentiments cannot be discounted. Those claiming British and mixed British-European ancestry tend overall to be more moderate in nationalist outlook although a slight tendency is evidenced for students of British origin to be higher in D-Independence and Anti-Americanism. Those of European ancestry tend generally to be lowest in nationalist sentiment.

Socio-economic Status and Nationalist Orientations

Several writers (Hoffer, 1951; Lipset, 1960) have suggested that individuals who are members of the lower middle and working classes are more susceptible to the appeals of social movements. Delameter *et al*. (1969) found lower SES respondents in their study to be more symbolically oriented or patriotic. Rosenblatt (1964) suggests that nascent

TABLE 5
Socio-economic Status by Nationalist Outlook

	High N-Loyalty	High N-Idealization	High D-Independence	High Anti-Americanism	High D-Power
Parents' Education					
Grade school	57.9%	77.0%	74.2%	47.2%	48.1%
Some high school	62.1	79.8	73.9	47.9	43.1
High school graduate	59.5	76.4	73.4	45.9	44.0
Some university	52.4	74.1	71.4	48.3	51.3
University graduate	46.0	66.2	66.9	40.3	53.3
Chi square (X^2) =	17.3	13.4	3.4	3.2	7.9
Significance (P) =	.01	.01	ns	ns	ns
Father's Occupation (Blishen)					
Low status	62.2	77.2	72.5	47.5	57.0
2	59.5	76.5	73.9	47.6	54.2
3	52.7	76.9	76.3	44.8	50.0
High status	49.7	74.3	66.5	45.5	47.7
Chi square (X^2) =	14.5	.7	6.0	1.0	5.9
Significance (P) =	.01	ns	ns	ns	ns
After School Plans					
Attend University	57.3	77.0	74.8	46.8	49.3
Attend Trade or Business School	71.1	84.2	74.2	37.9	70.1
Intend to work	63.7	76.6	71.8	51.0	60.6
Intend to travel	43.8	64.6	83.3	56.3	56.1
Other	41.0	68.9	72.1	54.1	59.5
Chi square (X^2) =	28.6	12.1	3.4	11.4	29.1
Significance (P) =	.001	.02	ns	.05	.001
Job Expectations					
Extremely good	60.0	80.0	70.2	50.7	51.1
Good	60.6	78.3	74.2	45.3	55.9
Poor	54.5	70.9	74.3	50.3	50.0
Extremely poor	38.9	59.3	68.5	59.3	51.1
Chi square (X^2) =	12.8	17.9	2.4	7.2	3.8
Significance (P) =	.01	.001	ns	ns	ns

nationalism and ethnocentrism tend to be greatest in those groups with the lowest level of living, groups with the most to gain (Katz, 1940) and in those social groupings with the most socioeconomic inequality or the most rigid barriers to socio-economic mobility. Much of this literature seems to be based upon a view of nationalism as encompassing authoritarianism, a conceptual position which is unsatisfactory in our view as a base for making inferences regarding all of the aspects of nationalism central to our syndrome.

These theoretical expectations, which we term "the social disadvantage" model of nationalism, could apply at best, we reasoned, to our more traditional indicators of nationalism and possibly Anti-Americanism because of its xenophobic nature. Two indicators of SES of the family of origin are examined: parents' education and father's occupation (using Blishen ratings of occupational status). Simultaneously, two indicators of probable future SES are considered: after school plans, and the perceived chances of getting a good job (job expectation).

Parents' education is significantly associated with N-Loyalty and N-Idealization (table 5). In each case, students whose parents have grade-school education only tend to be less nationalistic than those whose parents have some high school, after which point nationalistic sentiment drops steadily as parental education increases. Students whose parents are university graduates are least likely to exhibit strong N-Loyalty and N-Idealization sentiments. At the same time, these students are least likely to exhibit Anti-Americanism and D-Independence sentiments although these relationships are not significant. In general this pattern supports the social disadvantage model of nationalism. Examination of relations between nationalism dimensions and *father's occupational status*, however, (Table 5) shows significant correspondent results in the case of N-Loyalty only. There we see that as father's occupational status increases, the percentage high in N-Loyalty declines steadily from 62.2 per cent to 49.7 per cent. It is interesting, however, that consistent trends in the other sub-tables show low occupational status to be associated in each case with the more nationalistic perspective.

After-school plans is the best SES predictor of nationalist sentiment, relating significantly to all dimensions except D-Independence. Those anticipating entry into trade or business schools were highest in N-Loyalty, N-Idealization, and D-Power, but least Anti-American. Those planning to work tend to reflect in a somewhat more moderate manner the sentiments exhibited by those bound for trade or business schools. Those planning to travel or attend university tend to be least nationalistic. Once again, these results seem to support the social disadvantage model of nationalism. *Job expectation* provides much more complex results, perhaps because of elements of optimism and pessimism tapped by the question. In any case the results here are somewhat contrary to those for Parents' Education, Father's Occupation, and After School Plans. As was the case for each of those variables, Job Expectation is related to N-Loyalty and N-Idealization, but the relationship is reversed. Of those viewing their chances of getting a job as "extremely good," 60 per cent are high in N-Loyalty, and 80 per cent are high in N-Idealization. Of those who viewed their job chances as "extremely poor," however, only 38.9 per cent are high in N-Loyalty and only 59.3 per cent are high in N-Idealization. In the case of job expectations, the socially advantaged position seems to heighten nationalist sentiments. Only in the case of Anti-Americanism does the nationalistic response seem more characteristic of the disadvantaged. There, about 59.3 per cent of the students who see their job chances as "extremely poor" could be classified high in Anti-Americanism compared with about 46 per cent Anti-American overall. These results do not present a totally clear picture regarding the effects of SES on nationalist sentiments. The social disadvantage model is generally supported by the broad set of SES indicators, but we must view its relevance as greater for traditional nationalist sentiments than for D-Independence and Anti-Americanism. Further, we must note the apparent reinforcement or reward effects of high SES or high SES expectations on nationalist sentiments. These seem to suggest that the social disadvantage model is a potentially powerful, but only partial, explanation of the ways in which social statuses affect the emergence of nationalist outlooks.

Discussion

Our analysis in this section has shown nationalistic orientations to be interconnected with a broad range of independent variables. We find such indicators as sex, religion, ethnicity, and socio-economic status to be useful predictors of nationalist sentiments. But we are satisfied neither with the extent to which the findings noted here have been explained nor with the extent to which the emergence of nationalist sentiments has been accounted for. It is evident that our independent variables can account for only a portion of the variance of each of our nationalism indicators. Further research—both of a developmental and explanatory sort on the emergence of nationalist sentiment and research extending our understanding of nationalism's interrelation with political as well as personality variables—is clearly called for.

Conclusion

Summary

In this paper we have: (1) discussed the importance of studying contemporary Canadian nationalism and attempted to link its study to the study of nationalism in general; (2) presented our conceptualization of Canadian nationalism and outlined the method by which we derived its multi-dimensional characterization; (3) explored the prevalence of nationalist sentiment along these dimensions for a large sample of Ontario adolescents; and (4) explored the relationships between these sentiments and selected independent variables.

A brief recapitulation of our findings may be useful in concluding the paper. Most importantly, we found the following: (1) that four key dimensions can be distinguished as encompassing contemporary Canadian nationalist sentiment: National Loyalty, National Idealization, Desire for National Independence, and Anti-Americanism; (2) that these sentiments, along with that tapped by an a priori indicator of Desire for National Power, were relevant for and prevalent among our adolescent sample; (3) that in terms of overall stance, our sample of Ontario youth was highly nationalistic in outlook, particularly in national idealization, desire for independence from American influence, and in desire for national power; (4) that nationalist sentiments appeared to form a psychological syndrome including all of the five dimensions of nationalist outlook; and (5) that nationalist sentiments were strongly related to indicators of social circumstance and socio-economic status.

Future Research

Our research leaves a number of puzzling questions which should prove to be of interest to future researchers. Of these, questions as to the generalizability of our findings are clearly most important. Is nationalist sentiment as prevalent among young people across Canada as it is in our Ontario-wide sample? This question is important both for understanding more thoroughly the extent and depth of young peoples' nationalist feelings and for appraising its implications for Canadian national politics. Obviously the mood of nationalism detected here gains in significance if it is paralleled in other parts of Canada. The generalizability of our findings to all Canadians is uncertain. We would expect to find evidence of considerable nationalist feeling among Canadian adults, but we would expect it to be less intense than the sentiment we have found in our adolescent sample. We are also left with the puzzle of how our results are to be related to nationalism in

Quebec. We suspect that our scales are robust enough to survive implementation in a survey of Canadian nationalist sentiment among Quebec youth, but we are quite uncertain as to how prevalent such sentiment would be. The problem, moreover, of studying a nationalism within a nationalism (that is, Quebec nationalism) is challenging and complex. Determining the degree to which Quebec nationalism and Canadian nationalism are mutually exclusive alternatives among general populations of Quebec young people would be a fascinating undertaking indeed and one of great importance to public policy. We will leave these anticipations and questions for future research since we can do little more than speculate with the data at hand. (See Hargrove, 1970; and Forbes, 1972a).

Additionally, we need to better understand the extent to which the nationalist sentiments uncovered here are *behaviourally* significant. Are the young people we have classified as "nationalistic" capable of being aroused or likely to be aroused to nationalist action? Contemporary social-psychological theory provides no clear answer to this question. Clarifying this link between sentiment and behaviour seems a central priority for studies of Canadian nationalism as it is for behavioural science in general. This is especially true because the understanding of linkages between sentiment and behaviour is a necessary prerequisite to understanding more complex linkage processes in the political system.

Understanding the way in which the development of nationalist sentiments is interwoven with political outlook and the political socialization process as a whole provides another central concern in the study of nationalism. Similarly important is the role of personality in the emergence of nationalist sentiments. Future research needs to investigate more carefully the roles of political experience and outlook and personality in the learning of nationalistic sentiments. We also need to better understand the effects of these factors on processes of opinion linkage and aggregation.

The Potential of Canadian Nationalism

While our study is one of young people who are largely excluded from formal or effective roles in the political system (because of their age), certain implications of our results for the future of Canadian nationalism can not be neglected.

The fact that nationalistic sentiment is widely prevalent among these young people suggests that there may be a more broadly based potential for an on-going nationalist social movement in Canada than has hitherto been recognized by politicians, journalists, or social scientists. We find Ontario adolescents to exhibit a pattern of nationalistic outlooks which can conservatively be characterized as "ripe" for arousal or mobilization. Whether this sentiment will, in fact, ever be activated, or whether once activated it will be directed into a nationalist movement is dependent upon social and political events which we cannot foresee.

It may well be that the sentiments expressed by our sample of adolescents are only indicative of the "youth culture," and that these values will change as the adolescents mature. But these data seem to reflect a concern with problems far too conventional to be labelled "counter-culture" (see Reich, 1970), and in any case, our data regarding developmental patterns show the outlooks exhibited to be fairly stable among all age groups. It is more probable that this pattern of outlook portends a turning of public opinion towards more nationalistic positions as additional groups of young people assume effective political roles. There is, we would argue, a high potential for mobilization of this opinion into new mass movements. This potential is bound to be heightened if its spirit is not adopted by present day political parties and other institutions.

Notes

[1] More recently (August, 1972), the Waffle itself has launched a new organization, the Movement for an Independent Socialist Canada.

[2] This is perhaps best typified by the controversy aroused in August 1972 over the hiring of an American as police chief of the City of Calgary.

[3] Primarily this is because such forecasting requires models of individual behaviour and within-nation and inter-nation linkages far more complex than those available to social science today. More pertinently, however, our study is one of nationalist sentiment only and not one of action or behaviour supporting nationalist goals.

[4] B. Christiansen, *Attitudes Towards Foreign Affairs As a Function of Personality* (Oslo: Oslo University Press, 1959), p. 230.

[a] Hans Kohn, Nationalism, Its Meaning and History (New York, 1955), p.

[b] Bjorn Christiansen, Attitudes Towards Foreign Affairs as a Function of Personality (Oslo, 1959), p.

[c] L.W. Doob, "South Tyrol: An Introduction to the Psychological Syndrome of Nationalism," *Public Opinion Quarterly*, Volume 26 (1962)

[d] K.W. Terhume "Nationalism Among Foreign and American Students: An exploratory study," *Journal of Conflict Resolution*, Volume 8, No. 3 (1964), p.

[e] Symmons—Symonolewicz, Modern Nationalism: Towards a Consensus in Theory (New York, 1968), p.

[5] Altogether 118 items dealing with national and international attitudes were included in the university student pre-tests. Of these 35 items were selected for the final questionnaire administered to high-school students. All of these

items were in an agree-disagree format with the following response choices: "strongly agree," "agree," "neither agree nor disagree," "disagree," "strongly disagree."

[6]To avoid confusion as to the level of analysis involved herein (especially confusion between notions of nationalism as relating to individual belief system, national consciousness, and national movement) we will for the most part use the term *nationalist sentiment* in lieu of *nationalism*. This usage should not be taken as either necessitating or disallowing the role of nationalist sentiment in the emergence of nationalist behaviour or, at the societal level, nationalist movements.

[7]This list was adapted from Deutsch (1968), regarding which the sample was told that it represented an estimate of how the countries indicated would compare for national power in 1990. The respondents were asked to insert "Canada" into the list at the point "which represents where you would like Canada to be in 1990." This list was as follows, from highest in projected power to lowest: China, United States, Soviet Union, Japan, West Germany, Britain, France.

[8]Two scales derived from these questions merit comment: Supra-nationalism and Militarism. Supranationalism was dealt with throughout the nationalism scale development procedure primarily because of its apparent logical oppositeness to nationalism. We wished to determine if our adolescents reflected any clear response to notions of world government and world unity which matched whatever nationalistic outlooks they had. Militarism was included to determine whether whatever Canadian nationalist sentiment was found tended to assume a militaristic quality. These indicators were delineated by factor analysis. Elaboration on the measurement of these and other indicators included in the study may be obtained by writing to the authors.

[9]Some additional missing data were encountered, especially in the final section of the questionnaire, which related to foreign policy. This was because of limited testing time allowed in some schools, and the inability of some slower students to complete the questionnaire in the time allotted.

[10]The cutting-point on each scale was the scale score anticipated for a "hypothetical maximally uncertain student" who could neither reject nor accept any nationalist position indicated by our items, and who instead always checked the uncertain response category. Students whose scale scores fell above this point were more likely to endorse than to reject nationalist items; students whose scale scores fell below this point were more likely to reject than endorse nationalist items.

[11]Only when X^2 is significant at $P = .05$ will results be considered as significant, but particular levels of significance obtained will be reported. All correlations reported in the remainder of the paper are *Gamma* correlations. All data processing was completed using the CDC 6400 version of the Statistical Package for the Social Sciences (Nie *et al.*, 1970).

[12]As will be noted below, D-Power is most closely related to traditional nationalist sentiments such as N-Loyalty and N-Idealization. This fits in well with expectations regarding D-Power which we would derive from Terhune (1964). The fact that D-Power seems consequential and distinct from D-Independence has interesting implications for the characterization of Canadian nationalism, not the least of which are the repercussions of that desire's

frustration. In this connection we would expect its repercussions to be most dramatic in intranational political arenas.

[13]Such tendency towards consistency of organization of attitudes is usually thought to indicate greater permanence or endurance of the attitudes and greater centrality to the individual's belief system as a whole. Patterning and endurance of a belief system should mean that as the number of objects or situations the belief system can encompass increases, the probability will increase that the belief system will become manifest in behaviour and action (Rokeach, 1968).

[14]Correlations of the nationalism dimensions with Supranationalism and Militarism were also examined, to see what light these associations might cast upon nationalistic outlook. Supranationalism was found *not* to correlate with the nationalism dimensions. Only the correlation with Anti-Americanism was of interest (Gamma = .13). These non-correlations between nationalist and supranationalist outlook correspond closely to previous findings of Terhune (1965) and Forbes (1972b) where nationalism was found to be unrelated to internationalism—a puzzling confirmation of previous research. Militarism is significantly correlated with only one indicator of nationalist sentiment, N-Loyalty—a finding generally consistent with N-Loyalty's conventional and near "super patriotic" content.

[15]The significance of this pattern of prevalence and belief organization is magnified by consideration of the lack of *alternatives* for mobilization. Our analysis of prevalence, combined with insight gained from the scale development procedure, leads us to view the nationalist position as opposed to no coherent positive alternative. This is reflected in the dissatisfaction of our sample with "continentalist" alternatives. It is also reflected in the samples' rejection of Supranationalist sentiments (only 9.1% could be categorized as strong Supranationalists).

Bibliography

Alvik, Trond. "The Development of Views on Conflict, War, and Peace Among School Children," *Journal of Peace Research*, Vol. 2 (1968), p. 171-195.

Baker, D.G. "Political Socialization: Parameters and Predispositions," *Polity*, Vol. 4 (Summer 1971).

Blishen, B.R. "A Socio-Economic Index for Occupations in Canada," *Canadian Review of Sociology and Anthropology*, Vol. 4 (Feb. 1967), p. 41-53.

Block, Jack. *The Challenge of Response Sets* (New York: Appleton-Century-Crofts, 1965).

Burgess, P.M. and Hofstetter, C. R. "The 'Student Movement': Ideology and Reality," *Midwest Journal of Political Science* (Nov. 1971).

Christiansen, Bjorn. *Attitudes Towards Foreign Affairs as a Function of Personality* (Oslo: Oslo University Press, 1959).

Clarkson, S.E., ed. *An Independent Foreign Policy for Canada?* (Toronto: McClelland and Stewart, 1968).

Converse, P.E. "The Nature of Belief Systems in Mass Publics," in David Apter, ed., *Ideology and Discontent* (New York: The Free Press, 1962).

Cooper, Peter. "The Development of the Concept of War," *Journal of Peace Research*, Vol. 1 (1965), p. 1-16.

Dawson, R.E., and Prewitt, Kenneth. *Political Socialization* (Boston: Little, Brown, 1969).

Delamater, John, Katz, Daniel and Kelman, H.C., "On the Nature of National Involvement: A Preliminary Study," *Journal of Conflict Resolution*, Vol. 13, No. 3 (1969), p. 320-357.

Dennis, Jack. "Major Problems of Political Socialization Research," *Midwest Journal of Political Science*, Vol. 12 (Feb. 1968).

Deutsch, K. "On the Concepts of Politics and Power," in J.N. Rosenau, *International Politics and Foreign Policy*, (New York: Free Press, 1968).

Doob, L.W. "South Tyrol: An Introduction to the Psychological Syndrome of Nationalism," *Public Opinion Quarterly*, Vol. 26 (1962), p. 172-184.

Doob, L.W. *Patriotism and Nationalism: Their Psychological Foundations* (New Haven: Yale University Press, 1964).

Ferguson, L.W. "The Isolation and Measurement of Nationalism," *Journal of Social Psychology*, Vol. 16 (1942), p. 215-228.

Forbes, H.D. "Some Correlates of Nationalism Among Quebec Youth in 1968," (Paper presented to the Annual Meetings of the Canadian Political Science Association, McGill University, Montreal, 1972a).

Forbes, H.D. "English Canada's Nationalism." (Unpublished manuscript, University of Toronto, 1972b).

Greenstein, F.I. *Children and Politics* (New Haven: Yale University Press, 1965).

Halleck, S.L. "Hypotheses on Student Unrest," in J. Foster and D. Long, eds., *Protest: Student Activism in America* (New York: William Morrow, 1967).

Hargrove, E.C. "Nationality, Values and Change: Young Elites in French Canada," *Comparative Politics*, Vol. 2 (Apr. 1970), p. 473-512.

Harvey, T.G. "A multi-Dimensional Analysis of Patterns of Adolescent Political Socialization," (unpublished manuscript, 1967).

Harvey, T.G. "Comment on Response Biases in Field Studies of Mental Illness," *American Sociological Review* (June, 1971), p. 510-512.

Harvey, T.G. "Political Socialization Research: Problems and Prospects," (Paper presented to the Annual Meetings of the Canadian Political Science Association, McGill University, Montreal, 1972).

Harvey, T.G. and Vance, W.G.R., "The Measurement and Appraisal of Canadian Nationalist Sentiment," Mimeo. (University of Western Ontario, 1972).

Jackson, J.S. "The Political Behavior and Socio-Economic Backgrounds of Black Students: The Antecedents of Protest," *Midwest Journal of Political Science*, Vol. 15 (Nov. 1971).

Katz, Daniel. "The Psychology of Nationalism," in J.P. Guilford, ed., *Fields of Psychology* (New York: Van Nostrand, 1940).

Katz, Daniel. "Nationalism and Strategies of International Conflict Resolution," in H.C. Kelman, ed., *International Behavior* (New York: Holt, 1965).

Kohn, Hans. *Nationalism, Its Meaning and History* (New York: Van Nostrand, 1955).

Lambert, W.E. and Klineberg, Otto. *Children's Views of Foreign Peoples* (New York: Appleton-Century-Crofts, 1967).

Lawson, E.D. "Canadian Social Attitude Scores and Correlates," *Journal of Social Psychology*, Vol. 69 (1966), p. 327-335.

Lipset, S.M. *Political Man: The Social Bases of Politics* (Garden City: Doubleday, 1960).

Lipset, S.M. and Altback, P. "Student Politics and Higher Education in the United States," in S.M. Lipset, ed., *Student Politics* (New York: Basic Books, 1967).

Nie, Norman, Bent, D.H. and Hull, C. H. *Statistical Package for the Social Sciences* (New York: McGraw-Hill, 1970).

Piaget, Jean, and Weil, Anne-Marie. "The Development in Children of the Idea of the Homeland and of Relations with Other Countries," in R.S. Sigel, ed., *Learning About Politics: A Reader in Political Socialization* (New York: Random House, 1970).

Reich, C.A. *The Greening of America* (New York: Random House, 1970).

Rokeach, Milton. *Beliefs, Attitudes and Values* (San Francisco: Chandler Publishing Co., 1968).

Rokeach, Milton. *The Open and Closed Mind* (New York: Basic Books, 1960).

Rorer, L.G. "The Great Response Style Myth," *Psychological Bulletin*, Vol. 63 (1965), p. 129-129-156.

Rosenblatt, P.C. "Origins and Effects of Group Ethnocentrism and Nationalism," *Journal of Conflict Resolution*, Vol. 8, No. 2 (1964), p. 131-146.

Royal Bank. *A Conspectus of Canada* (Montreal: The Royal Bank of Canada, 1967).

Rummel, R.J. *Applied Factor Analysis* (Evanston: Northwestern University Press, 1970).

Russel, Peter, ed. *Nationalism in Canada* (Toronto: McGraw-Hill, 1966).

Sartori, Giovanni. "Politics, Ideology, and Belief Systems," *American Political Science Review*, Vol. 2 (June 1969), p. 398-411.

Symmons-Symonolewicz, Konstantin. *Modern Nationalism: Towards a Consensus in Theory* (New York: Czas, 1968).

Terhune, K.W. "Nationalism Among Foreign and American Students: An Exploratory Study," *Journal of Conflict Resolution*, Vol. 8, No. 3 (1964), p. 256-270.

Terhune, K.W. "Nationalist Aspiration, Loyalty, and Internationalism," *Journal of Peace Research*, Vol. 3 (1965), p. 277-287.

Toch, Hans. *The Social Psychology of Social Movements* (New York: Bobbs Merrill, 1965).

Vance, W.G.R. "The Structure of Adolescent Nationalistic Outlooks," (Unpublished M. A. Thesis, University of Western Ontario, 1971).

10.

Political Socialization of French and English Canadian Youth: Socialization into Discord*

Paul G. Lamy

IN the most extensive study of political socialization in Canada to date carried out for the Royal Commission on Bilingualism and Biculturalism (Johnstone, 1969), there is considerable evidence that the French and English develop divergent orientations to the political and social system at an early age, and that on some important dimensions, the two groups are further apart in young adulthood than in adolescence. The thrust of this study by Johnstone, then, is that the political socialization process seems to produce a change toward greater dissensus with age between French and English. He reports that at an early age both French and English youth see their differences about the country's future as a greater threat to national unity than differences between other social aggregates. The young respondents in this national sample perceive the differences in political attitudes between the two linguistic groups to be serious and to concern the central elements of the political system:

> The more interesting differences . . . were on the statements reflecting national goals for Canada—the kind of government they want Canada to have and the type of country they want Canada to be in the future. . . . (T)he Anglophones and the "Others" saw the two groups as oriented in quite different directions, while the Francophones were much more evenly divided in their opinions. . . . (W)hile English and French Canadians are seen as having much in common, the points on which they are seen to differ are serious ones.
>   (A)greement on similarity was highest among the 13- and 14-year-olds, and trhe lowest among either the oldest age group or the second oldest.[1]

*An earlier draft of this paper was read at the Meetings of the Learned Societies of Canada, Sessions of the Canadian Sociology and Anthropology Association, Summer 1970. I wish to thank John Johnstone and Maurice Pinard for their useful comments on this earlier draft.

These perceptions of differences on the part of Canadian youth appear to be based on sound empirical grounds. For instance, concerning orientations towards the major levels of government Johnstone reports:

> The older groups gave progressively higher positive ratings to their provincial governments. These trends are continuous among both language groups, and among the Francophones they are accompanied by consistently increasing negative feelings toward the federal government.[2]

And again, orientations toward bilingualism, an extremely salient political issue in Canadian life, vary with age in a way which sees young members of both linguistic groups entering adulthood further apart on this issue than younger age groups:

> As Anglophones pass through adolescence their tolerance for bilingualism appears to decrease while over the same years Francophones come to feel even more strongly about the position of their language in Canadian society. Members of the two cultures thus enter adulthood a good deal further apart in their views on bilingualism than when they entered adolescence.[3]

Apart from orientations toward the federal government, Johnstone's study does not provide for further measures of actual as opposed to perceived differences between French and English on such issues as national symbols and institutions, historically important foreign powers, alternative political arrangements, and feelings of the ethnolinguistic groups toward each other. Johnstone's study does touch upon some of these issues in a passing way. It was found that more French than English favoured a new flag, while more of the English favoured a flag having historical symbolism.[4] It was also found that considerably more English respondents named Britain as Canada's best friend though a majority of both language groups at all age levels saw the United States as Canada's best friend.[5] Johnstone's study, then, is more successful at indicating perceived differences between French and English than in dealing with actual differences in political orientation.

Another aspect of Johnstone's study is that it "is somewhat more heavily focussed on beliefs and impressions than on attitudes and sentiments—that is, on cognitive rather than affective reactions."[6] Studies of political socialization have found that affective reactions to political objects usually precede the more cognitive ones. Greenstein, for instance, notes:

Evaluations and "affective knowledge" about political leaders precede the factual information on which one might assume they would be based.[7]

Divergence on cognitive dimensions between English and French of the kinds found by Johnstone may very well come later than related divergences on affective dimensions of political attitude objects. If this were the case, the apparent trend toward growing divergence in mid-adolescence and young adulthood on the part of the English and French may all but disappear on the affective dimensions; it is the lack of divergence in the youngest age group on the cognitive dimensions which accentuates the apparent changes among the older age groups. Hess and Torney maintain that:

> children first think of political objects as good or bad; later, more complex information and orientation may be acquired. . . .
>
> Evaluations of political objects in gross good-bad terms are expressed earlier than more differentiated beliefs, probably because of the importance of the evaluation dimension in semantic assessment of objects and concepts and because the child has had more external contact with evaluation of his own behavior as good or bad. . . .[8]

It was therefore hypothesized that cleavages on broad affective dimensions of attitude between English and French would manifest themselves at an earlier age than the cleavages found on cognitive dimensions by Johnstone.

In partial test of the hypothesis that differences between French and English in their affective orientations to political attitude objects emerge early in life and carry over into young adulthood, self-administered questionnaires were given to a sample of 1251 Quebec French-speaking and Ontario English-speaking elementary and high school students eleven to twenty years of age.[9] The respondents were required to rate on three semantic differential scales the following concepts: The Queen, English Canadians, the Federal Government, Bilingualism, Canadians who are of neither British nor French origin, Quebec Independence Movements, English-Canadian Separatists, France, Quebec Separatists, Great Britain, Republic, Monarchy, United States, French Canadians, Ontario Government, Quebec Government, Biculturalism.[10]

The French were expected to show significantly less positive affect toward such attitude objects as the Queen, monarchy, federal government, and Great Britain than the English. The English were expected to show less positive affect to the provincial level of government, bilingualism, biculturalism, republic, and France than the French. The English were expected to show negative affect to Quebec independence movements and Quebec separatists, whereas the French were expected to show some degree of positive affect to these concepts. The divergence between English and French, then, is hypothesized to encompass not only national symbols and institutions, but also foreign affairs and the very existence of the political system itself.

Johnstone reports that while the French and English see each other as having much in common, they perceive each other to differ on important dimensions, and it is the English who are more likely to perceive such differences.[11] Rokeach and Mezei argue that "differences in belief on important issues are a more powerful determinant of prejudice or discrimination than differences in race or ethnic membership."[12] As perceived attitude dissimilarity on important dimensions between French and English coincides with ethno-linguistic cleavages, it is hypothesized that both English and French would show a degree of negative affect toward one another and that this would be most pronounced on the part of the English who perceive the greatest dissimilarity between the two groups.

Ethnicity and Political Socialization in Canada

This study found that ethnic origin is an important independent variable and that the use of linguistic group rather than ethnicity as the independent variable conceals important differences between those of British and those of "Other" (i.e. neither British nor French) origin. As will be seen in the subsequent pages, those of French and British origin were the most different in their patterns of affective orientations toward levels of government, national symbols and institutions, and historically important foreign powers. Those of "Other" origin feel somewhere between the French and the British on many issues, though in their overall pattern of affective orientations they tended to be more similar to the British than the French. Both this study and that of Johnstone which has been referred to extensively in previous pages seem to support Porter's view:

> Strong emphasis on ethnic pluralism . . . has stood in the way of creating a coherent social structure supported by a commonly held set of values and beliefs, a consensus, that is about what Canada is and what it means to be Canadian.[13]

However, it is doubtful whether the lack of a common set of values and beliefs can be attributed solely to ethnic pluralism. In Switzerland, there is a strong emphasis on ethnic pluralism, yet there appears to exist a common set of beliefs and values underlying a stable political structure. Naroll (1963) sees a set of core values underlying the ethnic pluralism of the Swiss. Heiman, in comparing the Swiss situation to the Canadian one, notes:

> Whether he is of French-Swiss, German-Swiss or Italian-Swiss background, the citizen of that country subscribes to one common political tradition. Such is not the case in Canada.[14]

The existence of ethnic pluralism itself, then, seems an insufficient explanation for the lack of a common political tradition in Canada.

Affect toward levels of government

Affect toward the federal government as measured by the "t" score decreased more sharply with age among both the French and Others than among the British[15] (see Table 1). This decline in positive affect on many political concepts is to be expected and is consistent with previous studies of political socialization such as that of Greenstein:

> . . . items dealing with political efficacy suggest that children are far more positive in their political orientations than adults.[16]

The French were the least favourably oriented to the federal government in the seventeen to twenty age group. The "t" score of the French was 8.31 on this concept compared to a "t" of 20.38 for the British and 16.75 for the Others. This contrasts with a "t" of 22.95, 23.35, and 30.77 respectively for these same groups at the eleven to thirteen age level. The English fourteen- to sixteen year-olds of both ethnic categories[17] were systematically less positive to all levels of government than the seventeen- to twenty-year-olds, for some reason, and this tendency to lower positive scores was repeated on several other concepts. However, in the case of the French, there is a steady decline in affect toward the federal government and as this affect decreases, the standard deviation from the mean score increases. As the "t" declines from 22.95 to 20.19 and 8.31, the standard deviation goes up from .82 to 1.15 and 1.50. While there is a slight trend for the standard deviation from the English (i.e. British and Other origins) mean scores to rise as affect toward the federal government declines, it is not nearly so great.

While the affect all groups show toward the provincial government declines with age, as it did in the case of the federal government, the affect of the English toward this level of government declines and

TABLE 1

AFFECT TOWARD LEVELS OF GOVERNMENT

	FRENCH				BRITISH				OTHERS			
	Mean	Standard Deviation	t*	N**	Mean	Standard Deviation	t	N	Mean	Standard Deviation	t	N
11 - 13-year-olds												
Federal Government	1.84	.82	22.95	93	1.84	.75	23.35	87	1.81	.69	30.77	135
Ontario Government	2.82	1.41	9.97	101	1.66	1.08	22.57	100	1.44	.76	36.37	153
Quebec Government	1.76	1.11	21.64	103	2.56	1.45	11.93	99	2.48	1.42	15.70	152
14 - 16-year-olds												
Federal Government	2.19	1.15	20.19	143	1.96	1.23	9.01	24	1.82	.80	15.05	38
Ontario Government	3.10	1.42	9.81	169	2.42	1.44	7.91	36	2.09	1.24	11.63	46
Quebec Government	1.98	1.24	23.81	172	2.97	1.42	5.17	36	3.41	1.60	3.15	46
17 - 20-year-olds												
Federal Government	2.43	1.50	8.31	42	1.74	.84	20.38	68	1.83	.98	16.75	58
Ontario Government	2.80	1.34	7.33	50	2.58	1.42	11.63	95	2.40	1.25	12.11	72
Quebec Government	2.12	1.27	11.79	50	3.44	1.53	4.39	95	3.23	1.33	5.75	74

* t is explained in footnote 15.

** N is the number of cases.

levels off in the middle (fourteen to sixteen) age groups, whereas the affect of the French toward the provincial government declines only among seventeen- to twenty-year-olds. This is in contrast to the steady decline in affect on the part of the French toward the federal government. While all groups in young adulthood show a strikingly similar degree of affect toward the provincial level of government (the French, British, and Others have "t" scores of 11.79, 11.63, and 12.11 respectively),the French show more positive affect to the provincial level than to the federal. The English of both ethnic categories show the opposite tendency, that is, they have more positive affect toward the federal than toward the provincial level of government. Only the Others at the eleven- to thirteen-year-old level show more positive affect to the provincial level of government than they do to the federal level with a "t" of 36.37 for the former and 30.77 for the latter. The French at the youngest age level were more favourable to the federal level of government than the provincial level—a "t" of 22.95 against a "t" of 21.64. The fourteen- to sixteen-year-olds and the seventeen- to twenty-year-olds switch to a higher positive score for the provincial level with the "t" for this level at 23.81 and 11.79 compared to a "t" for the federal level of 20.19 and 8.31.

Affect Toward National Symbols and Institutions

Surprisingly, at all age levels, all groups show slightly more positive affect to the concept of republic than to that of the monarchy (see Table 2). Affect toward the monarchy and the Queen declines sharply with age among all groups, but the French and Others in the oldest age group actually show negative affect toward the monarchy, in the case of the latter, and to both the monarchy and the Queen, in the case of the former. At the oldest age level, all groups show more positive affect to the concept of republic than to either the monarchy or the Queen. As one would expect, the British are more favourable than any other group to the Queen and monarchy. The French, however, show increasing heterogeneity of affect as group affect toward the Queen and the monarchy declines and affect toward republic rises relative to the latter concepts. This heterogeneity of affect on the part of the French is attested to by the standard deviations which are the highest of any group on these concepts. It would appear that Canadian youth may have quite different orientations to some of our national symbols and institutions than do their elders. The finding that among seventeen- to twenty-year-olds of all ethnic categories positive affect is higher toward the concept of republic than toward the Queen or the monarchy was not expected, and if such orientations are maintained into adulthood, it may

TABLE 2

AFFECT TOWARD NATIONAL SYMBOLS AND INSTITUTIONS

	FRENCH				BRITISH				OTHERS			
	Mean	Standard Deviation	t	N	Mean	Standard Deviation	t	N	Mean	Standard Deviation	t	N
11 - 13-year-olds												
Queen	1.89	1.21	19.75	106	1.88	1.22	18.88	96	1.92	1.27	23.04	156
Monarchy	3.04	1.51	7.90	102	2.97	1.72	7.59	93	2.86	1.58	10.92	145
Republic	2.51	1.33	11.04	73	2.61	1.39	8.44	51	2.22	1.34	15.27	91
14 - 16-year-olds												
Queen	3.40	1.99	5.62	175	3.14	1.29	4.55	36	3.02	1.48	5.45	46
Monarchy	3.90	1.83	1.01	172	3.44	1.44	2.77	36	3.89	1.70	.57	45
Republic	3.10	1.75	6.84	101	2.76	1.71	3.89	17	2.22	.85	9.27	23
17 - 20-year-olds												
Queen	4.22	1.66	-1.21	50	3.08	1.41	7.51	95	3.77	1.63	1.55	74
Monarchy	4.58	1.82	-3.04	50	3.78	1.66	1.68	94	4.51	1.75	-3.27	73
Republic	2.91	1.79	4.80	35	2.55	1.26	9.83	58	2.21	.92	12.93	48

indicate there may be a change in the role and importance of these symbols and institutions in Canadian political life.

Affect Toward Historically Important Foreign Powers

As hypothesized, the French at all age levels, and especially in the two oldest age categories, were more favourable to France than to Great Britain (see Table 3). The British were more favourable to Great Britain than to France at all age levels, and the seventeen- to twenty-year-olds gave a negative "t" score to this concept. Those of Other origin were more favourable to Britain than to France, which obtained a negative "t" score from the two oldest age groups. When the "t" scores on the concept of the United States are compared with those on Great Britain and France, it is interesting to note that only the British give greater positive affect to the same country—Great Britain—across all age categories. Those of "Other" origin, while originally more favourable to Great Britain than to the United States, show more positive affect toward the United States than to Great Britain in the two oldest age groups. The French, too, originally more favourable to France than to the United States, become more positive in their affect toward the United States in the two oldest age categories. One is tempted to conjecture here that socialization at the elementary school level, which emphasizes the historical contributions of Great Britain in the case of the English, and France in the case of the French, is being eroded as the children are exposed to other agents of political socialization

Affect Toward Bilingualism and Biculturalism

As expected, the attitudes of the French toward bilingualism and biculturalism are very positive and remain so over all age categories (see Table 4). Among the seventeen- to twenty-year-old French, bilingualism obtains the highest "t" score of any concept on the questionnaire except for "French Canadians." The "t" score for bilingualism is 18.06 and for French Canadians, 20.60. The attitudes of the English of both ethnic categories are less consistent across age groups, but if anything affect toward both these concepts tends to rise with age rather than decline. Johnstone found that the more specific the behavioural implications of bilingualism are, the less the English were in favour of it; also, the older they were, the less commitment they showed to bilingualism generally. However, Johnstone was dealing with behavioural aspects of bilingualism and this study is dealing with affective dimensions of attitude. In line with Johnstone's findings, though,

TABLE 3

AFFECT TOWARD HISTORICALLY IMPORTANT FOREIGN POWERS

	FRENCH				BRITISH				OTHERS			
	Mean	Standard Deviation	t	N	Mean	Standard Deviation	t	N	Mean	Standard Deviation	t	N
11 - 13-year-olds												
Great Britain	2.74	1.37	10.97	104	2.05	1.18	17.99	100	2.21	1.31	19.49	155
France	2.44	1.45	13.18	104	3.15	1.38	7.23	100	3.12	1.51	8.84	154
United States	2.56	1.44	12.26	104	2.75	1.45	10.40	101	2.51	1.49	15.11	153
14 - 16-year-olds												
Great Britain	3.49	1.56	5.37	172	2.25	1.20	9.57	36	2.93	1.27	6.41	46
France	2.81	1.58	12.48	173	3.89	1.60	.53	36	4.07	1.62	-.35	45
United States	2.53	1.71	14.84	173	3.03	1.59	4.62	36	2.80	1.42	6.75	45
17 - 20-year-olds												
Great Britain	3.38	1.60	3.46	50	2.55	1.31	12.37	95	3.08	1.31	6.90	74
France	2.84	1.58	6.52	50	4.20	1.45	-1.62	95	4.08	1.39	-.59	74
United States	2.32	1.38	10.12	50	2.84	1.55	9.06	95	2.53	1.24	11.37	74

NATIONALISM AND THE CANADIAN DUALITY   273

is the fact that the more diffuse concept of biculturalism outstripped the affective popularity of the more specific concept of bilingualism among the English of both ethnic categories. The French, on the other hand, consistently rate bilingualism more favourably than biculturalism, and the gap between the affect accorded bilingualism and that accorded biculturalism widens at each higher age level. The English of both ethnic categories also show far less homogeneity of affect toward bilingualism than did the French. There is an appreciable rise in the standard deviations of the English on this concept, and this increases with age. In the older age groups the English rate the more diffuse concept of biculturalism higher than bilingualism, and as age increases they become more divided in their affect toward bilingualism. The trend among the French is in the opposite direction.

Orientations Toward Separatist Movements and Separatists

The affect of the French toward both independence movements and separatists, other than the English-Canadian variety, becomes increasingly positive with age, a tendency which is all the more significant given the trend to lower positive affect on most concepts on the part of all ethnic categories as age increases (see Table 5). On the other hand, the standard deviations of the French scores on these concepts was high across all age groups, indicating a greater degree of heterogeneity. What is more striking is that affect toward Quebec separatists changes from negative affect to positive affect as age increases. This is the only instance in all ethnic categories where a concept which received negative affect at the youngest age level received positive affect from a higher age category. From a low "t" of 1.84 among the eleven- to thirteen-year-olds, positive affect toward independence movements rises to 5.39 and 4.69 in the two oldest age groups. The affect toward Quebec separatists rises from -1.65 to -.32 and then to 3.81 among the oldest group. Both the British and the Others are more negative toward all these concepts the higher the age level. All groups showed negative affect to English-Canadian separatists, the French probably because the attitudes of such people toward the French are well known, and the English perhaps because separatists are separatists no matter what language they speak.

French and English Affect Toward Each Other

At all age levels and in all ethnic categories, French-English relations are designated as the most important single issue on an open-ended

TABLE 4

AFFECT TOWARD BILINGUALISM AND BICULTURALISM

	FRENCH				BRITISH				OTHERS			
	Mean	Standard Deviation	t	N	Mean	Standard Deviation	t	N	Mean	Standard Deviation	t	N
11 - 13-year-olds												
Bilingualism	1.88	1.27	19.19	104	2.82	1.58	9.15	95	2.91	1.68	10.16	146
Biculturalism	2.27	.88	15.86	74	2.84	1.50	7.05	55	2.85	1.52	8.39	81
14 - 16-year-olds												
Bilingualism	1.91	1.48	22.63	173	3.26	1.90	3.11	34	3.02	1.78	4.92	45
Biculturalism	2.43	1.18	16.56	127	2.67	1.30	6.07	27	3.03	1.53	4.85	38
17 - 20-year-olds												
Bilingualism	1.48	.97	18.06	50	2.38	1.89	11.40	94	2.29	1.78	10.96	73
Biculturalism	2.30	.78	11.75	37	2.38	1.15	14.07	87	2.26	.96	14.71	69

TABLE 5

AFFECT TOWARD INDEPENDENCE MOVEMENTS AND SEPARATISTS

	FRENCH				BRITISH				OTHERS			
	Mean	Standard Deviation	t	N	Mean	Standard Deviation	t	N	Mean	Standard Deviation	t	N
11 - 13-year-olds												
Quebec Independence Movements	3.74	1.79	1.84	87	4.48	1.62	-3.45	83	4.45	1.67	-4.04	132
Quebec Separatists	4.23	1.55	-1.69	82	4.27	1.35	-1.99	75	4.42	1.45	-3.69	112
English-Canadian Separatists	4.61	1.67	-4.78	104	4.52	1.57	-4.05	97	4.40	1.74	-3.75	152
14 - 16-year-olds												
Quebec Independence Movements	3.41	1.74	5.39	146	4.97	1.18	-4.79	29	4.71	1.61	-3.25	34
Quebec Separatists	4.03	1.71	-.32	147	4.67	1.06	-3.54	30	4.74	1.31	-3.97	38
English-Canadian Separatists	4.52	1.80	-5.10	173	5.23	1.31	-6.36	35	4.84	1.57	-4.53	45
17 - 20-year-olds												
Quebec Independence Movements	3.00	1.75	4.96	43	5.07	1.17	-9.08	84	5.13	1.05	-9.11	68
Quebec Separatists	3.31	1.47	3.81	45	4.77	1.10	-6.86	87	4.57	1.17	-4.41	70
English-Canadian Separatists	4.65	1.81	-3.40	49	5.47	1.22	-12.86	94	5.08	1.44	-7.75	74

question concerning the major problem facing the country (see Table 6). In spite of these perceptions on the part of the respondents, and contrary to the prediction from attitude similarity theory, the expected negative affect of each group toward the other did not occur. (see Table 7). Both the French and the British showed less positive affect toward the Others than they did toward each other. The Others showed more positive affect toward themselves than they showed toward either the English or the French, whom they rated about the same, except at the youngest age level where English Canadians were rated higher than both Canadians of other origin and the French. The English of British origin were only slightly less positive in their affect to French Canadians than they were to English Canadians. Those of Other origin at the two oldest age levels were only slightly less positive in affect to both French and English Canadians than they were to Canadians of other origin. However, the ''t'' score of the French on English Canadians was only about a third as high as their score on French Canadians. Their ''t'' score on Canadians of other origin was even lower. Significantly, the affect of the French toward the English Canadians declines with age whereas affect toward the Others rises with age. Those of British origin show greater affect to both French Canadians and Others with increasing age. The Others show decreasing affect to both English and French Canadians in favour of Others, and at the seventeen- to twenty-year-old level, they show the same amount of positive affect to both charter groups.

TABLE 6

**Perceptions of biggest problem facing Canada
By Ethnic Group**

(percentages)

	French	British	Others
French-English Relations	37	43	45
Canada-Wide Political Problems	22	23	22
Economic Problems	18	10	09
Social and Environmental Problems	17	14	18
American Problems	04	08	05
Other Problems	02	01	01
No. of Cases:	328	230	264
Chi Square: .05	V: .11		

TABLE 7

AFFECT OF ETHNOLINGUISTIC GROUPS TOWARDS EACH OTHER

	FRENCH				BRITISH				OTHERS			
	Mean	Standard Deviation	t	N	Mean	Standard Deviation	t	N	Mean	Standard Deviation	t	N
11 - 13-year-olds												
English Canadians	2.73	1.40	10.90	103	2.52	1.14	17.26	155	2.30	1.19	15.56	100
French Canadians	1.95	.59	26.63	100	2.54	1.08	15.79	126	2.61	1.28	11.28	84
Canadians of neither French nor English origin.	3.71	1.35	3.56	102	2.81	1.40	12.47	154	3.06	1.39	7.88	98
14 - 16-year-olds												
English Canadians	2.94	1.55	11.24	175	2.80	1.19	7.45	46	1.92	1.00	12.52	36
French Canadians	1.95	.45	38.66	159	2.70	1.49	6.13	33	2.58	1.03	7.80	31
Canadians of neither French nor English origin.	3.54	1.42	5.06	172	2.49	1.04	9.96	45	3.00	1.33	5.20	36
17 - 20-year-olds												
English Canadians	2.80	1.56	6.78	50	2.65	1.30	10.21	74	2.41	1.38	13.19	95
French Canadians	1.90	.51	20.60	49	2.66	1.01	10.23	59	2.67	1.11	11.16	78
Canadians of neither French nor English origin.	3.04	1.43	5.63	50	2.28	1.32	12.85	74	2.57	1.42	11.71	95

Conclusions

It was found, contrary to what was expected, that divergences on affective dimensions of political attitude between French and English Canadians do not appear to develop prior to the kinds of divergences on cognitive dimensions found by Johnstone. Comparing the findings of both this study and that of Johnstone, it appears that divergences emerge contemporaneously on both cognitive and affective dimensions related to levels of government, national symbols and institutions, foreign affairs, and ethnic relations (Johnstone, 1969). This study found that while the French and English diverge increasingly with age in these areas, the French become more divided in their patterns of affective orientations than do the English of British or Other origin. But among the English, affective orientations to political attitude objects differed substantially according to ethnic origin.

Several tendencies discernible in the data are foreboding. The French show more positive affect toward the provincial than the federal level of government in young adulthood. The English display the opposite pattern. As age increases, affect toward independence movements and separatists rises among the French. Among the French, affect toward biculturalism declines with age, and the gap between the affect toward bilingualism vis-à-vis biculturalism increases at each age category. Positive affect toward the English declines steadily with age. These trends seem to indicate the growth of a nationalist orientation among the French in late adolescence and young adulthood. However, the French are a much more divided group in young adulthood than are the English in terms of their orientations to key political phenomena.

As far as the results of this study can be projected beyond the samples of French- and English-Canadian youth used, it can be said that there are significant cleavages between French and English on concepts which seem fundamental to the existence and stability of the present Canadian political system, and these divergences emerge particularly in late adolescence and young adulthood. These findings are in the general direction of those of Johnstone's study which utilized a national random sample. What is clear from both of these studies is that on many important attitudinal dimensions, the French and English are more alike in early or pre-adolescence than they are in late adolescence and young adulthood. Political socialization in Canada, then, seems to be for young French and English Canadians a process of socialization into discord, or, in the words of Johnstone, "the adolescent years, at least for Canadian young people, could be characterized as the period of emergent sectionalism."[18]

Notes

[1] J.C. Johnstone, *Young People's Images of Canadian Society*. Study of the Royal Commission on Bilingualism and Biculturalism (Ottawa: Information Canada, 1969), p. 2-29.

[2] Ibid., p. 20.

[3] Ibid., p. XVI.

[4] Ibid., p. 11-13.

[5] Ibid., p. 14-16.

[6] Ibid., p. XII.

[7] F.I. Greenstein, *Children and Politics* (New Haven: Yale University Press, 1965), p. 35.

[8] R.D. Hess and J.V. Torney, *The Development of Political Attitudes in Children* (New York: Doubleday, 1968), p. 29-30.

[9] The pre-tested, back-translated questionnaires were administered in one elementary and two French language secondary schools in Shiwinigan, Quebec, and in two elementary and three secondary schools in St. Catharines, Ontario, in mid-1968. As the Quebec and Ontario school systems are somewhat different, grades seven, nine and eleven were used for the French, and grades nine, eleven, and thirteen for the English. In each system, the grade containing the largest number of twelve-and thirteen-year-olds was used as a starting point with every second grade thereafter being included in the sample.

[10] The semantic differential is a scale composed of polar adjectives with a number of semantic spaces, usually seven, interposed between the adjectives. A simplified version of the standard introduction to the semantic differential was used. A thorough discussion of this scale and applications of it are contained in Charles E. Osgood, *et al.*, *The Measurement of Meaning* (Urbana: University of Illinois Press, 1957). The basic procedure calls upon respondents to indicate the relationship of a particular concept to one or the other bipolar adjectives by marking one of the spaces in this manner:

GOOD — : _X_ : — : — : — : — : — BAD

The mid-point on the scale is a neutral position. The scales used for all the concepts mentioned in the text of the paper are comprised of the following sets of bipolar adjectives with known evaluative loadings: good-bad, important-unimportant, wise-foolish. Responses in the direction of good, important, and wise are indicative of positive affect, and responses in the direction of bad, unimportant, and foolish are affectively negative. Scores on the three scales were summed into a "t" score for each concept. The "t" score is discussed in note 15.

[12] M. Rokeach and L. Mezei, "Race and Shared Belief or Factors in Social Choice," *Science*, Vol. 151 (1966), p. 167.

[13]J. Porter, "Canadian Character in the Twentieth Century," *Annals of the American Academy of Political and Social Science* (1967), p. 49.

[14]G. Heiman, "The 19th Century Legacy: Nationalism or Patriotism," in P. Russell, ed., *Nationalism in Canada* (Toronto: McGraw-Hill, 1966), p. 338.

[15]The data dealing with affect toward the various levels of government is presented in Table 1. The "t" score is an application of Student's "t" to the semantic differential scale. As adapted here, the "t" is a means of representing the extent of positive or negative affect accorded each concept on the three semantic differential scales on which it was judged. If a concept obtains a negative "t" score, this indicates negative affect, and if the "t" score is positive, it indicates positive affect. The formula for the "t" score is (X - u) $\sqrt{}$ N/s and it assumes an underlying normal distribution. Affect toward a concept, then, is positive or negative to the degree that the mean (X) varies from the assumed neutral mean (u) which is equal to four since this is the mid-point of the seven-point bipolar adjectival scales which were used. "N" refers to the number of cases and "s" to the standard deviation.

[16]Greenstein, *op. cit.*, p. 36.

[17]The "English" refer to those of British and Other origin combined. There were only a few respondents of British or Other origin who turned up in the sample from the French-speaking Catholic school system, and these were dropped from the analysis.

[18]Johnstone, *op. cit.*, p. 22.

Bibliography

Greenstein, F.I. *Children and Politics* (New Haven: Yale University Press, 1965).

Heiman, G. "The 19th Century Legacy: Nationalism or Patriotism," in P. Russell, ed., *Nationalism in Canada* (Toronto: McGraw-Hill, 1966).

Hess, Robert D. and Torney, Judith V. *The Development of Political Attitudes in Children* (New York: Doubleday, 1968).

Johnstone, John C. *Young People's Images of Canadian Society*. Studies of the Royal Commission on Bilingualism and Biculturalism (Ottawa: Information Canada, 1969).

Naroll, Raoul. "Some Problems for Research in Switzerland," *American Ethnological Society Proceedings* (1963), p. 4-9.

Porter, John. "Canadian Character in the Twentieth Century," *Annals of the American Academy of Political and Social Science* (1967), p. 370.

Rokeach, M. and Mezei, L. "Race and Shared Belief or Factors in Social Choice," *Science*, Vol. 151 (1966), p. 167-172.